1-2-3® Release 4 for
QuickStart

Pat Freeland

1-2-3 Release 4 for Windows QuickStart

Library of Congress Catalog No.: 93-87382

ISBN: 1-56529-618-4

96 95 94   6 5 4 3 2 1

Interpretation of the printing code: the rightmost double-digit number is the year of the book's printing; the rightmost single-digit number, the number of the book's printing. For example, a printing code of 94-1 shows that the first printing of the book occurred in 1994.

Screen reproductions in this book were created using Collage Plus from Inner Media, Inc., Hollis, N.H.

1-2-3 Release 4 for Windows QuickStart covers 1-2-3 for Windows Release 4.

Publisher: David P. Ewing

Director of Publishing: Michael Miller

Managing Editor: Corinne Walls

Marketing Manager: Ray Robinson

About the Author

Pat Freeland is a design-verification engineer with Lotus Development
Corporation and a former public-school teacher and software trainer.
He has written articles for *Lotus Magazine* and written or contributed to
several books on using computer software. He lives with his wife, two
children, and two dogs in Hingham, Massachusetts, near Boston.

Publishing Manager

Charles O. Stewart III

Acquisitions Editor

Nancy Stevenson

Product Director

Jim Minatel

Production Editors

Donald R. Eamon
Kathy Simpson

Copy Editor

Linda Seifert

Technical Editor

Michael Watson

Editorial Assistant

Jill L. Stanley

Book Designer

Amy Peppler-Adams

Illustrator

Kathy Hanley

Cover Designer

Dan Armstrong

Production Team

Gary Adair
Jeff Baker
Angela Bannon
Danielle Bird
Charlotte Clapp
Steph Davis
Anne Dickerson
Karen Dodson
Brook Farling
Teresa Forrester
Joelynn Gifford
Carla Hall
Bob LaRoche
Tim Montgomery
Nanci Sears Perry
Dennis Sheehan
Carol Stamile
Michael Thomas
Tina Trettin
Sue VandeWalle
Mary Beth Wakefield
Donna Winter
Michelle Worthington
Lillian Yates

Indexers

Rebecca Mayfield
Craig Small

Acknowledgments

To Vicki, Michael, and Cavi: thanks for your patience, love, and support. You're the best.

Trademark Acknowledgments

Que Corporation has made every effort to supply trademark information about company names, products, and services mentioned in this book. Trademarks indicated below were derived from various sources. Que Corporation cannot attest to the accuracy of this information.

Lotus, 1-2-3, Lotus Notes, Freelance, cc:Mail for Windows, and Symphony are registered trademarks of Lotus Development Corporation. Ami Pro is a trademark of Lotus Development Corporation.

Microsoft, Microsoft Windows, MS-DOS, and Multiplan are registered trademarks of Microsoft Corporation.

dBASE and Paradox are registered trademarks of Borland International, Inc.

IBM is a registered trademark of International Business Machines Corporation.

DIF Enable is a trademark of Enable Software.

SuperCalc is a registered trademark of Computer Associates International, Inc.

Contents at a Glance

Table of Contents

4 Modifying Data in a Worksheet   75

5 Changing the Appearance of a Worksheet   105

8 Charting Data   179

12 Customizing 1-2-3 for Windows   257

13 Making Use of Advanced Spreadsheet Features 275

Introduction

Lotus 1-2-3, long known as one of the most popular of all software programs, takes full advantage of the Microsoft Windows environment, providing a dazzling set of useful features. *1-2-3 Release 4 for Windows QuickStart* is one of the fastest and easiest ways to learn the advanced features as well as the basics of this powerful tool. *1-2-3 Release 4 for Windows QuickStart* uses a step-by-step tutorial format intended to quickly make you a productive 1-2-3 for Windows user.

Who Should Use This Book

If you are a new spreadsheet user, *1-2-3 Release 4 for Windows QuickStart* will help you become productive quickly. If you are an experienced computer user who is new to the Windows environment, *1-2-3 Release 4 for Windows QuickStart* will help you learn 1-2-3 in the Windows environment. If you are upgrading from 1-2-3 for Windows Release 1 or 1.1, you will find this book useful for learning the new features of Release 4.

What's New in 1-2-3 Release 4 for Windows

New to 1-2-3 Release 4 for Windows are streamlined procedures for common operations, including many new SmartIcons and cell formatting from the status bar.

New macro commands and functions expand your ability to create sophisticated worksheets.

Now you can not only perform many actions on cells and ranges, but also highlight groups of ranges, called collections, for speedier changes in larger areas.

Version Manager enables you to store several different entries in one cell and then group specific entries in several cells into scenarios for evaluating alternatives.

You can create multiple worksheets in a file. The tab at the top of each worksheet enables you to give the worksheet a name as well as a letter.

1-2-3 Release 4 for Windows QuickStart shows you how to use all these new features, plus the following:

- In-cell editing, which enables you to make changes right in the cell.

- Eight SmartIcon palettes, each of which you can customize to streamline common actions.

- Buttons that you can add to a worksheet and associate with macros to make launching macros easier.

- Special @function selector and navigator SmartIcons to speed the process of writing formulas and moving to named ranges.

- The capability to create and edit charts and drawn objects right in the worksheet.

- Customization commands that enable you to set defaults and customize workspace settings.

- A simplified query table that provides for quick querying and sorting of in-worksheet and external databases.

- DDE (Dynamic Data Exchange) and OLE (Object Linking and Embedding), which make data and text exchange between 1-2-3 for Windows and other Windows applications easy.

- A spell checker to verify correct spelling in all cells.

- Fill by **E**xample, which enables you to fill a range with items in a sequence.

- A palette of 256 colors and a selection of 16 patterns with which you can enhance charts, drawn objects, and cells.

How This Book Is Organized

1-2-3 Release 4 for Windows QuickStart is a tutorial developed with easy-to-follow, step-by-step instructions. All chapters follow the same format. First, new commands or procedures are described briefly. Next, procedures are presented in numbered steps to guide you through the required mouse actions or keystrokes. In most cases, illustrations show how the screen should look during and after a certain action.

Throughout each chapter, notes and cautions provide shortcuts, additional information, and warnings about possible pitfalls. Sections called "If You Have Problems" alert you to possible problems and provide suggestions for solving them. Key terms in the margin clarify terminology. A summary table appears at the end of each chapter, providing instructions for executing the commands covered throughout the chapter. Also included at the end of each chapter is an optional exercise designed to reinforce your understanding of the concepts presented in the chapter.

The chapters are organized into three parts.

Part I: Getting To Know 1-2-3 for Windows

Chapter 1, "Getting Started," introduces 1-2-3 for Windows basics, including a description of the Windows environment; how to start Windows and 1-2-3; the basics of the screen; opening, closing, and saving files; using **U**ndo; and exiting the application. The chapter also covers the help feature.

Chapter 2, "1-2-3 Release 4 for Windows Basics," teaches you the basic skills required for using 1-2-3 for Windows: moving around a worksheet, accessing commands, selecting data, and using keyboard shortcuts.

Part II: Building Worksheets

Chapter 3, "Building a Worksheet," covers entering labels, values, and formulas; differentiating between labels and values; using **F**ill and Fill by **E**xample; and adding worksheets to a file.

Chapter 4, "Modifying Data in a Worksheet," deals with changing the contents of cells and making room for new data. Included are editing cell contents, copying and moving, finding and replacing, checking spelling, deleting data, and changing the size of rows and columns.

Chapter 5, "Changing the Appearance of a Worksheet," explains how to convert a worksheet into a finished product by using number formats, realigned labels, font and text enhancements, colors, lines, patterns, and drawn objects.

Chapter 6, "Using Basic Functions," covers how to write these powerful formulas and how to customize the readily available list of functions available with the @function selector SmartIcon.

Part III: Getting the Most from 1-2-3 for Windows

Chapter 7, "Printing a Worksheet," discusses changing the printer setup, defining print titles, setting up the page, inserting page breaks, previewing a worksheet, and printing a report.

Chapter 8, "Charting Data," teaches you the basics of creating a chart, changing a chart type, and editing and enhancing a chart. The chapter also covers the uses of the various types of charts.

Chapter 9, "Working with Multiple Worksheets and Multiple Documents," explains how to open several files, navigate among multiple worksheets and files, use data from other files, display several documents on-screen, split the screen, and use named ranges.

Chapter 10, "Managing Data," shows you how to create, sort, search, and query databases, as well as how to set up criteria.

Chapter 11, "Using Macros," describes how to write a macro, record keystrokes for a macro, debug a macro, and associate macros with buttons.

Chapter 12, "Customizing 1-2-3 for Windows," deals with the ways you can tailor the program's appearance and performance, including changing the screen display and default settings, customizing the SmartIcon palette, and creating your own Fill by Example sequences.

Chapter 13, "Making Use of Advanced Spreadsheet Features," covers the creation of text boxes, the use of Version Manager, ensuring worksheet security, and auditing the worksheet to analyze formulas.

Chapter 14, "Advanced Analysis Tools," shows you how to analyze your data by using what-if tables and Solver.

Chapter 15, "Working with Other Windows Applications," discusses running multiple applications under Windows, opening files from other programs, exchanging data between Windows applications, using SmartSuite and the Bonus Pack, and sending electronic mail from 1-2-3 for Windows.

Where to Find More Help

After you learn the basics covered in this book, you may want to explore some advanced features of *1-2-3 Release 4 for Windows*. These features include outlining, advanced charting, and creating custom dialog boxes with the Dialog Editor.

Que Corporation offers a complete line of books designed to meet the needs of all computer users. Other 1-2-3 for Windows books include *Using 1-2-3 Release 4 for Windows, Special Edition*, and *1-2-3 for Windows Quick Reference*. You also can use the program's on-line help feature, which is explained in Chapter 1, "Getting Started."

Conventions Used in This Book

As you can in all Windows applications, you can either use the mouse or the keyboard for most operations. In some cases, you may need to use key combinations. In this book, a key combination is joined by a comma or a plus sign (+). Alt+*letter*, for example, means "Hold down the Alt key, press the letter key, and then release both keys."

When a picture of a SmartIcon appears next to a numbered step or narrative, it means that you can click that SmartIcon instead of choosing the command listed in the step.

When you use the mouse to operate 1-2-3 for Windows, you can perform four kinds of actions:

Action	Technique
Click	Place the mouse pointer on the item you want to select, and click the left mouse button.
Double-click	Place the mouse pointer on the item you want to select, and click the left mouse button twice in rapid succession.

(continues)

(continued)

Action	Technique
Drag	Place the mouse pointer on the item you want to select, and hold down the left mouse button as you move the mouse.
Shift+click	Hold down the Shift key as you click the item you want to select.

This book uses the following special typefaces:

Typeface	Meaning
Italic type	This font is used for terms that are being defined and for optional items in functions.
Boldface type	This font is used for things you type, such as commands and functions. It also indicates the underlined letter in menu and dialog-box choices, which you can use to access commands from the keyboard.
Monospace font	This font is used to represent system messages, screen messages, and on-screen results of functions.

System Requirements for Running 1-2-3 Release 4 for Windows

To provide optimum performance for 1-2-3 for Windows, your computer and software should meet or exceed the following requirements:

Hardware Requirements

- IBM or IBM-compatible computer with an 80286, 80386, or 80486 processor

- A hard disk with 8M to 13M of space

- 640K or more of conventional memory

- At least 4M of RAM

- A color or gray-scale EGA, VGA, or IBM 8514 monitor

- A mouse (optional but highly recommended)

Software Requirements

- Microsoft Windows Version 3.0 or higher

- MS-DOS Version 3.3 or higher

Visual Index

This index contains sample worksheets and figures that illustrate some of the capabilities you have with 1-2-3 Release 4 for Windows. Each sample has labels that briefly describe the relevant tasks and refer you to the appropriate sections of the book.

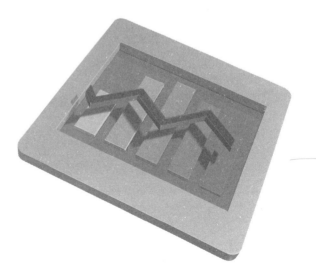

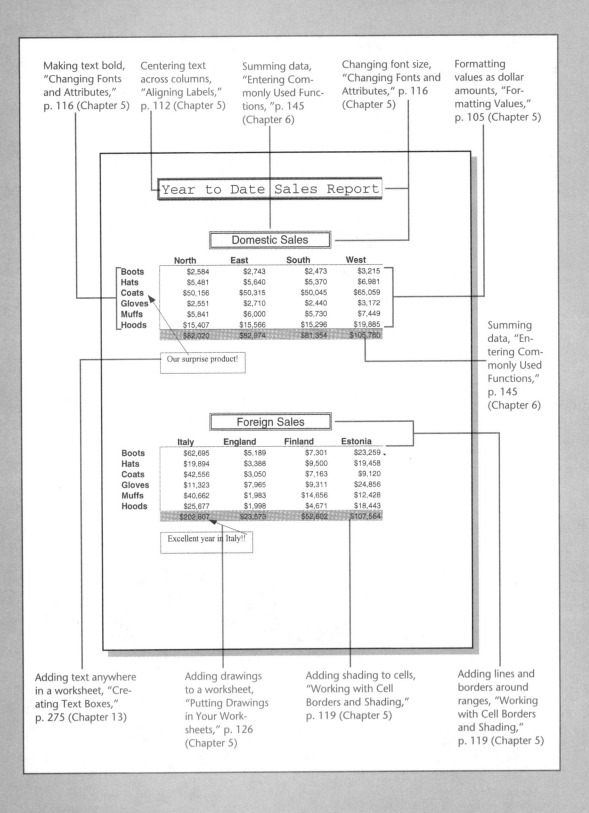

Making text bold, "Changing Fonts and Attributes," p. 116 (Chapter 5)

Centering text across columns, "Aligning Labels," p. 112 (Chapter 5)

Summing data, "Entering Commonly Used Functions, "p. 145 (Chapter 6)

Changing font size, "Changing Fonts and Attributes," p. 116 (Chapter 5)

Formatting values as dollar amounts, "Formatting Values," p. 105 (Chapter 5)

Year to Date Sales Report

Domestic Sales

	North	East	South	West
Boots	$2,584	$2,743	$2,473	$3,215
Hats	$5,481	$5,640	$5,370	$6,981
Coats	$50,156	$50,315	$50,045	$65,059
Gloves	$2,551	$2,710	$2,440	$3,172
Muffs	$5,841	$6,000	$5,730	$7,449
Hoods	$15,407	$15,566	$15,296	$19,885
	$82,020	$82,974	$81,354	$105,760

Our surprise product!

Summing data, "Entering Commonly Used Functions," p. 145 (Chapter 6)

Foreign Sales

	Italy	England	Finland	Estonia
Boots	$62,695	$5,189	$7,301	$23,259
Hats	$19,894	$3,388	$9,500	$19,458
Coats	$42,556	$3,050	$7,163	$9,120
Gloves	$11,323	$7,965	$9,311	$24,856
Muffs	$40,662	$1,983	$14,656	$12,428
Hoods	$25,677	$1,998	$4,671	$18,443
	$202,807	$23,573	$52,602	$107,564

Excellent year in Italy!!

Adding text anywhere in a worksheet, "Creating Text Boxes," p. 275 (Chapter 13)

Adding drawings to a worksheet, "Putting Drawings in Your Worksheets," p. 126 (Chapter 5)

Adding shading to cells, "Working with Cell Borders and Shading," p. 119 (Chapter 5)

Adding lines and borders around ranges, "Working with Cell Borders and Shading," p. 119 (Chapter 5)

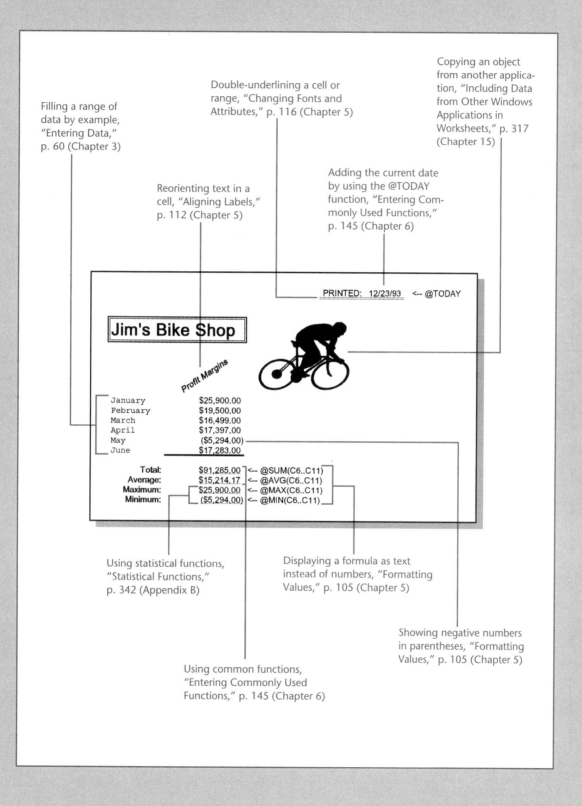

Filling a range of data by example, "Entering Data," p. 60 (Chapter 3)

Double-underlining a cell or range, "Changing Fonts and Attributes," p. 116 (Chapter 5)

Copying an object from another application, "Including Data from Other Windows Applications in Worksheets," p. 317 (Chapter 15)

Reorienting text in a cell, "Aligning Labels," p. 112 (Chapter 5)

Adding the current date by using the @TODAY function, "Entering Commonly Used Functions," p. 145 (Chapter 6)

PRINTED: 12/23/93   <-- @TODAY

Jim's Bike Shop

Profit Margins

January	$25,900.00
February	$19,500.00
March	$16,499.00
April	$17,397.00
May	($5,294.00)
June	$17,283.00

Total:	$91,285.00	<-- @SUM(C6..C11)
Average:	$15,214.17	<-- @AVG(C6..C11)
Maximum:	$25,900.00	<-- @MAX(C6..C11)
Minimum:	($5,294.00)	<-- @MIN(C6..C11)

Using statistical functions, "Statistical Functions," p. 342 (Appendix B)

Displaying a formula as text instead of numbers, "Formatting Values," p. 105 (Chapter 5)

Showing negative numbers in parentheses, "Formatting Values," p. 105 (Chapter 5)

Using common functions, "Entering Commonly Used Functions," p. 145 (Chapter 6)

Using page num-
bers in headers or
footers, "Changing
the Page Setup,"
p. 158 (Chapter 7)

Adding dates and times as headers or footers,
"Changing the Page Setup," p. 158 (Chapter 7)

12/23/93									05:17 PM

YEAR	MAKE	MODEL	COLOR	MILES	DRIVE	CYLS	DISP	TRANS	REGIST	STATE
1973	VOLKSWAGEN	BEETLE	ORANGE	48,000	REAR	4	1.3	4-SP	324MCW	MA
1984	TOYOTA	PICKUP TRUCK	DK BLUE	48,000	REAR	4	2.1	5-SP	AD9635	MA
1985	CHRYSLER	FIFTH AVENUE	DK GREY	18,000	REAR	8	5.2	AUTO/OD	CZY146	MA
1976	LANCIA	BETA	MAROON	46,321	FRONT	4	1.8	5-SP	CZB73	MA
1982	SUBARU	WAGON	BEIGE	37,000	ALL	4	1.8	5-SP 4WD	MYA167	MA
1984	VOLKSWAGEN	JETTA	MAROON	23,153	FRONT	4	1.9	5-SP	181945	NH
1975	VOLKSWAGEN	RABBIT	RED	116,000	FRONT	4	1.6	4-SP	145MKP	TX
1978	BMW	3.0 CSI	LT BLUE	67,450	REAR	6	3	5-SP	BUMW	FL
1972	SAAB	SONNET	ORANGE	103,495	FRONT	4	1.4	4-SP	IXLR8	CA
1985	AUDI	4000S QUATTRO	DK GREY	10,653	ALL	5	2.3	AUTO 4WD	AUDIDO	TX
1972	MERCEDES-BENZ	250	BROWN	89,035	REAR	6	2.5	AUTO	BK5006	RI
1985	HONDA	ACCORD SE-I	BEIGE	16,595	FRONT	4	2	AUTO OD	PIE576	CT
1973	FIAT	128 SEDAN	YELLOW	112,000	FRONT	4	1.2	4-SP	197754	NH
1975	VOLVO	BERTONE COUPE	SILVER	76,000	REAR	4	2.2	4-SP OD	FLATTOP	CA
1976	MERCEDES-BENZ	250 SL CONV	YELLOW	79,341	REAR	6	2.5	AUTO	PPL554	TX
1975	VOLKSWAGEN	BEETLE CONV	BEIGE	92,790	REAR	4	1.6	4-SP	BUGG	VT
1979	FIAT	124 SPYDER CONV	RED	99,640	REAR	4	2	5-SP	650DFG	FL
1973	MG	B-GT	GREEN	89,000	REAR	4	2	4-SP OD	109975	NH
1971	TRIUMPH	SPITFIRE CONV	WHITE	103,000	REAR	4	1.6	4-SP	DWE785	OK
1980	NISSAN	300ZX	BLUE	49,000	REAR	6	3	AUTO	980DQP	MA
1977	HONDA	CIVIC FE	BROWN	88,050	FRONT	4	1.3	5-SP	POD567	MI
1979	VOLKSWAGEN	SCIROCCO	GREEN	70,495	FRONT	4	1.8	5-SP	OMG620	ME
1981	BMW	318I	SILVER	58,000	REAR	4	1.8	5-SP	SHARO	CA
1979	MERCEDES-BENZ	300 SD	RED	87,000	REAR	6	3	AUTO	10SNE1	OH
1983	SAAB	900 TURBO	WHITE	42,970	FRONT	4	2	5-SP	19IM458	CA
1986	SAAB	9000 TURBO	BLACK	500	FRONT	4	2.3	5-SP	NEW790	MA
1976	TRIUMPH	STAG CONV	WHITE	76,530	REAR	6	2.7	4-SP OD	LMM423	MN
1973	VOLVO	1800 ES	RED	91,000	REAR	6	2.9	4-SP OD	SAINT	CT
1976	BMW	BAVARIA	MAROON	79,500	REAR	6	3	AUTO	JFF538	TN
1983	PEUGEOT	505 STI	BLACK	61,000	REAR	4	2.2	5-SP	LIN505	ME
1978	MERCEDES-BENZ	240 TD WAGON	YELLOW	90,000	REAR	4	2.4	4-SP	MBENZ	CA

Page - 1

Printing in landscape (wide) orientation,
"Changing the Page Setup," p. 158 (Chapter 7)

Creating a chart, "Creating an Automatic Chart from Worksheet Data," p. 181 (Chapter 8)

Formatting data with a set of predefined styles, "Naming and Using Styles," p. 122 (Chapter 5)

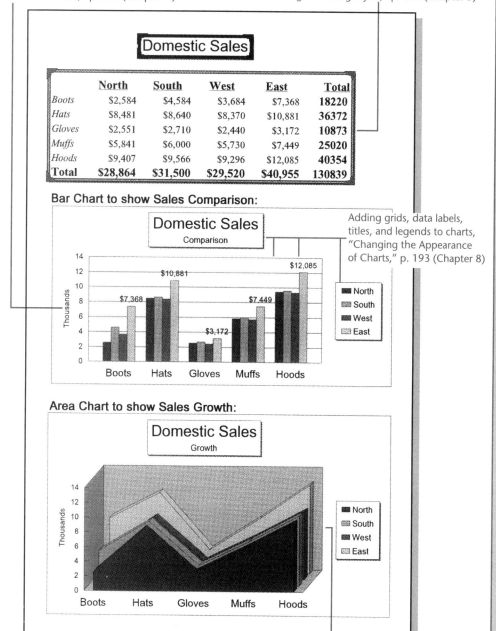

Domestic Sales

	North	South	West	East	Total
Boots	$2,584	$4,584	$3,684	$7,368	**18220**
Hats	$8,481	$8,640	$8,370	$10,881	**36372**
Gloves	$2,551	$2,710	$2,440	$3,172	**10873**
Muffs	$5,841	$6,000	$5,730	$7,449	**25020**
Hoods	$9,407	$9,566	$9,296	$12,085	**40354**
Total	**$28,864**	**$31,500**	**$29,520**	**$40,955**	130839

Bar Chart to show Sales Comparison:

Adding grids, data labels, titles, and legends to charts, "Changing the Appearance of Charts," p. 193 (Chapter 8)

Area Chart to show Sales Growth:

Changing to a different chart type, "Changing the Chart Type," p. 186 (Chapter 8)

Changing the font, "Changing Fonts and Attributes," p. 116 (Chapter 5)

Setting up a database, "Creating a Database," p. 224 (Chapter 10)

Entering database field names, "Creating a Database," p. 224 (Chapter 10)

CARS_NH.WK4

Chuck's Garage

YEAR	MAKE	MODEL	COLOR	MILES	STATE	PRICE
1973	VOLKSWAGEN	BEETLE	ORANGE	48,000	MA	$1,500
1984	TOYOTA	PICKUP TRUCK	DK BLUE	48,000	MA	$4,959
1985	CHRYSLER	FIFTH AVENUE	DK GREY	18,000	MA	$11,199
1976	LANCIA	BETA	MAROON	46,321	MA	$1,795
1982	SUBARU	WAGON	BEIGE	37,000	MA	$3,979
1984	VOLKSWAGEN	JETTA	MAROON	23,153	NH	$7,695
1975	VOLKSWAGEN	RABBIT	RED	116,000	TX	$895
1978	BMW	3.0 CSI	LT BLUE	67,450	FL	$10,095
1972	SAAB	SONNET	ORANGE	103,495	CA	$2,395
1985	AUDI	4000S QUATTRO	DK GREY	10,653	NH	$16,595
1972	MERCEDES-BENZ	250	BROWN	89,035	RI	$6,995
1985	HONDA	ACCORD SE-I	BEIGE	16,595	CT	$11,955
1973	FIAT	128 SEDAN	YELLOW	112,000	NH	$595
1975	VOLVO	BERTONE COUPE	SILVER	76,000	CA	$9,895
1976	MERCEDES-BENZ	250 SL CONV	YELLOW	79,341	TX	$10,050
1975	VOLKSWAGEN	BEETLE CONV	BEIGE	92,790	VT	$6,795
1979	FIAT	124 SPYDER CONV	RED	99,640	FL	$5,900
1973	MG	B-GT	GREEN	89,000	NH	$4,390
1971	TRIUMPH	SPITFIRE CONV	WHITE	103,000	OK	$1,095
1980	NISSAN	300ZX	BLUE	49,000	NH	$11,075
1977	HONDA	CIVIC FE	BROWN	88,050	MI	$895

CARS FROM NEW HAMPSHIRE ONLY:

YEAR	MAKE	MODEL	COLOR	MILES	STATE	PRICE
1984	VOLKSWAGEN	JETTA	MAROON	23,153	NH	$7,695
1985	AUDI	4000S QUATTRO	DK GREY	10,653	NH	$16,595
1973	FIAT	128 SEDAN	YELLOW	112,000	NH	$595
1973	MG	B-GT	GREEN	89,000	NH	$4,390
1980	NISSAN	300ZX	BLUE	49,000	NH	$11,075

23-Dec-93

Entering records in a database, "Creating a Database," p. 224 (Chapter 10)

Finding database records based on specific criteria, "Using Query Tables to Sort, Find, Extract, and Delete Records," p. 232 (Chapter 10)

Entering macro code, "Writing Command Macros," p. 247 (Chapter 11)

Assigning a macro to a button, "Creating a Macro Button," p. 251 (Chapter 11)

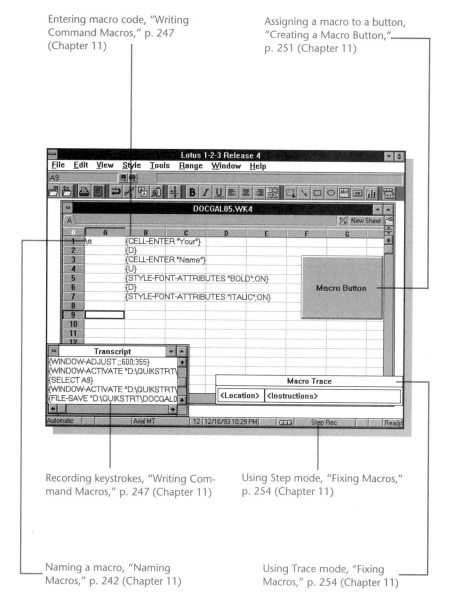

Recording keystrokes, "Writing Command Macros," p. 247 (Chapter 11)

Using Step mode, "Fixing Macros," p. 254 (Chapter 11)

Naming a macro, "Naming Macros," p. 242 (Chapter 11)

Using Trace mode, "Fixing Macros," p. 254 (Chapter 11)

Writing formulas for constraints,
"Using Solver," p. 295 (Chapter 14)

Entering initial estimates in adjustable
cells, "Using Solver," p. 295 (Chapter 14)

Setting up a Solver problem,
"Using Solver," p. 295 (Chapter 14)

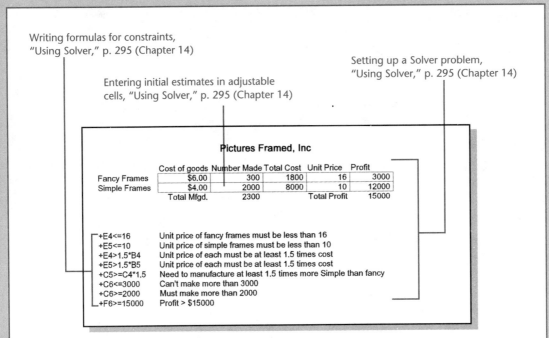

Pictures Framed, Inc

	Cost of goods	Number Made	Total Cost	Unit Price	Profit
Fancy Frames	$6.00	300	1800	16	3000
Simple Frames	$4.00	2000	8000	10	12000
	Total Mfgd.	2300		Total Profit	15000

+E4<=16	Unit price of fancy frames must be less than 16
+E5<=10	Unit price of simple frames must be less than 10
+E4>1.5*B4	Unit price of each must be at least 1.5 times cost
+E5>1.5*B5	Unit price of each must be at least 1.5 times cost
+C5>=C4*1.5	Need to manufacture at least 1.5 times more Simple than fancy
+C6<=3000	Can't make more than 3000
+C6>=2000	Must make more than 2000
+F6>=15000	Profit > $15000

Running Solver to find optimal solutions,
"Using Solver," p. 295 (Chapter 14)

Pictures Framed, Inc

	Cost of goods	Number Made	Total Cost	Unit Price	Profit
Fancy Frames	$6.00	1200	7200	16	12000
Simple Frames	$4.00	1800	7200	10	10800
	Total Mfgd.	3000		Total Profit	22800

+E4<=16	Unit price of fancy frames must be less than 16
+E5<=10	Unit price of simple frames must be less than 10
+E4>1.5*B4	Unit price of each must be at least 1.5 times cost
+E5>1.5*B5	Unit price of each must be at least 1.5 times cost
+C5>=C4*1.5	Need to manufacture at least 1.5 times more Simple than fancy
+C6<=3000	Can't make more than 3000
+C6>=2000	Must make more than 2000
+F6>=15000	Profit > $15000

Printing a Solver report to analyze a solution,
"Using Solver," p. 295 (Chapter 14)

Solver Table Report - Answer table
Worksheet: G:\6184\DATA\CH14EX2.WK4
Solved: 23-Dec-93 05:51 PM

Optimal cell

Cell	Name	Lowest value	Highest value	Optimal (#1)	2	3	4	5
A:F6	Profit Total Profit	15000	22800	22800	15600	15000	15000	15000

Adjustable cells

Cell	Name	Lowest value	Highest value	Optimal (#1)	2	3	4	5
A:C4	Number Made Fancy Frames	300	1200	1200	1200	300	1125	1154
A:C5	Number Made Simple Frames	1731	2000	1800	1800	2000	1875	1731
A:E4	Unit Price Fancy Frames	16	16	16	16	16	16	16
A:E5	Unit Price Simple Frames	6	10	10	6	10	6	6

Supporting formula cells

Cell	Name	Lowest value	Highest value	Optimal (#1)	2	3	4	5
A:D4	Total Cost Fancy Frames	1800	7200	7200	7200	1800	6750	6923
A:F4	Profit Fancy Frames	3000	12000	12000	12000	3000	11250	11538
A:D5	Total Cost Simple Frames	6923	8000	7200	7200	8000	7500	6923
A:F5	Profit Simple Frames	3462	12000	10800	3600	12000	3750	3462
A:C6	Number Made Total Mfgd.	2300	3000	3000	3000	2300	3000	2885

Creating scenarios and versions based on possible data changes, "Using Version Manager," p. 276 (Chapter 13)

Expenditures by Quarter for the current year

Minimum Expenditures:

	Qtr 1	Qtr 2	Qtr 3	Qtr 4
Salaries	$18,000	$17,500	$16,000	$19,750
Administration	1,250	1,425	1,675	1,000
Advertising	1,900	2,200	1,800	1,000
Totals:	$21,150	$21,125	$19,475	$21,750

Grand Total: $83,500

Expenditures by Quarter for the current year

Most Realistic:

	Qtr 1	Qtr 2	Qtr 3	Qtr 4
Salaries	$20,000	$21,000	$19,000	$22,500
Administration	1,400	1,650	1,975	1,300
Advertising	2,200	2,500	2,100	2,400
Totals:	$23,600	$25,150	$23,075	$26,200

Grand Total: $98,025

Expenditures by Quarter for the current year

Maximum Expenditures:

	Qtr 1	Qtr 2	Qtr 3	Qtr 4
Salaries	$22,500	$23,000	$22,750	$24,650
Administration	1,675	1,950	2,300	1,475
Advertising	2,500	2,700	2,300	2,500
Totals:	$26,675	$27,650	$27,350	$28,625

Grand Total: $110,300

Part I
Getting To Know 1-2-3 for Windows

Chapter 1

Getting Started

This chapter is designed to acquaint you with 1-2-3 Release 4 for Windows, and assumes that you have installed the product on your hard disk and are ready to start the program. If you need help with installation, please read Appendix A, "Installing 1-2-3 Release 4 for Windows."

If you are a new user, this chapter is a valuable starting point. If you are an experienced spreadsheet user, you will find some useful pointers and tips in this chapter.

This chapter covers the following topics:

- Starting 1-2-3 for Windows
- Starting a new file
- Opening an existing file
- Saving a file to disk
- Closing a file
- Using the Help feature
- Exiting 1-2-3 for Windows

Starting the Program

After you install 1-2-3 Release 4 for Windows, you see an icon that represents the program in the Lotus Applications program group in the Program Manager window.

This is the Windows Program Manager window with the icon for 1-2-3 Release 4 for Windows highlighted.

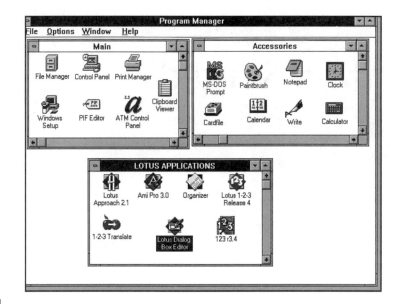

Double-clicking
Pressing the left mouse button twice in rapid succession.

To start the program, place the mouse pointer on the icon and *double-click*.

If you have problems...

If the program doesn't start when you double-click the icon, be sure that you are not moving the mouse pointer when clicking, and be sure that you click rapidly. Simply clicking once and then clicking again a few seconds later is not the same as double-clicking.

Touring the Screen

After you start 1-2-3 for Windows, make sure that the program's window fills the screen. It is easier to work with a program when you can see as much of it as possible, because other information on-screen can distract you. Click the Maximize button (the up arrow) in the upper right corner of the 1-2-3 window to cause this window to occupy the whole screen.

This is the screen you see when you start 1-2-3 Release 4 for Windows and then click the Maximize button. Notice that the Restore button replaces the Maximize button.

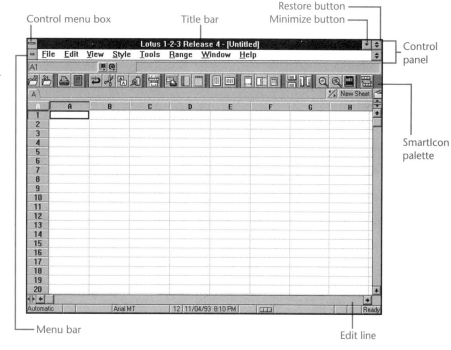

The first three lines of the 1-2-3 for Windows screen are the *control panel*, which consists of the title bar, the menu bar, and the edit line.

The Title Bar

The top line of all application windows is the *title bar*, which shows the name of the program and—when a document or file was retrieved—the name of the file. At the left end of the title bar, you see the Control menu box. Double-clicking this box is the fastest way to close an application. Clicking this box once opens the drop-down menu associated with the box.

At the right end of the title bar, you see the Minimize and Maximize or Restore buttons, represented by the down, up, and double arrows, respectively. Two of the three buttons are always visible.

Active window
The window that has a darker title bar than the others. The active window is the one in which you can enter text and execute commands.

Only one application window is active at a time, and within an application, only one document or spreadsheet is active. When several windows are visible on-screen, the title bar of the active window is darker than the title bars of other windows.

The Menu Bar

Below the title bar is the *menu bar*, which contains the program's main menus. **R**ange changes to a different menu, such as **C**hart, if a chart is selected.

The Edit Line

The third line of the 1-2-3 for Windows screen is the *edit line*, which contains the following four items:

■ The active cell

■ The navigator icon

■ The @function selector icon

■ The contents of the active cell

The navigator icon

Active cell   The @function selector icon   Contents of the active cell

The 1-2-3 for
Windows edit line.

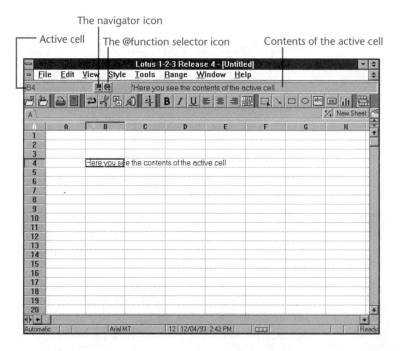

Active cell

The cell in which the cell pointer currently is placed. Pressing an arrow key or clicking another cell changes the active cell. The active cell's address is shown in the third line of the 1-2-3 for Windows screen.

The left end of the edit line shows the location, or *address*, of the *active cell* in the worksheet. If you currently are using only one worksheet, the edit line displays the address of the active cell as the column letter and row number. If the *cell pointer* is in the top left cell of the worksheet, for example, the edit line shows A1. When a *range* in the worksheet is highlighted, the top left and bottom right cells of the range are listed with two dots between the cells—for example, A1..C8.

1

Cell pointer
The box that frames one cell and makes that cell the active cell.

Range
A rectangular group of cells. When a range is highlighted, the addresses of the top left and bottom right cells appear in the third line of the 1-2-3 for Windows screen, with two periods between the two addresses.

Any file can contain 256 worksheets. Each worksheet uses a letter or letter combination as a default name (A through IV). When you have more than one worksheet, the cell address is preceded by the worksheet's letter or name—for example, A:A1, CF:IV8000, or CHARTS:A9.

Next to the active cell's address, you see two small icons. The icon on the left is the *navigator icon*. You use this icon (which is described more fully in Chapter 9, "Working with Multiple Worksheets and Multiple Documents") to move to named ranges in a worksheet. Next to the navigator icon is the *@function selector icon*, which you use to select and enter a function into a cell. The @function selector icon is described in Chapter 6, "Using Basic Functions."

The majority of the edit line contains the contents of the active cell. When the cell contains a value or a label, the actual contents appear in the edit line. When the cell contains a formula, however, the result of the formula appears in the cell and the formula itself appears in the edit line.

The SmartIcon Palette

The fourth line of the 1-2-3 for Windows screen is the *SmartIcon palette*. *SmartIcons* are little pictures that represent actions you can perform—generally, the most common actions you perform in the normal course of using 1-2-3 for Windows. Clicking a SmartIcon once with the left mouse button causes the action that it represents to take place.

Note: *To find out what a given SmartIcon does, place the mouse pointer on the SmartIcon and hold down the right mouse button. The title bar displays a brief description of the icon's function.*

 The last icon on the right is special in that it enables you to display the other seven SmartIcon palettes, one at a time, in order. Some actions are so common that SmartIcons for those actions appear in more than one palette. The first eight SmartIcons appear in every palette because they represent the most common actions performed in 1-2-3 for Windows: retrieving files, saving files, printing, print previewing, undoing the last action, cutting, copying, and pasting.

The Worksheet Tabs

Below the SmartIcon palette is a space for the *worksheet tabs*. (If a worksheet is not maximized, it has its own title bar, in which case the tabs appear below the title bar.)

A file can have more than one worksheet so that data can be arranged in layers. Each worksheet is designated by a letter, the topmost being A. This letter appears on a tab that extends up from the worksheet itself. You can change the letter on a tab by double-clicking it and then typing a more descriptive name, called a *label*.

A file with several worksheets, each with a descriptive name.

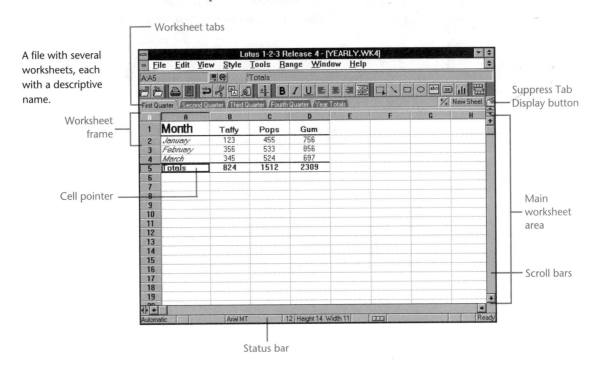

Status bar

You can have a total 256 worksheets in a spreadsheet file, so some of the tabs will not be visible on-screen, especially if you changed the letters on the tabs to labels. Near the right end of the line containing the worksheet tabs is a pair of arrowheads separated by a slash mark. Clicking these arrowheads brings the nonvisible tabs into view. Clicking the right arrow, for example, displays the worksheets whose tabs have higher letters.

At the end of the line containing the worksheet tabs is a small picture of three folders. Click this button once to suppress display of the worksheet tabs. Click again to display the tabs again.

Chicken Pockets

20-35 min.   4   (350°F)

3 oz. Cream cheese, softened
3 T margerine, melted
2 c. cooked chicken, cubed
1/4 t. salt
1/8 t. pepper
2 T milk
1 T onion, minced
1 - 8 oz package crescent rolls
3/4 c. crushed seasoned croutons

Blend cream cheese + 2 Tblsp.
of melted margerine. Add
next 5 ingrediants.
Separate rolls into 4
rectangles. Place 1/2 cup
meat mixture into center
of each. Fold up points
+ press seams together.
Brush with rest of margerine
and sprinkle tops with
crushed croutons.

Bake @ 350°F for 20-25 min.
until golden brown.

1

The Main Worksheet Area

The largest part of the screen—the *worksheet area*—is where you do most of your work. The *worksheet frame* at the left and at the top of the screen contains the row numbers and column letters for the current sheet.

The Scroll Bars

Along the right side and at the bottom of the worksheet area are the *scroll bars*. In each scroll bar is a small box. Click and drag the box within the scroll bar to move the focus of the screen to another area of the worksheet. Dragging the box in the vertical scroll bar, for example, moves the worksheet up or down to display the area above or below the current screen.

Note: *Using the scroll bars does not change the active cell. When you scroll to a distant section of a worksheet, you leave the cell pointer behind. Remember to click a visible cell after using the scroll bars before you enter data.*

At the left end of the horizontal scroll bar and at the top of the vertical scroll bar is a small box containing arrowheads pointing away from parallel lines. Clicking and dragging these boxes splits the active worksheet into two separate sections called panes. For more information on using panes, see Chapter 9, "Working with Multiple Worksheets and Multiple Documents."

The Status Bar

The bottom line of the 1-2-3 for Windows screen is the *status bar*. The individual sections of the bar tell you something about the active cell or the status of the program. Clicking certain sections of the status bar enables you to change certain cells.

The status bar at the bottom of the 1-2-3 for Windows screen.

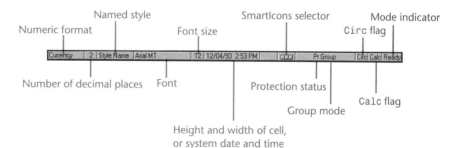

The following list briefly describes the sections of the status bar. More complete descriptions of these sections appear in later chapters of this book.

- *Numeric format:* the way a value appears in the cell. The number 300 can be formatted to look like $300.00, for example.

- *Decimal places:* the number of decimal places included in the number in the current cell. Decimal places and numeric formats are discussed in Chapter 5, "Changing the Appearance of a Worksheet."

- *Named style:* has contents only when a named style is applied.

- *Font* and *font size:* the type style and size applied to data in the current cell.

- *Cell height and width* or *date and time:* click this section of the status bar to change the contents back and forth between date/time and height/width.

- *SmartIcons selector:* click this selector (sometimes called "the icon icon") to display a different SmartIcon palette.

- *Worksheet status:* indicates when such changes as Group mode or protection are in effect.

- *Circ indicator:* indicates that a circular formula exists in the worksheet.

- *Calc flag:* indicates that the formulas in the worksheet have not recalculated since data was changed.

- *Mode indicator:* shows what the program is doing at the present time. The most important modes are described in the following table.

Mode	Meaning
Ready	You can enter data or execute commands
Point	You need to highlight a range for a command (or you are in the process of highlighting a range)
Menu	A menu item has been selected, a menu selection is about to be implemented, or a menu is open

Mode	Meaning
Wait	An operation is taking place; you cannot execute further commands or input data until the operation is finished
Edit	Either you voluntarily entered Edit mode, or you made a mistake in a cell entry and 1-2-3 for Windows placed you in Edit mode to fix the mistake

Starting, Saving, and Retrieving Files

The work you do on-screen remains there until you erase it or until you exit the program. When either event occurs, you lose the information on-screen unless you save your work. Work that you save becomes a *file*.

Before you save work, the title bar contains the word Untitled, indicating that the work exists only on-screen and has not been saved to disk. After you save the work, the title bar displays the file name you used and the extension WK4 (the extension automatically assigned to 1-2-3 Release 4 for Windows data files).

Starting a New File

Caution
Don't wait until you have entered a great deal of data to save your work. Saving is easier and quicker than re-entering data after a power loss or a careless mistake erases all your work.

When you start 1-2-3 for Windows, you see a blank, untitled worksheet. You can enter data in this worksheet and then save it as a new file. If, during a working session, you want to start another new file, choose **F**ile, **N**ew. A new blank, untitled worksheet appears.

Note: *Choosing* **F**ile, **N**ew *does not affect the data on which you were working. Both the current worksheet and the new worksheet are active, and you can move back and forth between them. (Working with multiple files is covered in Chapter 9, "Working with Multiple Worksheets and Multiple Documents.")*

Opening a File

After you save a worksheet, you can retrieve it for updating. (Remember to save the worksheet again after you update it so that the new data becomes a permanent part of the file.)

You can retrieve, or *open*, a file in either of two ways. To open a file:

1. Click the File Open SmartIcon or choose **F**ile, **O**pen. The Open File dialog box appears.

The Open File
dialog box, with
the drop-down
Drives list box
showing all
available disk
drives.

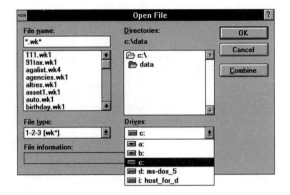

2. If the current drive or directory is not where the file that you want
    to open is located, you need to change the drive and/or directory.
    Click the Dri**v**es drop-down box and then select the proper disk
    drive. Click the **D**irectories box and then select the directory that
    contains the file you want to open.

3. After you select a directory, a list of 1-2-3 for Windows files in that
    directory appears in the File **N**ame list box. Double-click the name
    of the file you want, or highlight the file name and then press En-
    ter.

    Alternatively, type the name of the file in the File **N**ame text box
    and then press Enter.

Note: *The bottom of the drop-down* **F**ile *menu lists the files you have retrieved
most recently, including those retrieved in previous work sessions. By default,
this list is up to five files long. (You can list more files than five; for details, see
Chapter 12, "Customizing 1-2-3 for Windows.") To open a recently used file,
choose* **F**ile *and then click the file name at the bottom of the menu.*

The **F**ile menu, including the five most recently opened files, is different for each user and may be different every time you choose **F**ile.

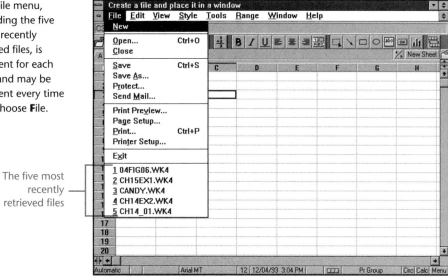

The five most recently retrieved files

Saving a File

To avoid losing data that you have entered, get into the habit of saving your work early and often.

The first time you save a file, you must name it. Thereafter, saving takes very little time. To save a file for the first time:

1. Click the Save File SmartIcon or choose **F**ile, **S**ave. The Save As dialog box appears.

The Save As dialog box.

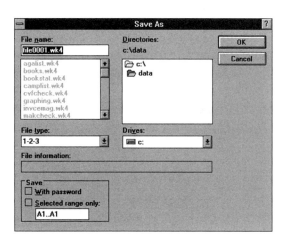

2. Select the drive and directory where you want to save the file if you don't want to use the listed drive.

   Note: *The Save As dialog box is similar to the Open dialog box. If you need help choosing directories or drives in this dialog box, see the preceding section.*

3. Type a name in the File **N**ame text box. You don't need to type the file extension (WK4); 1-2-3 Release 4 for Windows adds the extension for you.

4. Choose OK.

Follow these rules when you name a file:

■ Don't use more than eight characters. You can use fewer than eight, but if you use more, you will get an error message.

■ Don't put spaces in file names. (The name MY FILE, for example, is not acceptable because of the space; use an underscore character, as in MY_FILE, instead.)

■ Don't use the following symbols:

   . " / \ [ ] : | < > + = ; * ? ,

Caution
If you are saving to a floppy disk, leave the disk in the drive until the drive light goes out. Removing the disk too soon makes it impossible to retrieve the file the next time you want to work with it.

To save a file that you already have saved, click the Save File SmartIcon or choose **F**ile, **S**ave.

After either of these actions, the file is saved to the disk and directory to which it was saved the first time or from which it was retrieved.

Any time you save a file, you overwrite the preceding version of the file on disk. Normally, this is exactly what you want to do. But if you change a worksheet and don't want the changes to be permanent, don't save the file. The only time 1-2-3 for Windows warns you that you are using an existing file name is when you choose **F**ile, Save **A**s and enter a file name that has already been used.

Saving a File with a Different Name, Location, or Format

Sometimes, you want to save a file in a different way. For example, you may want to save a file to a floppy disk so that you can take the disk to another computer and continue working on the file there. You also might decide that a file needs a different name than the one you saved it under.

When you want to save a file to a new location or change a file name:

1. Choose **F**ile, Save **A**s. The Save As dialog box appears—the same one that you see when you save a file for the first time.

2. Change the drive, directory, or file name.

3. Choose OK.

You also can use the **F**ile, Save **A**s command to save a portion of a file. You might have a large worksheet file that contains several kinds of data on your company's employees, for example, and you might want to create a new file containing only employee names.

To save part of a worksheet under a different name:

1. Highlight the range of cells that you want to include in the new file.

2. Choose **F**ile, Save **A**s.

3. Give the file a different name, and (if you want to save the file to another location) select a different drive or directory.

4. If you forgot to highlight a range in step 1, choose **S**elected Range Only at the bottom of the Save As dialog box and then type the top left and bottom right cells of the range you want to save, using two periods to separate the cell addresses. (If you are saving cells A1 to B12, for example, you would type **A1..B12**.)

5. Choose OK.

Closing a File

After a file has been saved, you may want to clear it from the screen. To close a file, choose **F**ile, **C**lose or double-click the Control menu button.

If you have saved the work that is on-screen, the data disappears from the screen. If you have not saved your work, a Close dialog box appears, displaying three options:

- **Y**es saves and then closes the file, if the file already has been saved. If the file has not been saved before, the Save As dialog box appears. Choose the proper drive and directory, name the file, and then choose OK.

- **N**o erases the work from the screen without saving it and then closes the file.

- Cancel stops the close operation and returns you to the worksheet.

Getting Help

The help feature in 1-2-3 for Windows is called *context-sensitive* because you can call up help for the command or function that you currently are using. Any time you want to get help on any subject, choose **H**elp, **C**ontents or press F1. The main help screen appears.

The main help screen.

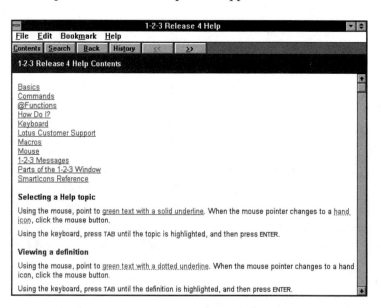

1

All help screens contain two elements that you can use to access further help:

■ Text with a solid underline is a cross-reference to more help. When you click the underlined text, a new help screen appears, displaying information specific to the text that you clicked.

■ Text with a dotted underline is connected to a definition. Click the underlined text to display a definition of the word or phrase; click again to close the definition.

Under the help screen's menu bar are several buttons that help you navigate the help system:

■ *Contents*. This button displays the main help screen.

■ *Search*. This button displays a dialog box in which you can type a word or phrase for which you want help. (If you need help with copying, for example, type **copy**.) A list of topics containing the word or phrase that you typed appears in the list box below the text box. Choose **S**how Topics or double-click a specific topic; a list of related topics appears at the bottom of the dialog box. Choose **G**o To or double-click one of the choices to display a new help screen containing help on the subject you chose.

Note: *You also can search for a help topic by choosing* **H**elp, **S**earch *from the main menu.*

Type a subject in the **W**ord box to see available help topics for that subject.

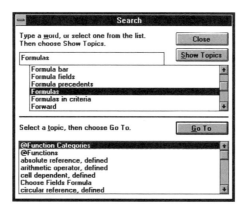

■ **B***ack*. This button returns you to the preceding help screen.

■ *History*. This button displays a record of the last 40 help topics that you viewed. Click << or >> to move back or forward through the history, one help topic at a time.

Other items in the **H**elp drop-down menu include **U**sing Help (a guide to the help system), **K**eyboard (information on how to use the keyboard in 1-2-3 for Windows), and **H**ow Do I (a list of common activities for which further help is available). **F**or Upgraders lists the new features in 1-2-3 Release 4 for Windows, and **T**utorial is a series of lessons on using the program.

Printing, Copying, and Marking Help Topics

Below the help screen's title bar is the main help menu. This menu contains commands for printing a file (you might find it useful to have a printout of a help topic to which you often refer), copying a help screen (you might want to copy the help information to a document in another program), and adding a bookmark (to make a topic easier to find).

To print a help topic, choose **F**ile, **P**rint Topic from the help-screen menu.

To copy text to the Clipboard for pasting into a document:

1. Choose **E**dit, **C**opy. The Copy dialog box appears.

2. Select the text to be copied.

When you choose **E**dit, **C**opy in a help screen, this dialog box appears, enabling you to select text to be copied.

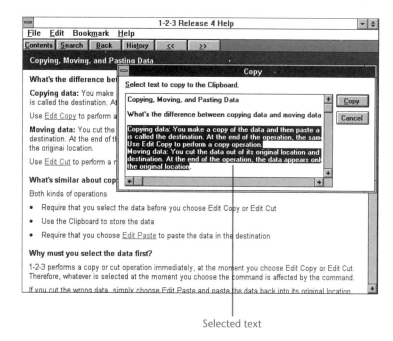

Selected text

3. Choose **C**opy.

You now can switch to a document in another application and paste in the copied text, using whatever command is appropriate in that application (usually the **E**dit, **P**aste command).

To create a bookmark:

1. Choose Book**m**ark, **D**efine. The Bookmark Define dialog box appears.

2. A suggested name appears in the Book**m**ark Name text box. To accept this name, choose OK. To use another name, type that name in the text box and then choose OK.

To jump quickly to a topic for which you have created a bookmark, choose Book**m**ark. The names of all of the bookmarks you have created appear in the menu. Select the name of the bookmark that you want to find.

Using Context-Sensitive Help

You might be in the middle of performing an action in 1-2-3 for Windows when you realize that you aren't sure about how to proceed. Context-sensitive help is useful at such a time.

Suppose that you chose **S**tyle, **L**ines & Color, and now need more information before you continue. The top right corner of the Lines & Color dialog box contains a question mark. To display context-sensitive help for that topic, click the question mark or press the F1 (Help) key.

The **S**tyle, **L**ines & Color help screen.

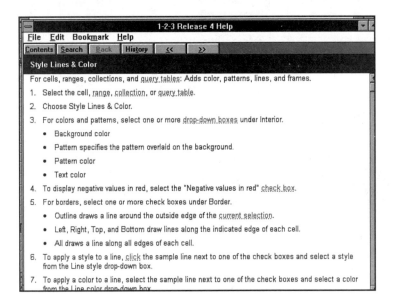

Exiting the Program

Caution

Never turn off your computer without first properly exiting all active programs, including Windows. This practice ensures that you don't forget to save your work.

Located in the top left corner of every window is the control button. The easiest and fastest way to exit any Windows program is to double-click this button. To use the menu to exit the program, choose **F**ile, **E**xit.

If you have saved the work that appears on-screen, the program terminates, and the Program Manager or File Manager window reappears. If you have not saved your work, 1-2-3 for Windows asks whether you want to save your work before exiting. Choosing **Y**es saves all active files that have names and then closes the program. (If the work on-screen has not been saved, the Save As dialog box appears.) Choosing **N**o closes the program and erases any work left on-screen.

Summary

To	Do This
Start 1-2-3 for Windows	Double-click the 1-2-3 for Windows icon in the Windows Program Manager
Save a file	Choose **F**ile, **S**ave
Open a file	Choose **F**ile, **O**pen
Close a file	Choose **F**ile, **C**lose
Get help	Choose **H**elp or press F1
Get help on a command	Start the command; then press F1
Exit 1-2-3 for Windows	Choose **F**ile, E**x**it

On Your Own

Estimated time: 10 minutes

1. Start 1-2-3 for Windows.

2. Save the blank worksheet on-screen with the name BLANK.

3. Close the file named BLANK.

4. Retrieve BLANK.WK4.

5. Create a new worksheet.

6. Suppress display of worksheet tabs; then redisplay them.

7. Enter the help feature, and get help for the **C**opy command.

Chapter 2

1-2-3 Release 4 for Windows Basics

Before you start entering data and formulas and executing commands, it makes sense to master the techniques for accomplishing those tasks. This chapter is a guide to performing basic activities in 1-2-3 for Windows.

This chapter covers the following topics:

- Executing commands
- Understanding the user interface (the way the menus, icons, and dialog boxes work)
- Canceling and undoing commands
- Selecting items in the worksheet
- Navigating the work area

Executing Commands

Command

An action represented by an item in a menu, a SmartIcon, or a section of the status bar.

You can use several methods to execute a *command* in 1-2-3 for Windows. You can access most commands with either the mouse or the keyboard. As you work with the program, you will discover that you don't use the keyboard or mouse exclusively; instead, you will use a combination of the two methods, depending on your working habits and the type of work you do. You will decide which method to use with each type of command as you grow more comfortable with the software and discover what works best for you.

Note: *We recommend that you get a mouse if you don't already have one. Windows products are designed for the mouse, and this book assumes that you have one. Many operations in Windows products in general and in 1-2-3 for Windows in particular are much easier and faster when you use a mouse.*

Because you can use many different methods to accomplish the same task, you could easily get confused if this book listed all possible methods of accomplishing every step of every task. For that reason, the primary method shown throughout the book will be menu commands, which you can access with either the mouse or the keyboard. When you can achieve significant time savings by using other methods—such as SmartIcons, shortcut menus, and function keys—the book will mention those methods too.

Undo is an example of a command that you can execute in several ways:

Method	Procedure
Menu command	Choose **E**dit, **U**ndo
SmartIcon	Click the Undo icon
Keyboard	Press Ctrl+Z shortcut or press Alt+Backspace

The method you find easiest is a matter of personal style or habit.

The next several sections discuss in detail how to use different methods of using commands.

Using the Menus

The primary way to access all the commands in 1-2-3 for Windows is through the menus. The menus are designed to be used with a mouse or the keyboard. If you use the mouse, click an item in the main menu. If you use the keyboard, press the Alt key and the underlined letter of the command you want.

Note: *The letters that are underlined in the menus are shown boldfaced in this book to make them easier to see.*

Note: *Use the Alt key with main-menu items and with dialog-box items that have underlined letters. Don't use the Alt key with items in drop-down or cascade menus.*

Drop-down menu

A menu of commands that appears to drop down from a menu item when that item is chosen. The drop-down menu enables you to make further choices about the action you want to perform.

Cascade menu

A list of options that appears when an item in a drop-down menu is chosen.

The main menu contains eight items, each of which relates to a specific area of commands in 1-2-3 for Windows. **F**ile, for example, contains commands for retrieving, printing, and saving worksheets; **V**iew is used to change the nature of the screen display.

At times, the main menu changes slightly. When you select a chart on-screen, for example, **R**ange is replaced by **C**hart.

Selecting main-menu items calls to the screen a *drop-down menu*. Choosing an item from a drop-down menu completes the action you want to perform or calls to the screen another series of options. These options appear in either a *cascade menu* or a *dialog box*. To choose a menu option from a cascade menu, click the option with the mouse or press the key corresponding to the option's underlined letter (without using the Alt key).

Note: *Dialog boxes are covered later in this chapter.*

Menu items that are followed by an ellipsis call a dialog box to the screen. Items with an arrowhead call a cascade menu to the screen.

The **R**ange drop-down menu.

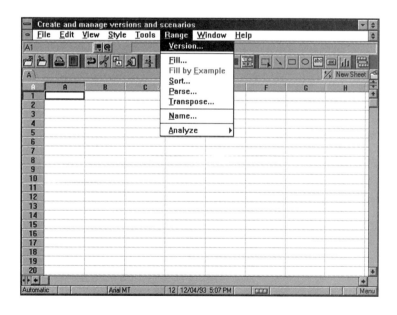

2

The **R**ange **A**nalyze menu, an example of a cascade menu.

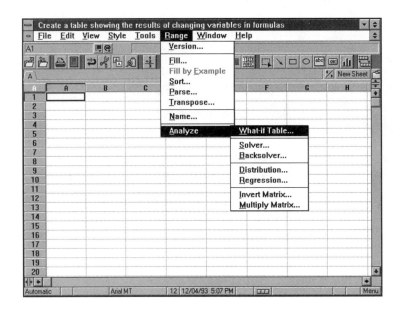

Using SmartIcons

Many common tasks are easier when you use the SmartIcon palette. Rather than remember a menu command or function key, all you have to do is click the SmartIcon. Some SmartIcons (such as Save, Cut, and Paste) execute a command immediately. Other SmartIcons (such as Open and Print) take you to the dialog box associated with the command, just as the command would.

To see a different SmartIcon palette:

Click the icon at the right end of the current palette. The next SmartIcon palette appears. Click the icon until the palette that you want to see appears.

or

Click the SmartIcons selector in the status bar, and then choose a SmartIcon palette from the list.

The SmartIcon palette list, called to the screen with the SmartIcons selector in the status bar.

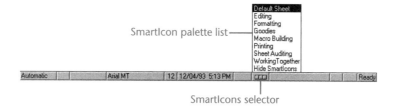

SmartIcon palette list

SmartIcons selector

2

Using Classic Menus

Many users of 1-2-3 for Windows may be familiar with the two so-called "classic menus," which contained commands for the DOS version of 1-2-3. One classic menu generally affects data and performance and is called to the screen when you press the slash key (/). The other classic menu generally affects the appearance of cells, adding such features as colors, lines, or fonts, and is called to the screen when you press the colon key (:).

The 1-2-3 classic menu.

You can perform most actions in the classic menus by using the techniques described in this chapter. Several items in those menus are obsolete, however, and you will want to perform many actions that you cannot access through a classic menu. Classic menus are mentioned here only for recent converts to the Windows environment from DOS who occasionally might prefer to use methods that have become second nature to them. We do not recommend that users new to 1-2-3 for Windows use the classic menus.

Using Quick Menus

Quick menu

A menu, called to the screen with the right mouse button, that contains commands relating to whatever object is selected.

Normally, you make choices by clicking an item with the left mouse button. When various screen objects are selected, the right mouse button calls to the screen a menu containing commands for the selected object. This *quick menu* contains the commands that most commonly are performed on that object. If, for example, you select a chart and then press the right mouse button, a quick menu appears, displaying commands that you can use in charts. If you select a range of cells and then click the right mouse button, a different quick menu appears.

The quick menu associated with a range of cells.

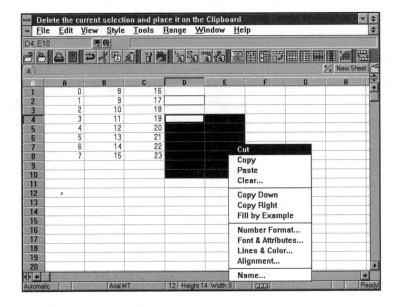

Using the Status Bar

The status bar across the bottom of the screen has several sections that contain information about the current cell. You can use these sections to change the characteristic reflected in that section. In the following figure, the status bar was used to change the number format in the selected range.

Using the status bar to make changes in the selected range.

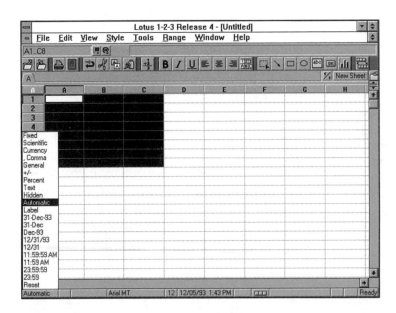

Note: Although menus are useful and icons are fast, the fastest way to make many changes is to use the status bar.

Using Function Keys

The function keys labeled F1 through F10 perform specific functions in 1-2-3 for Windows. In some cases, these keys duplicate commands and actions that are available through the menus and SmartIcons. Whenever a particular function key is useful for performing a certain task, this book will mention the key.

Note: One of the advantages of 1-2-3 for Windows is that you do not need to memorize function keys or worry about losing the function-key template for your keyboard. With the menu commands, you can use function keys as you see fit.

Using Keyboard Shortcuts

Keyboard shortcuts are keystrokes or combinations of keystrokes that you can use to execute certain commands without using a menu. When you choose a menu item, the keyboard accelerators appear in the drop-down menu as a reminder. If you want to undo your last action, for example, you might choose **Edit**, **Undo**. Notice that next to **Undo** in the **Edit** menu is the keyboard shortcut: Ctrl+Z.

If you have problems...

A plus sign between the names of two keys, as in Ctrl+Z, means that you must press both keys at the same time. The correct way to press two keys is to press the first key (Ctrl) and hold it down while you tap the second key (Z). If you poise both hands above the keyboard and drop them onto the proper keys at the same time, the finger aimed at the Z key might get there first, in which case you would type a Z on-screen instead of calling up the **U**ndo command.

Note: The menu in 1-2-3 for Windows shows the keyboard shortcut for Insert as Ctrl + and for Delete as Ctrl –. The correct way to show the combination is Ctrl++ and Ctrl+–.

Working in Dialog Boxes

Dialog boxes
Framed areas that appear when you choose certain menu items, containing options for making further menu choices.

Regardless of which method you use to start them, many commands open *dialog boxes*. To make changes in a dialog box and, therefore, in a 1-2-3 for Windows worksheet, you need to understand how dialog boxes work.

The following figures show typical dialog boxes.

The **S**tyle, **A**lignment dialog box, with several common dialog-box elements.

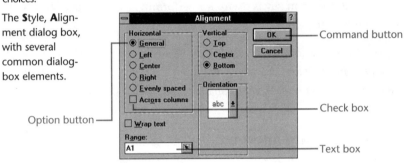

Option button

Command button

Check box

Text box

The **S**tyle, **F**ont & Attributes dialog box, with other elements of dialog boxes.

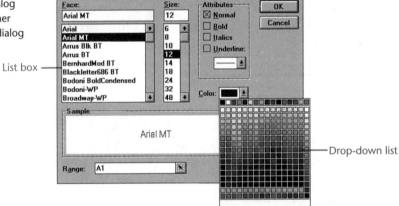

List box

Drop-down list

When a dialog box appears, you can:

- *Choose only one option button in each group.* A dot in the middle indicates that the item is selected.

- *Choose any and all check boxes.* An X in the box means that the item it represents is selected.

- *Type text in a text box.* In a **R**ange text box, for example, you can type the cell addresses of the range you want to select, or you can click the arrow next to the box and then select the range in the worksheet.

- *Click a command button.* Choosing OK puts all your choices into effect and dismisses the dialog box. Choosing Close or Cancel dismisses the dialog box without making any of the changes that you chose.

- *Highlight an item.* Highlighting an item in a list box or drop-down list box selects that item.

2

Changing Your Mind about Commands

The time will come when you choose a command and then realize that your choice is not what you intended. You also might complete an action and then realize that you did the wrong thing. In the first case, you need to cancel the command; in the latter case, you need to undo what you did.

Canceling a Command

You can stop a command in several ways:

- When a drop-down or cascade menu is on-screen, simply click anywhere in the worksheet area away from the menu. This action returns the program's focus to the worksheet and dismisses the menu. Keep in mind that the cell that you click becomes the new active cell.

- When a dialog box is on-screen, click the Cancel or Close button once, or double-click the *Control menu box* (the minus sign in the top left corner of the dialog box). The dialog box closes, and 1-2-3 for Windows ignores any selections you made in the dialog box. If several dialog boxes are on-screen, you must close each of them individually.

- When a dialog box is on-screen, use the Ctrl+Break keystroke. Hold down the Ctrl key, and then tap the Break key (the word *Break* usually appears on the side of the Pause key). All dialog boxes and menus close, and the program's focus returns to the current worksheet.

- Press Esc once per menu level. For example, **R**ange **A**nalyze requires three Esc keystrokes.

Undoing a Command

You can undo many—but not all—commands and actions, and you can use several methods to undo an event.

 The first method is to click the Undo SmartIcon. (Because you often will want to undo an action, Undo appears in every SmartIcon palette.)

Another way to undo an action is to choose **E**dit, **U**ndo from the main menu. You also can use either of two keyboard shortcuts: Ctrl+Z and Alt+Backspace.

Note: *You can use the* **U***ndo command only once at any given time. You cannot undo an action and then reverse the undo operation.*

If you have problems...

You might notice that the word *Undo* in the **E**dit menu occasionally is grayed out, meaning that the command temporarily is inactive. **U**ndo becomes inactive when the most recent command is one that cannot be undone or when you have just used **U**ndo. Because you can use **U**ndo only once after you perform an action, the command becomes inactive until you perform another action.

Caution

If **U**ndo doesn't always work for you, remember that the command undoes only the last action you performed. Use the command immediately if you make a mistake.

Several actions cannot be undone. You cannot, for example, undo a print command; once the paper is moving through the printer, the **U**ndo command is useless. Other actions that cannot be undone are:

- The commands associated with charts

- The menus associated with Control menu boxes (the minus sign in the top left corner of a window)

- **F**ile, **S**ave and **F**ile, Save **A**s operations

- Commands that affect a source of data external to 1-2-3 to Windows

- Formula recalculations

- Cell-pointer movements

- Window-scrolling commands

- A previous **U**ndo operation

Making Selections

Selecting
Designating an item on-screen. You select an item so that you can perform some action on it. Sometimes the term *highlighting* is used instead of selecting.

The method of performing commands in Windows usually involves *selecting* the object to be affected and then executing the command. An example is copying a group of cells to the Clipboard; you first select the cells to be copied and then execute the **C**opy command. The contents of the cells are copied to the Clipboard, ready to be pasted elsewhere.

The way you select an item depends on the item, as shown in the following list:

- *Cell.* To select a cell, go to the cell.

Shift+clicking
Holding down the Shift key while clicking the left mouse button.

- *Range.* To select a range with the mouse, click and drag the mouse pointer from one corner of the range to the other, and then release the mouse button. An alternative method is to place the cell pointer at one end of the range, scroll to the opposite corner (without moving the cell pointer), and then *Shift+click* the opposite corner of the range.

A blank worksheet with the range B5..E17 selected.

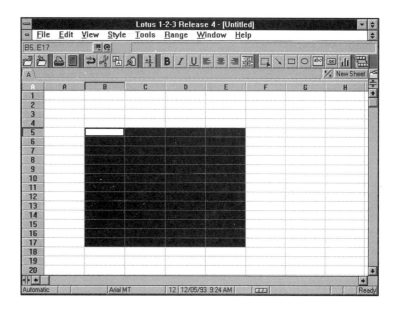

3-D range
A selected range that extends across several worksheets. In the range A:C1..B:F10, A and B refer to the worksheets.

- *3-D range.* To select a 3-D range, select the range in the first worksheet and then Shift+click the tab of the last worksheet in which the range falls. If you select cells A1 to B5 in worksheet A and then Shift+click the tab of worksheet C, for example, you high-light cells A1 to B5 in worksheets A, B, and C. (If you don't hold down the Shift key, you cancel the selection.)

A worksheet with a
selected range.

The worksheet names in
the selected range indicate
that a 3-D range is selected

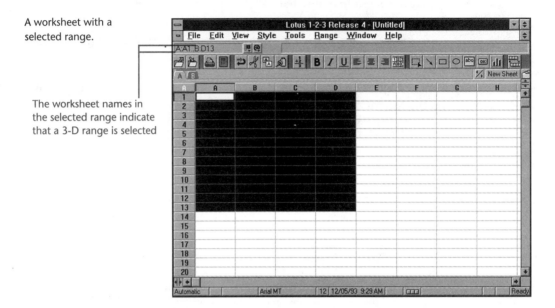

- *Column or row*. To select a column or row, click the column letter or row number in the worksheet frame.

- *Worksheet*. To select an entire worksheet, click the letter in the corner of the worksheet frame.

- *Collection*. The capability to select a *collection*—a group of ranges—is a new feature of 1-2-3 Release 4 for Windows. In earlier versions of the program, you can select only one range at a time. Release 4 enables you to select several ranges and then execute a command (or a series of commands) that affects all cells in the collection.

To select a collection:

1. Select the first cell or range.

2. Hold down the Ctrl key while making additional selections of worksheets, rows, columns, cells, or ranges with the mouse.

When you select a collection, you can perform most commands on all the items in that collection. Certain commands, such as **R**ange, **F**ill, do not work with collections.

A worksheet with a collection selected.

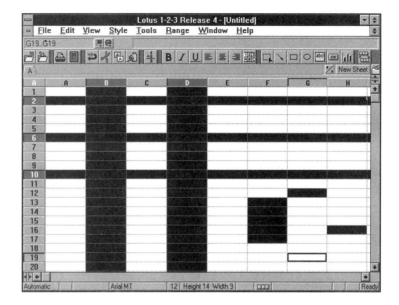

Navigating the Worksheet

Navigating means moving the cell pointer to another location. You normally move the cell pointer by pressing the arrow key for the direction in which you want the pointer to move.

If you have problems...

Most keyboards contain two sets of keys that move the cell pointer: the gray arrow keys, which always move the cell pointer; and the numeric-keypad arrow keys, which perform two functions. If the Num Lock key is pressed, the numeric-keypad arrow keys enter numbers; if Num Lock is not pressed, you can use those keys to move the cell pointer.

If you want to use the numeric keypad to move the cell pointer, make sure that Num Lock is off.

For small moves, using an arrow key makes perfect sense. If you want to move the pointer 200 cells to the right, however, pressing the right-arrow key 199 times would be a huge waste of time. For larger moves, you can use the keystrokes listed in Table 2.1.

Table 2.1 Cell-Pointer Keystrokes	
Keystroke	**Destination**
Arrow key	One cell in the direction of the arrow
Tab or Ctrl+right arrow	One screen to the right
Shift+Tab or Ctrl+left arrow	One screen to the left
PgUp	One screen up
PgDn	One screen down
Home	Cell A1 of the current worksheet
Ctrl+PgUp	The following worksheet
Ctrl+PgDn	The preceding worksheet
Ctrl+Home	Cell A:A1 of the first worksheet of the current file

The fastest way to move the cell pointer to a distant cell is to use the **G**o To command. You can use this command to go to any cell, named range, or object in a worksheet.

To use this command:

1. Choose **E**dit, **G**o To, or press F5. The Go To dialog box appears.

2. To go to a cell or range, type the cell reference in the text box below the **T**ype of Item drop-down list.

   To go to a chart, object, or query table, select that type of item in the **T**ype of Item drop-down list; then type the name of the object in the text box below that list or select the name of the object in the list box below the text box.

Use the **T**ype of Item list box to go to charts, drawn objects, or charts that are in an open file.

3. Choose OK. The selection indicator moves to the cell, range, or object that you entered in the Go To dialog box, and that item is selected.

Summary

To	Do This
See a different SmartIcon palette	Click the SmartIcon palette list icon in the status bar; then click the name of the palette you want
Execute a menu command	Click the menu item or press Alt+the underlined letter
See the quick menu for a selected item	Select the item and then press the right mouse button
Escape from a menu	Press Esc
Dismiss a dialog box	Press Ctrl+Break or click the Cancel button
Undo a mistake	Click the Undo SmartIcon
Select a range	Click and drag across the cells in the range
Select a collection	Select the first range in the collection; then select subsequent ranges while holding down the Ctrl key

On Your Own

Estimated time: 5 minutes

1. Display the Editing SmartIcon palette.

2. Select a range and call the quick menu for the range to the screen.

3. Select a menu item and then escape from the menu.

4. Call the **S**tyle, **F**ont & Attributes dialog box to the screen and then dismiss it.

5. Enter your name in a cell, and then undo that entry.

6. Select a collection consisting of a cell, a row, a column, and a range.

Part II
Building Worksheets

Chapter 3

Building a Worksheet

Having mastered the basics and gotten a feel for the way 1-2-3 for Windows works, the time has come for you to learn how to put meaningful data in worksheets.

This chapter discusses the types of cell entries and techniques for entering them, and then explores ways to change the way the program looks to meet your needs and preferences.

This chapter covers the following topics:

- Planning the layout of a worksheet

- Understanding the difference between labels and values

- Understanding the techniques for writing formulas

- Changing the appearance of the screen

- Changing the appearance of parts of the screen

Planning the Layout

Before you start to enter data into your worksheet, plan the arrangement of that data. Plan for the eventual addition of charts, more data, or additional types of data.

Also decide how your audience will see the material. If the material is to be printed for distribution, arrange the data so that you can place page breaks in logical places. If the material is to be viewed on-screen, make sure that all relevant data is visible or logically arranged so that each screen of data is complete.

Naturally, you can insert columns and rows; you also can move and copy data. Sometimes, however, moving data corrupts formulas, and rearranging data might be more confusing than planning its initial placement.

Entering Data

The most important task you will perform in 1-2-3 for Windows is entering data into cells. This task is simple, but because you can enter data in several ways—and also enter several types of data—the information in this section of the chapter is important.

Following is the simplest way to enter data into a cell:

1. Place the cell pointer on the cell where you want to enter the data.

2. Type the cell entry, using the Backspace key as necessary to correct mistakes.

3. When the entry is correct, press Enter or a directional arrow key to complete the data entry in that cell.

  When you start to type or edit a cell entry, two new icons appear in the edit line: a checkmark and an X. Clicking the X cancels the edit or the entry and leaves the current cell contents unchanged. Clicking the checkmark enters the new or edited contents into the cell.

Note: *Pressing the Enter key or clicking the checkmark icon places the typed data in the cell and leaves the cell pointer right where it is. Pressing an arrow key enters the data and moves the cell pointer to the next cell in which you want to enter data. This action performs the dual function of entering the text and moving the cell pointer.*

 If you are typing data in a cell and decide not to enter that data, press Esc to terminate the creation of the data without entering it into the cell.

Understanding Types of Data

Values
Cell entries that show only numbers.

Labels
Cell entries that can include any combination of letters and numbers.

The data that you enter into cells can be any of three types: *values, labels,* and *formulas*.

Following is a list of the differences between values and labels:

■ Labels can spill out of a cell to the right as far as necessary to display everything you type. A value must fill a cell left to right. If a

Formulas
Cell entries that process data, often from other cells, and return an answer.

value is too big for the cell, the entire value appears as asterisks if the number format is not set to Scientific or Automatic.

- Labels can be anything that you type. Values must be formulas or numbers (not numbers followed by letters).

- You can use values in numerical formulas; you cannot use labels, which have a value of zero.

- If something appears in a cell to the right of a long label, only part of the label will be visible. By contrast, you either see all of a value, or you see asterisks.

- Values can be numerically formatted; labels cannot.

The moment you type a letter or one of these symbols—' " ^ or \— the cell entry becomes a label. By the same token, the moment you type a number or one of these symbols— + – (@ # . or $—the cell entry becomes a value.

Creating a Cell Entry

Cursor
The vertical bar that appears when you are creating or editing a cell entry and that shows where the character will be added or deleted.

To create a cell entry, simply start typing. As you type, notice that the characters you type appear in two places: the edit line near the top of the 1-2-3 for Windows screen, and in the cell where the cell pointer is located.

If you make a typographical error, use the Backspace key to move the *cursor* to the left, erasing the mistake; then type the correct characters.

As you enter data, you may discover that the cell pointer is in the wrong cell. If the cell where the pointer is located already contains data, be careful not to press Enter; if you do, the new data will replace the old. To stop typing a cell entry in the wrong place, press Esc.

Using Bound Boxes

Caution
Do not use the arrow keys to move around the text while you type a new cell entry. If you press any of these keys, 1-2-3 for Win-dows deposits the typed text in the cell and moves the cell pointer to an-other cell (if possible).

A *bound box* is a preselected range into which you intend to enter data.

To enter data into a bound box:

1. Create a bound box by selecting the range into which you want to enter the data.

2. Type the cell entries, pressing Enter after each entry. Pressing Enter moves the cell pointer to the next cell in the range and enters the data into the preceding cell.

A bound box—
A1..A7—into which
you enter data one
cell at a time,
pressing Enter after
each cell entry.

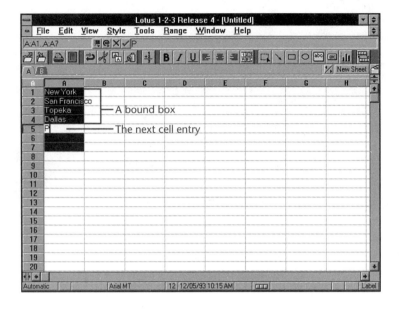

3. Press any arrow key to deselect the bound box.

Filling a Range by Example

A new feature in 1-2-3 Release 4 for Windows is the Fill by **E**xample command, which enables you to fill a range with data in a series.

Another way to use Fill by **E**xample is to type numbers in two cells to establish a sequence, and then use Fill by **E**xample to extend the sequence to more cells. For example, if you enter **10** in one cell and **20** in the next cell, and then choose **R**ange, Fill by **E**xample, the highlighted range will contain 10, 20, 30, 40, and so on.

Note: *The command uses only the first two cells to establish the sequence. If you enter data in more than two cells, Fill by **E**xample overwrites the additional data.*

The simplest example of a series is a series of numbers. But 1-2-3 for Windows also recognizes months, letters, text with numbers, financial quarters, and days of the week as series.

In each column is a different example of filling by example.

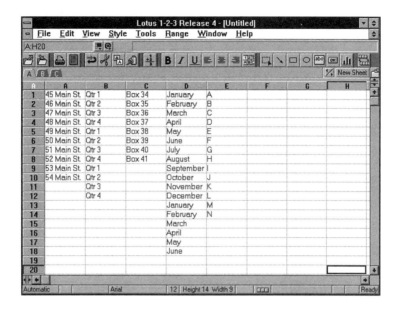

To use the Fill by **E**xample command:

1. Type the first item of a series in the first cell of the range to be filled.

2. Select a range that includes the cell in which you typed the entry and all empty cells to be filled.

Choose Fill by **E**xample to put the next dates in the highlighted cells.

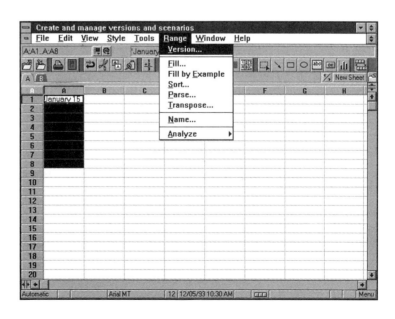

3. Choose **R**ange, Fill by **E**xample.

The result of
choosing Fill by
Example.

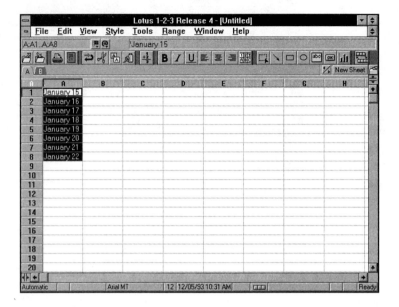

Cell entries that you can use for filling by example include months; days
of the week; and entries such as Quarter 1, Box 95, or 45 Main Street.

Chapter 12, "Customizing 1-2-3 for Windows," contains information
on how to create your own series, such as lists of employees or branch
offices.

Filling a Range

To fill designated cells with numbers, starting and ending with numbers
that you specify and at intervals that you determine, use **R**ange, **F**ill.

To fill a range with a series of values:

1. Select the range.

2. Choose **R**ange, **F**ill. The Fill dialog box appears.

The Fill dialog box.

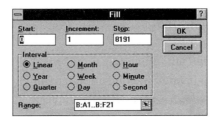

3. Enter the **S**tart number, the **I**ncrement value, and a St**o**p value at least as high as the highest number you want to enter into cells.

4. If necessary, select an interval choice.

5. Choose OK.

The result of a data fill with a **S**tart value of 10 and an **I**ncrement value of 10.

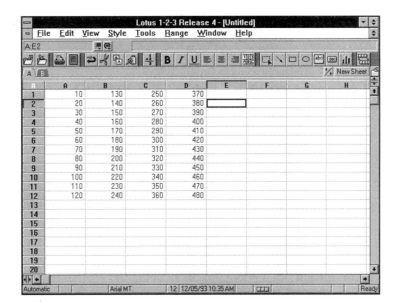

The **S**tart number is the smallest number in the numerical series to be entered. This number will appear in the top-left-corner cell of the high-lighted range.

The **I**ncrement number is the difference between successive numbers in the series. If you are counting from 1 to 10, naming every number, the increment is 1. If you are counting by twos, however, the increment is 2. If you are counting by halves, the increment is .5.

The Stop number is any number at least as high as the highest value you want to use in the range. Play it safe; use a high Stop number to ensure that the range is filled.

The interval is **L**inear by default. Changing the interval enables you to place dates or times in the designated range. Choosing **M**onth, for example, increments cell entries by one month. You could start with *Jan-94* and fill subsequent cells with *Feb-94, Mar-94,* and so on until all designated cells are filled.

Entering Formulas

Perhaps the most useful aspect of 1-2-3 for Windows is its capability to use formulas. A worksheet full of data would be of little use without built-in ways to calculate the significance of the data.

Chapter 6, "Using Basic Functions," contains information specific to functions (a type of formula). This section covers the basic skills and facts necessary to create valid formulas.

All formulas involve some of the following basic elements, the same way that an arithmetic problem does. Those elements include:

- *Operators*, which are symbols representing the arithmetic operation you want the formula to perform. Operators are + (addition), – (subtraction), * (multiplication), / (division), and ^ (exponentiation).

- The data or cells containing the data to be used in the calculation.

- In the case of functions, the @ symbol and the name of the function (for example, @SUM). For more information about functions, see Chapter 6, "Using Basic Functions."

- The *argument*, which is the information that the function will use.

The two major types of formulas are *numeric* and *string*. A numeric formula returns a value; a string formula returns a label, possibly a *concatenation* (chain) of labels from several cells.

These formulas— two numeric and one string—show both the formulas and the answers.

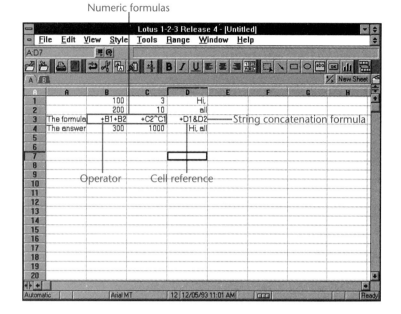

Numeric formulas

Understanding the Do's and Don'ts of Formula Writing

Some formulas are good; others are bad. To avoid writing a bad one:

- Place the cell pointer in the cell where you want the answer to appear. One of the most common mistakes people make in writing formulas is overlooking the need to position the cell pointer first.

- Don't use numbers in a formula if you can avoid it; use cell addresses instead. This concept (explained in the following section) is the most important rule in writing formulas.

- Don't do math in your head. The reason for letting 1-2-3 for Windows do the math is related to the reason why you should use cell addresses in formulas (explained in the following section).

- When a formula must start with a letter, use a plus sign (+) or equal sign (=) as the first character to trick 1-2-3 for Windows into thinking that the formula is a value. Otherwise, the program mistakes the formula for a label and places the formula, rather than its result, in the cell.

■ Don't use spaces in formulas. A formula may automatically turn into a label if you include spaces.

Understanding How Formulas Work

If you enter **100** in cell A1 and **200** in cell A2, you should use the formula +A1+A2, rather than 100+200, in cell A3. Changing the contents of A1 from 100 to 500 will be reflected in the formula that uses cell addresses (+A1+A2); the change will not be reflected in the formula that adds cell contents (100+200).

If you have problems...

If you entered exactly those characters—A1+A2—in cell A3, you probably were disappointed to see A1+A2 in the cell. You forgot to start a formula whose first character is a letter with a plus sign or an equal sign. Either symbol tricks 1-2-3 for Windows into thinking that you typed a value, and the text works as a valid formula.

Now change the number in either cell A1 and A2, or change the numbers in both. The formula in A3 returns the proper answer. If you do the math in your head, enter the result in a cell, and then change data in the worksheet, you must manually change every cell that should compute that number—a ridiculous waste of time.

Using Pointing in Formulas

Pointing

Moving the cell pointer to designate a cell or range during the writing of a formula or the execution of a command.

Although you can write a formula by typing every character, there is an alternative, known as *pointing*.

To write cell references in a formula by pointing:

1. Place the cell pointer in the cell in which you are writing the formula.

2. Begin typing the formula, starting with a plus sign (+), an equal sign (=), or the @ symbol followed by a function name.

3. Move the cell pointer to the cell you want to reference, and then press an operator (=, –, *, /, and so on).

4. Repeat step 3 for any additional cells you want to reference.

5. Press Enter.

As you move the cell pointer during the writing of the formula, the cell address of the current location of the cell pointer is included in the formula.

Making Display Changes

You can change the way you view your work in many ways. These changes don't affect the contents or the format of the worksheet—only what you see on-screen. Ways to change the worksheet and the format of the worksheet are covered in Chapter 4, "Modifying Data in a Worksheet," and Chapter 5, "Changing the Appearance of a Worksheet."

Making Permanent Display Changes

Three changes that you can make in the screen affect all files that you open thereafter and remain in effect when you exit and restart 1-2-3 for Windows. These changes are suppressing the display of the SmartIcons palette, the edit line, or the status bar. The main reason to suppress these parts of the screen is to gain additional space for displaying data.

To change the appearance of the screen for all files:

1. Choose **V**iew, Set View **P**references. The Set View Preferences dialog box appears.

   The options at the top of this dialog box affect the current file; changes you make here remain in effect if you save and reopen the file. The options at the bottom affect 1-2-3 for Windows defaults for all files; changes you make here remain in effect when you exit and restart the program.

The Set View Preferences dialog box.

The preferences in this box are for the current file only

The preferences in this box are for all files

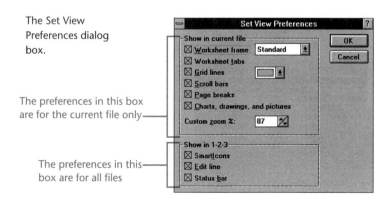

2. Select or deselect Smart**I**cons, **E**dit Line, or Status **B**ar to display or suppress these elements. (By default, all three elements are displayed.)

3. When you finish making selections, choose OK.

A 1-2-3 for Windows screen with display of the SmartIcons palette, the edit line, and the status bar suppressed.

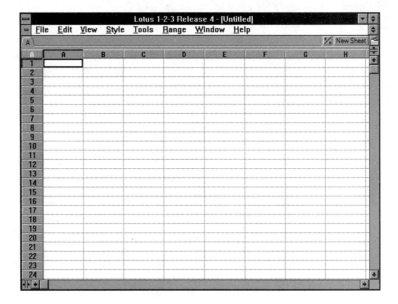

Changing the Appearance of the Current File

The top of the Set View Preferences dialog box contains options for changes that will appear in the current file even if you exit 1-2-3 for Windows and restart it later. The changes will be visible only in the current file. The pertinent options are:

■ *Worksheet Frame.* This option enables you to change the appearance of the area containing the row numbers and column letters, or to suppress display of the frame altogether.

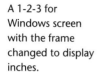

A 1-2-3 for
Windows screen
with the frame
changed to display
inches.

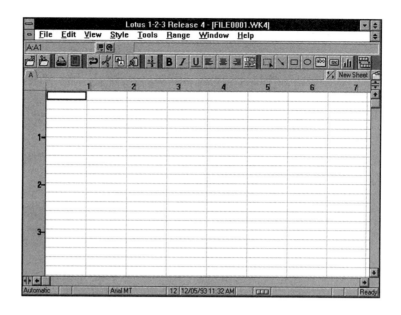

To suppress display of the frame, click the check box next to the
frame option to remove the X.

■ *Worksheet **T**abs.* Tabs, which normally contain letters, are visible
above each worksheet in a file. Clicking to remove the X in the
check box suppresses display of the tabs.

Note: *You probably will find it much faster to click the icon at the
right end of the tab line to suppress the display of worksheet tabs.*

■ *Grid Lines.* Grid lines are dotted vertical and horizontal lines that
are visible on-screen but not in printouts. Although grid lines give
you a clear idea of the limits of each cell, row, and column, they
can interfere with the display of data.

■ *Scroll Bars.* Scroll bars, which appear at the right and at the bottom
of the screen, enable you to move the focus of the screen. Suppressing their display gives you more worksheet area. If you don't have a
mouse, scroll bars are useless, so you might as well suppress them.

■ *P**age Breaks.* Page breaks normally appear on-screen as dotted lines.
If you plan to present your work on-screen rather than as a printout, the display of any page breaks that you inserted for later printing may be distracting.

■ *Charts, Drawings, and Pictures.* These elements are displayed by default. Aside from simply not wanting these elements to be visible, the main reason for suppressing display of graphic elements is to speed the performance of 1-2-3 for Windows. In slow or low-memory computers, redrawing the screen after data changes may take a long time. Suppressing display of charts makes redrawing charts unnecessary when you are entering large amounts of new data.

■ *Custom **Zoom** %.* This option permits you to enter settings ranging from 25 to 400 percent. The setting reflects the size of the display relative to its appearance when it is printed. Zoom does not affect the size of the printed data, only the screen display. This option is especially handy for users with failing eyesight who like to increase the size of the display. To change the zoom size, type a percentage number, or click the up or down arrowhead to increase or decrease the number.

Note: *Changing the zoom percentage does not affect the size of the printout.*

A 1-2-3 for Windows screen with 400 percent zoom.

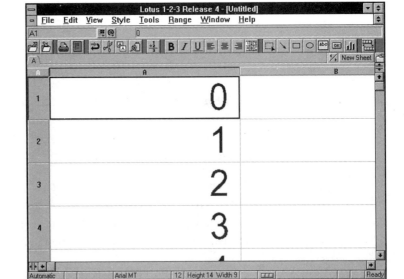

When you finish choosing options in the Set View Preferences dialog box, be sure to choose OK to confirm your changes. Choosing Cancel returns you to the preceding display.

Summary

To	Do This
Enter data into a cell	Type the data; then press Enter or an arrow key
Enter data in a bound box	Select a range; then type entries, pressing Enter after each entry
Fill a range with items in a series	Type the first entry; select a range including the first item; choose **R**ange, Fill by **E**xample
Fill a range with numbers	Select a range; choose **R**ange, **F**ill; and designate **S**tart, **I**ncrement, and St**o**p values
Change the appearance of the 1-2-3 for Windows screen	Choose **V**iew, Set View **P**references; change the last three items in the dialog box

On Your Own
Estimated time: 15 minutes

1. Enter the name **George Washington** in a cell.

2. Change the entry to **G. Washington**.

3. Select a range, and make it a bound box by entering a list of six people you know.

4. Enter **Room 205** in a cell, and then use the Fill by **E**xample command to fill nine more cells.

5. Fill a range with odd numbers, starting with 25.

6. Write a formula that adds some of those numbers.

7. Suppress display of the worksheet grid.

8. Change the zoom percentage to 125.

Chapter 4

Modifying Data in a Worksheet

You now know how to navigate; select; use the menus; and enter labels, values, and formulas. If that's all you need to know, you're finished reading this book. But if you need to know how to correct typing mistakes, fix formulas, or improve the appearance of your work on-screen, this chapter and the next one are important. This chapter deals with making changes in data and in the display of that data; the next chapter deals with making changes in the appearance of the worksheet and the data.

Specific topics covered in this chapter:

- Editing cell contents, including values, labels, and formulas
- Copying, moving, and deleting data
- Finding and replacing text in a worksheet
- Using the spell checker
- Widening and narrowing rows and columns
- Inserting and deleting rows and columns

Editing Cell Contents

When you notice that a cell's contents are wrong, misspelled, or inaccurate, you need to make a change. You can change cell contents by retyping the cell entry, thereby replacing the old contents. Often, however, retyping a cell entry takes longer than correcting the mistake. In such a case, you should edit the cell contents.

To correct a few characters in one cell entry:

1. Move to the cell that contains the mistake.

2. Enter Edit mode by double-clicking the cell or pressing F2.

3. The cell contents now are visible in the contents box in the edit line. You can edit the entry either in the cell or in the contents box.

   Use the contents box when only part of the entry is visible in the cell and you would have to scroll to bring more of the entry into view.

I-beam

The shape that the mouse pointer takes when 1-2-3 for Windows is in Edit mode. Clicking the I-beam at a position in the cell contents places the cursor at that position.

4. At the end of the cell entry is the blinking cursor. Move the cursor to the place in the entry you want to edit by pressing the left-arrow key. You also can use the mouse pointer, which changes in Edit mode to an *I-beam*. Click the place in the cell contents where you want to make a change. To select an entire word, double-click the word.

Note: *If you have difficulty seeing the text you want to edit in the worksheet area, you can use the I-beam to position the cursor in the cell contents box in the edit line.*

Editing a cell with a
long entry is easier
in the edit line.

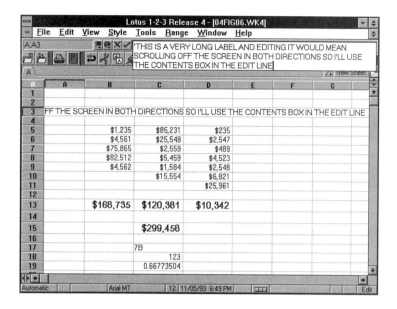

5. Press Del to erase the character at the insertion point or Backspace
to erase the character to the left of the insertion point. To delete an
entire selected word, press Del.

**If you have
problems...**

If you are deleting characters when you move to the left, you're using the
wrong key. To move the insertion point to the left, use the left-arrow key;
if you use the Backspace key, you delete all the characters as you backspace.
Also be careful of the way you use the Ctrl key. Ctrl+left arrow moves the
insertion point left one word at a time, but Ctrl+Backspace deletes the entire
word to the left of the insertion point.

6. With the insertion point at the place where you made a mistake,
correct the mistake.

7. To enter the corrected text into the cell, click another cell or the
checkmark icon, or press Enter.

Table 4.1 Editing Keystrokes	
Keystroke	**Action**
Left or right arrow	Moves insertion point one character to right or left
Up or down arrow	Completes edit and moves cell pointer up or down one cell
Backspace	Deletes character to left of insertion point
Del	Deletes character at insertion point
Ctrl+right or left arrow	Moves insertion point one word to left or right
Home	Moves insertion point to beginning of cell entry
End	Moves insertion point to end of cell entry
Esc	Clears entire entry from edit line
Esc, Esc	Returns to Ready mode without changing the current entry in the cell

Editing Formulas

A formula that is incorrectly written returns either ERR or a wrong answer. To rewrite a formula, go to the cell and type the new formula. You also can edit a formula (using the techniques described in the preceding section) rather than type it over again.

Understanding Absolute Cell References

In the following worksheet, C2 contains the amount of tax to be taken from the salaries: 10 percent. The formula +B4*C2 is in cell C4, and the amount is correct. But that is the only correct amount in column C.

Using absolute cell references in the tax formulas will correct the problem in this worksheet.

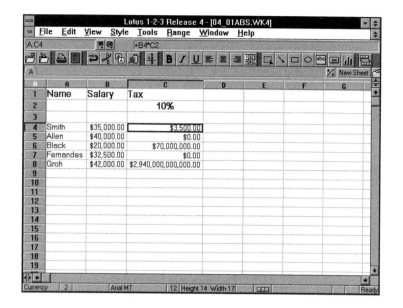

To understand the error, you must understand the concept of cell referencing. The formula entered into cell C4 multiplies the contents of B4 by the contents of C2. To the program, the formula says, "Get the contents from one cell to the left; multiply it by the contents from two cells above." Instead of referring to specific cells, the formula refers to cells *relative* to the formula's current position.

Relative cell reference

A formula, copied to a new location, that refers to the same cells relative to the new location as it did in the old location.

Copying a formula copies these *relative cell references* to other cells. Wherever the formula lands, it uses the values in the cell to the left and the values in the two cells above. The problem begins when you copy the formula from C4 to C5. The formula in C5 still looks one cell to the left for the salary and looks two cells up to multiply that figure by the tax percentage. Two cells up is an empty cell, so the tax figure is 0.

Note: *Copying data from one or more cells to other cells is explained later in this chapter.*

When the formula is copied to C8, it is still looking to the left for the salary and two cells up for the tax rate. The number two cells up is 70,000,000.

The solution lies in the way the original formula—+B4*C2—was written in cell C4. The tendency of the formula to look one cell to the left is fine; that should be a relative cell reference. The reference to cell C2, however, should not be relative; it should be an *absolute cell reference*. Dollar signs in a cell reference indicate that the cell reference is absolute. No matter where the formula is copied, it always will refer specifically to cell C2.

To make an existing cell reference absolute instead of relative:

1. Enter Edit mode.

2. Move the insertion point to the cell reference that you want to make absolute.

3. Press F4. Dollar signs appear in the cell reference, indicating that the reference now is absolute.

4. Continue pressing F4 to create a *mixed reference*.

5. Copy the corrected formula to other cells, as necessary.

6. Press Enter to complete the edit.

Absolute cell reference

A cell reference in a formula that refers to the same cell regardless of the place to which the formula is copied. Dollar signs before the worksheet letter, column letter, and row number make the reference absolute.

Mixed reference

A cell reference that is part absolute and part relative. $A1 means that the column reference is absolute, but the row number, 1, is relative.

Changing the reference to C2 from relative to absolute and then copying it to cells C5 through C8 corrected the problem of the incorrect tax amounts.

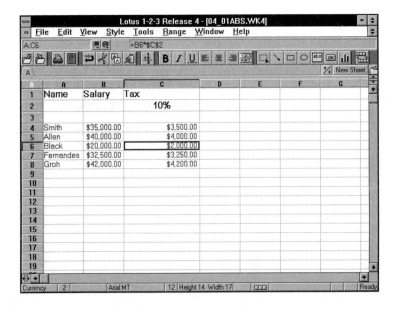

Eliminating Circular Cell References

Circular formula
A formula that includes a reference to the cell in which the formula was entered.

Whenever a *circular formula* exists anywhere in a worksheet, the word Circ appears near the right end of the status line. The word stays there regardless of which cell is the active cell, because a circular formula quickly returns a grossly inaccurate answer.

To understand a circular reference, look at the following figure. The cell pointer is in the cell that contains the circular formula. Notice that the formula (shown in the edit line) adds the three numbers above it but also includes its own cell. When you first enter the formula into a cell, the answer is correct. But whenever you enter or delete data anywhere in the worksheet, or whenever you execute a command, the formula recalculates, and the answer changes to add the current amount in the cell to itself. The more changes you make in the worksheet, the more inaccurate the answer becomes.

The result of writing a circular cell reference in a formula.

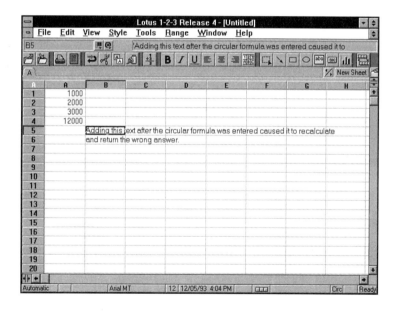

To remove a circular cell reference:

1. Click the word Circ in the status line. The cell pointer moves to the first cell that contains a circular formula.

2. Press F2 or double-click the cell to enter Edit mode.

3. Delete from the formula the reference to the current cell, and then change the formula so that it references the correct cell.

4. If you copied the formula to other cells, `Circ` will remain in the status line until you correct all circular formulas. Continue to click `Circ` and to delete circular references from all formulas.

Working with Precedence

Precedence

The order in which a formula performs mathematical operations.

Formulas in 1-2-3 for Windows do not always perform the functions from left to right. When a formula contains two or more mathematical operations, the program executes those operations in a specific sequence called the order of *precedence*. The program performs multiplication first, followed by division, addition, and subtraction.

The formula shown in the following figure did not take the rules of precedence into account. The formula first multiplied the tips amount—$50.00—by 10 percent and then added the salary figure to that amount. As a result, the tax is much too high.

The tax is much too high because the formula did not consider rules of precedence.

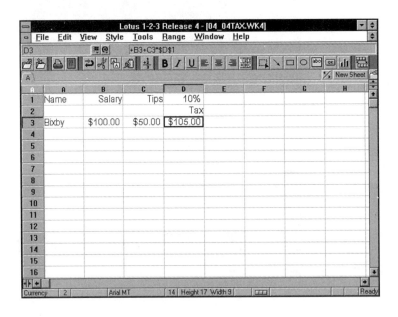

To force the formula to add the salary and the tip, and then multiply the result by the tax rate, put parentheses around the operation that you want 1-2-3 for Windows to perform first—in this case, the addition. The corrected formula is (+B3+C3)*D3. (The reference is absolute so that you can copy it to other cells.)

Table 4.2 Order of Precedence for Mathematical Operators in Formulas		
Operator	**Operation**	**Precedence**
^	Exponentiation	1
– +	Negative, positive value	2
* /	Multiplication, division	3
+ –	Addition, subtraction	4
= < >	Equal, not equal to	5
< >	Less than, greater than	5
<=	Less than or equal to	5
=>	Greater than or equal to	5
#NOT#	Logical NOT	6
#AND# #OR#	Logical AND, logical OR	7
&	String concatenation	7

Copying, Moving, and Clearing Data

When you enter data and then decide to place it somewhere else in the worksheet, you move that data. When you need an exact copy of some data you entered into a worksheet, copying it to the new location is much quicker than typing it a second time.

Copying also is useful when you write a formula that you need to use in several cells. Rather than write the formula again and again, write it once and then copy it to wherever it is needed. Keep in mind that cell references automatically adjust for the new locations when you copy a formula.

If you have problems...   You might notice a difference between moving and copying formulas. When you move a formula, the formula still refers to the cells that it referred to before you moved it. When you copy a formula, the formula refers to new cells relative to its new location. Therefore, when you copy or move formulas, you should check the results of the formula to be sure that they're what you expected.

Copying and Moving Data

1-2-3 for Windows makes use of its capability to work with Windows by using the *Clipboard* in copying and moving data. The data to be placed elsewhere must either be *copied* or *cut* to the Clipboard, and then *pasted* in a new location.

To copy a cell or range from one place to another:

1. Select the cell or range you want to copy.

2. Choose **Edit**, **C**opy, or choose Copy from the quick menu.

3. Position the cell pointer at the target location, and then choose **E**dit, **P**aste, or choose Paste from the quick menu.

    Note: *The target location can be in the current worksheet or in another open worksheet.*

If you have problems...   If the range being copied contains more cells than the target range does, some data may be overwritten. Use **U**ndo to reverse the error, and move some of the data out of the target range before trying the copy operation again.

To cut a cell or range from one place and move it to another:

1. Select the cell or range you want to move.

2. Choose **E**dit, Cu**t**, or choose Cut from the quick menu.

3. Position the cell pointer at the target location, and then choose **E**dit, **P**aste, or choose Paste from the quick menu.

Copying Quickly by Dragging

Clipboard

A section of memory set aside for storage of data or objects to be moved or copied to another location.

Copy

To place in the Clipboard a copy of the data or object to be placed elsewhere.

Cut

To remove from the worksheet and place in the Clipboard the data or object to be placed elsewhere.

Paste

To place in the worksheet a copy of the data or object that currently is in the Clipboard.

The techniques in this section bypass the Clipboard and enable you to copy a cell or range up, down, left, or right, or to copy a cell or range forward or backward to other worksheets.

To quick-copy cells:

1. Select the cell or cells you want to copy, and then extend the highlight in the direction you want to quick-copy.

2. To copy to the right or down, choose **E**dit, Copy Do**w**n or Copy **R**ight from the main menu or from the quick menu.

    To copy up or to the left, press Shift, and then choose **E**dit, Copy Up (**W**) or Copy Left (**R**) from the main menu or the quick menu. (The letters in parentheses are the keys to press if you are using the keyboard to copy left or up.)

4

Quick-copying
down.

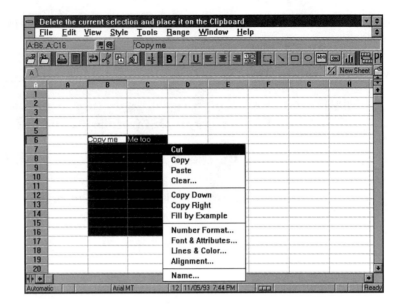

Caution

Cutting or copying
something to the
Clipboard replaces
the preceding item
in the Clipboard,
even if you switch
to another Windows
application and cut
or copy something
else to the Clip-
board.

To quickly copy a range from the current worksheet to the same range in
other worksheets in a file:

1. Select the range you want to copy to other worksheets.

2. Shift+click the tab of the last worksheet to which you want to copy
   the range.

3. Press Ctrl, and then choose **Edit**, Copy Fo**r**ward or **E**dit, Copy **B**ack
   from the main menu or the quick menu.

   Use Fo**r**ward to copy to worksheets lower in the alphabet than the
   source worksheet (from D to B, C, and A). Use **B**ack to copy to
   worksheets higher in the alphabet.

Caution

Be sure that you
make the correct
choice: Copy For-
ward or Copy Back.
Choosing the
wrong one will
delete the data
from the original
range.

1-2-3 for Windows copies the selected range to the same range in
all selected worksheets.

Clearing Data

Data in a worksheet that is no longer useful or is in the way must
be removed. You can remove the contents of one cell at a time by
entering new contents, but you need to use a command to empty a
cell completely.

To clear data:

1. Select the range you want to clear.

2. Choose **E**dit, Cl**e**ar. The Clear dialog box appears.

The Clear dialog
box.

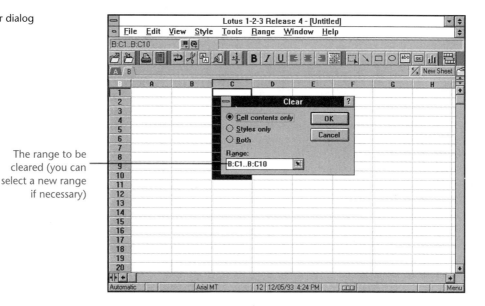

The range to be
cleared (you can
select a new range
if necessary)

3. Select which part of the cell or range you want to clear:

- Cell Contents Only clears only the contents of the cell.

- Styles Only clears changes made in the appearance of cells or
  their contents, including such enhancements as underlining,
  colors, and patterns.

- Both clears styles and contents from the selected cells.

4. Choose OK to clear the range.

**If you have
problems...**

Do not confuse the Cl**e**ar command in the **E**dit menu with Cu**t**. Cl**e**ar deletes
the selected item from the worksheet, but it does not use the Clipboard.
The item, once cleared, is gone. If you use Cl**e**ar by accident, immediately
use **U**ndo to reverse the error, and then Cu**t** the material to put it in the
Clipboard.

Note: *Use the Del key instead of* **E***dit,* **Cl***ear to clear cell contents. It's much faster.*

Pasting Text or Styles Only

Pasting means putting text and formatting enhancements in the target range. When you use the **E**dit, Paste **S**pecial command, you can choose to paste only the text portion of the Clipboard or only the styles in the cell, as well as both the styles and contents.

The word *style* in the Paste **S**pecial dialog box refers to changes to the appearance of the cell, such as cell background color or font changes.

The last option in the Paste **S**pecial dialog box is **F**ormulas as Values. When you choose this option, any formulas in the source range (the one being copied to the Clipboard) are pasted into the target range as answers rather than as formulas.

Caution

Using **E**dit, Paste **S**pecial, **F**ormulas as Values means that the cells where the formulas are pasted will not change if you change the under-lying data.

Finding and Replacing Data

When you need to find (and possibly replace) text or formulas in a worksheet, use the **E**dit menu. In searching for text, you must decide whether to search in cells with labels, in cells with formulas, or in both types of cells.

Note: *You cannot search for values in worksheets.*

Follow these steps to search (and replace) text:

1. If you want to restrict the search to a range, select the range.

2. Choose **E**dit, **F**ind & Replace. The Find & Replace dialog box appears.

The Find & Replace dialog box.

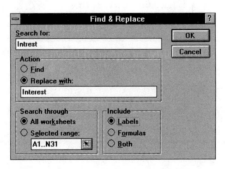

3. In the **S**earch For text box, type the text you want to find.

4. Choose Replace **W**ith, and then type the replacement text in the text box.

5. Choose All Wor**k**sheets or **Se**lected Range, depending on the scope of your search.

6. Choose **L**abels, **F**ormulas, or **B**oth, depending on the type of cells you want to search.

7. Choose OK to start the search.

8. If you chose to replace text, the cell pointer stops at the first cell containing the search text. A choice box appears, asking you to choose one of four items:

A find-and-replace operation is in progress, replacing *Volkswagen* with *VW*.

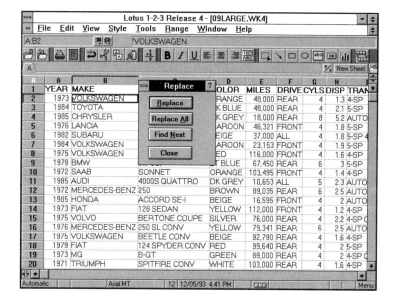

■ **R**eplace replaces the text in the current cell with the replacement text and goes on to the next cell that matches the search text.

■ Replace **A**ll immediately replaces the search text with replacement text in all cells that contain the search text.

■ Find **N**ext moves the cell pointer to the next cell containing the search text without replacing the text.

■ Close stops the search and closes the choice box.

■ If you chose to **F**ind text, the cell pointer stops on the first occurrence of the text. The program then displays a dialog box in which you can choose Find **N**ext to continue searching for more examples of the text or Close to stop the search.

9. After 1-2-3 for Windows has found all occurrences of the search text, a message box appears, indicating that the search is complete. Choose OK to close the box and return to the editing window.

Checking Spelling

The spell-checking feature, which is new in Release 4 of 1-2-3 for Windows, enables you to search your worksheets for misspelled words and to create a dictionary of your own additional words.

Checking for Spelling Errors
To check the spelling in a worksheet:

1. If you want to check spelling in a range, select it. Don't select a range if you want to check the entire worksheet.

2. Choose **T**ools, **S**pell Check. The Spell Check dialog box appears.

The main Spell Check dialog box.

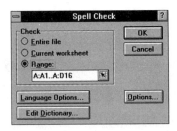

3. In the Check section, choose **E**ntire File to check every cell in all worksheets in the file, **C**urrent Worksheet to check every cell in the currently visible worksheet only, or **R**ange to limit the spell check to the selected cells only.

4. Choose OK to begin the spelling check.

When you choose OK, the spell checker checks every word in every cell in the file, in the current worksheet, or in the range you selected. When the spell checker finds a word that it does not recognize, it displays the following dialog box, in which you decide how to deal with the misspelling:

This dialog box appears when the spell checker finds what it thinks is a misspelled word.

Contents of cell with suspected misspelling are displayed here

Type the correct spelling here, or select a word from the list below and it will be displayed here

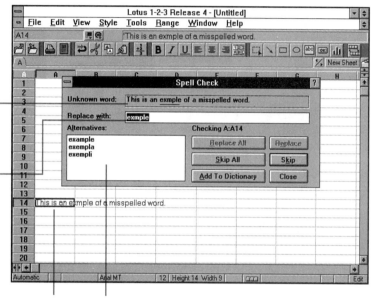

Cell with suspected misspelling   Possible correct spellings

Your options for dealing with a potential misspelling are:

- Select one of the words in the **A**lternatives box or edit the spelling in the Replace **W**ith text box. Then:

   Choose **R**eplace All to correct the same spelling error throughout the area being checked.

   or

   Choose R**e**place to correct the error in the current cell only.

   Note: *By default, the alternative spellings come only from the main dictionary, not from the user dictionary. You can change this setting.*

- **S**kip All occurrences of the spelling in the area being checked.

- S**k**ip the current cell only.

- If the word is one that you will use frequently, choose **A**dd To Dictionary to add the word to the user dictionary.

- Choose Close to stop further spell checking. Corrections that you have already made will remain in effect.

Changing Search Options

The following figure shows the ways you can modify the spell checker. Choose **T**ools, **S**pell Check, **O**ptions to open this dialog box.

The **T**ools, **S**pell Check, **O**ptions dialog box.

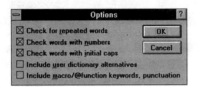

You might want to change the way the spell checker works. Choosing **O**ptions enables you to make the following changes:

- By default, the spell checker pauses and highlights repeated words. Deselect the Check for **R**epeated Words option to disable highlighting of repeated words.

- Deselect Check Words with **N**umbers to stop the spell checker from highlighting any letter/number combinations. If you use many letter/number combinations (in part numbers or employee numbers, for example), having every one of them highlighted will become annoying.

- **C**heck Words with Initial Caps refers to proper nouns. The spell checker will accept *Cincinnati*, which is a relatively common proper noun, but will stop on *Lucretia*. A list of employees who have unusual names will keep you busy for some time, as the spell checker catches all of them.

- Choose Include **U**ser Dictionary Alternatives to see alternatives from the user dictionary as well as from the main dictionary.

- Include **M**acro/Function Keywords, Punctuation instructs the spell checker to check the spelling of the words, abbreviations, and punctuation used in macros and functions.

Editing the User Dictionary

Whenever the spell checker finds a word that it does not recognize, it highlights the word. The spell checker recognizes only words that are in the main dictionary or the user dictionary.

You can add words one at a time to the user dictionary while checking spelling, or you can add a list of words quickly. Use the Edit **D**ictionary command at the bottom of the main Spell Check dialog box. Follow these steps:

1. Choose Edit **D**ictionary. The Edit Dictionary dialog box appears, displaying the list of words that you added in the **C**urrent Words list box.

The Edit Dictionary dialog box.

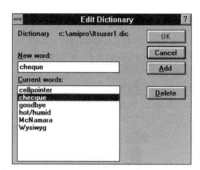

2. If a misspelled word appears in the list, select it and then choose **D**elete.

3. To add a word, type it in the **N**ew Word text box, and then choose **A**dd to place the new word in the list.

    If you want to add a list of words, type them one at time, choosing **A**dd after each one. The words are inserted into the **C**urrent Words list in alphabetical order.

4. Choose OK to close the dialog box and to make your new list the up-to-date user dictionary.

Working with Columns and Rows

By default, the width of a column is 9 characters, and the height of a row is 14 *points*. The data that you place in cells might require that the row or

Point

An increment for measuring the height of letters. An inch contains 72 points, so one point is 1/72 of an inch.

column be larger or smaller. You also might need to add columns or rows to accommodate new data or to hide a column or row containing sensitive data that others shouldn't see.

Note: *Columns are 9 units wide by default. A* unit *is about the width of a lowercase* a *in a 12-point font.*

Changing Row Height

When you change the font size of text in a row, 1-2-3 for Windows automatically adjusts the size of the row. At times, however, you might want to control the height of a row. (For details on changing fonts and font sizes, see Chapter 5, "Changing the Appearance of a Worksheet.")

Note: *Changing row heights normally is not necessary; 1-2-3 for Windows automatically adjusts row heights when you change fonts.*

The fastest and easiest way to shorten a row is to use the mouse, as follows:

1. Select the row or rows whose heights you want to change.

2. Place the mouse pointer on the frame. Notice that the pointer becomes a two-headed arrow when it is positioned on a grid line.

The mouse pointer has changed to a two-headed arrow in the frame.

Mouse pointer —

3. Click and drag the bottom of one row in the frame up to shorten the row or down to lengthen all selected rows. As you change the row height, notice that the current height appears in the edit line near the top of the screen.

When you are ready to reset the height of a row so that it's high enough for the largest font in the row:

1. Move the mouse pointer to the frame, and select the row or rows whose heights you want to reset.

2. Place the mouse pointer at the bottom of any selected row to make the pointer a double-headed arrow.

3. Double-click to reset all selected rows.

Note: *You can set several row heights to fit the largest font in each row by first selecting the rows and then double-clicking the bottom of any selected row in the border.*

If you need to adjust a row height to a precise value, you might want to use menu commands. To use the menu for adjusting row height:

1. Select all rows whose height you want to change.

2. Choose **S**tyle, **R**ow Height. The Row Height dialog box appears.

The Row Height dialog box.

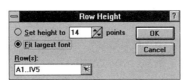

3. Choose **S**et Height To, and then change the number of points in the adjacent box.

    or

    Choose **F**it Largest Font so that 1-2-3 for Windows sets the height to accommodate the largest font in the row.

4. Choose OK to finish the command.

Changing Column Width

Although row heights change automatically when you change fonts, column widths do not automatically change. After you enter data in a column, you need to ensure that all data will be displayed correctly by adjusting column width as necessary.

Remember that long labels will appear to spill out of a cell into the adjacent cell as long as the adjacent cell is empty. Values, on the other hand, can be displayed only within the boundaries of the cell; if the column is too narrow, asterisks appear. Therefore, it is especially important to make sure that all values are being displayed properly and to widen the column if necessary.

To change a column width:

1. Select the column or columns whose widths you want to change.

2. Move the mouse pointer to the right edge of the column in the frame.

3. When the mouse pointer becomes a left and right arrow separated by a vertical line, click and drag the column boundary to the right to widen the column or left to narrow all selected columns.

The mouse pointer becomes a two-headed arrow.

Mouse pointer —

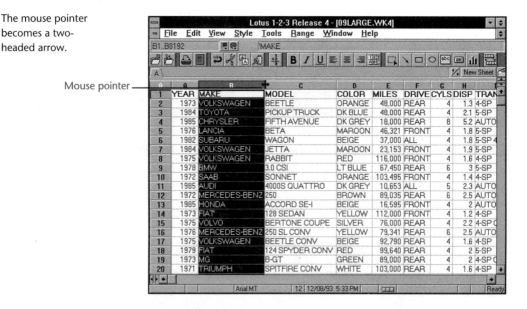

If you want to set the width of the column for the widest entry in the entire column:

1. Move the mouse pointer to the right edge of the column in the frame so that the mouse pointer becomes arrows separated by a vertical line.

2. Double-click the right edge of the column in the worksheet border.

If you have problems...

Fitting to the widest entry instructs 1-2-3 for Windows to adjust the column so that it is wide enough for the largest entry. At times, however, you don't want the column to be as wide as the widest entry in the column. To avoid making the column too wide, select only the cells whose entries should be used in setting the width. Then follow the preceding steps.

4

Note: *You can set several column widths to fit the widest entry in each column by selecting the columns first and then double-clicking the right edge of any of the selected columns in the border.*

As with rows, you might need more precision in setting column widths than you can achieve with a mouse. To use the menus to change column widths:

1. Choose **S**tyle, **C**olumn Width. The Column Width dialog box appears.

2. Set the width by typing the number of characters in the **S**et Width To text box.

   Alternatively, choose **F**it to Widest Entry or **R**eset to Worksheet Default. The latter option sets the selected column or columns to the default column width (9 units, unless you changed the default).

3. Choose OK.

Hiding Columns and Rows

Columns or rows can contain data that is important in formulas but not important for those who will see the worksheet.

Note: *Hiding a column does not change the data in the column or formulas that use the data.*

By shortening columns and rows as described in previous sections, you can hide entire columns or rows and their data. In the worksheet frame, click and drag the right border of a column to the left until the column is hidden. Click and drag the bottom of a row up until the row disappears. The worksheet frame shows that a row or column is hidden by skipping its number or letter. If you hide column C, for example, the column letters in the frame will be A, B, D, E, and so on.

A worksheet with column C hidden.

Column C has been hidden

	A	B	D	E	F	G	H	I	J	K
1	YEAR	MAKE	COLOR	MILES	DRIVE	CYLS	DISP	TRANS	REGIST	STA
2	1973	VOLKSWAGEN	ORANGE	48,000	REAR	4	1.3	4-SP	324MCW	M
3	1984	TOYOTA	DK BLUE	48,000	REAR	4	2.1	5-SP	AD9635	M
4	1985	CHRYSLER	DK GREY	18,000	REAR	8	5.2	AUTO/OD	CZY146	M
5	1976	LANCIA	MAROON	46,321	FRONT	4	1.8	5-SP	CZB73	M
6	1982	SUBARU	BEIGE	37,000	ALL	4	1.8	5-SP 4WD	MYA167	M
7	1984	VOLKSWAGEN	MAROON	23,153	FRONT	4	1.9	5-SP	181945	NI
8	1975	VOLKSWAGEN	RED	116,000	FRONT	4	1.6	4-SP	145MKP	T
9	1978	BMW	LT BLUE	67,450	REAR	6	3	5-SP	BUMW	FI
10	1972	SAAB	ORANGE	103,495	FRONT	4	1.4	4-SP	IXLR8	C
11	1985	AUDI	DK GREY	10,653	ALL	5	2.3	AUTO 4WD	AUDIDO	T
12	1972	MERCEDES-BENZ	BROWN	89,035	REAR	6	2.5	AUTO	BK5006	R
13	1985	HONDA	BEIGE	16,595	FRONT	4	2	AUTO OD	PIE576	C
14	1973	FIAT	YELLOW	112,000	FRONT	4	1.2	4-SP	197754	NI
15	1975	VOLVO	SILVER	76,000	REAR	4	2.2	4-SP OD	FLATTOP	C
16	1976	MERCEDES-BENZ	YELLOW	79,341	REAR	6	2.5	AUTO	PPL554	T
17	1975	VOLKSWAGEN	BEIGE	92,790	REAR	4	1.6	4-SP	BUGG	V
18	1979	FIAT	RED	99,640	REAR	4	2	5-SP	650DFG	FI
19	1973	MG	GREEN	89,000	REAR	4	2	4-SP OD	109975	NI
20	1971	TRIUMPH	WHITE	103,000	REAR	4	1.6	4-SP	DWE785	O

Using **S**tyle, **H**ide, you can hide columns or worksheets (but not rows), as follows:

1. Select the columns or worksheets you want to hide.

2. Choose **S**tyle, **H**ide.

3. Choose **C**olumn or **S**heet (if you want to hide an entire worksheet), and then choose OK.

To redisplay a hidden range:

1. Select the columns or worksheets on either side of the hidden ones.

2. Choose **S**tyle, **H**ide.

3. Choose Sho**w**.

Another way to redisplay hidden columns:

1. Click and drag the right edge of the hidden column to the right until the column is the desired width.

2. Click and drag the right edge of the next hidden column, and so on until all hidden columns are redisplayed.

Inserting Rows and Columns

To insert a row or column:

1. Select the row or column adjacent to where you want to insert the new blank row or column.

A worksheet with a column selected for insertion of a new column

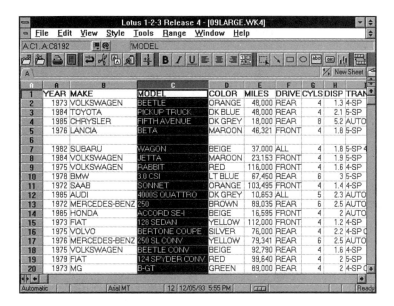

To insert a row, select the row below where you want the new row.

To insert a column, select the column to the right of where you want the new column.

If you want to insert more than one row or column, select as many adjacent rows or columns as you need blank rows or columns.

2. Choose **E**dit, **I**nsert. Blank rows or columns appear where the rows or columns were highlighted. Existing data is moved down far enough to make room for new empty rows or to the right to make room for new columns.

A worksheet with a blank column and a blank row inserted.

In the interest of speeding your work, be sure to select the column or row before you use the **E**dit, **I**nsert command. If the cell pointer is in one cell when you start the command, you must use the Insert dialog box to choose **R**ow or **C**olumn. When the columns or rows are already selected, no dialog box appears, and the insertion occurs immediately.

Inserting Part of a Row or Column

New to Release 4 of 1-2-3 for Windows is the capability to insert part of a row or a column. If you have two separate tables, one above the other, and only one table needs an extra blank column, you don't want to insert a column the entire length of the worksheet. The creator of the worksheet shown in the following figure forgot to enter data for the Northwest region. Inserting a column in the entire worksheet, however, would put an unwanted blank column in the Foreign Sales data.

This worksheet
needs part of a
column inserted.

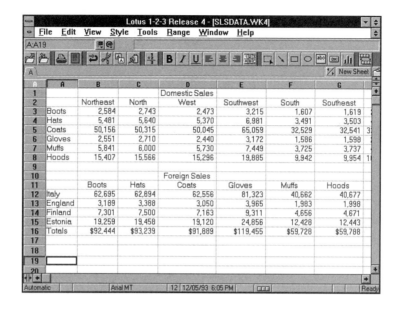

To insert part of a row or column:

1. Select the range into which you want to insert part of a new row or column.

2. Choose **Edit**, **Insert**. The Insert dialog box appears.

3. Choose **Column** or **Row**, and then choose **Insert** Selection.

Choose **Insert**
Selection to insert
part of a row or
column.

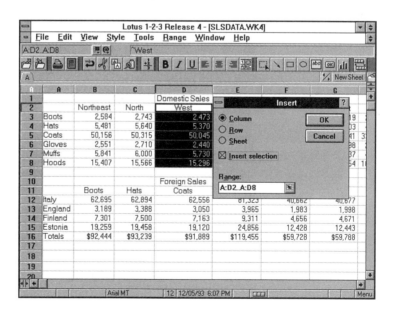

4. Choose OK to execute the command.

Deleting Rows and Columns

Deleting rows and columns involves techniques similar to those that you use to insert them. Follow these steps:

1. Select the rows or columns you want to delete.

2. Choose **E**dit, **D**elete.

Caution
If you select a column and then click the Delete Row SmartIcon, you will delete all rows in the worksheet.

Don't confuse **E**dit, **D**elete with **E**dit, Cu**t**. Deleting a row or column means removing not only the data, but also the column or row in which the data appeared. To clear the contents of a selected row or column, press Del, or choose **E**dit, **C**ut or **E**dit, **C**lear.

You can delete part of a row or part of a column by selecting the range of cells you want to delete and then choosing **E**dit, **D**elete. In the Delete dialog box, choose **R**ow or **C**olumn, as appropriate, and be sure to choose **D**elete Selection. Remember that the data *and* the cells in which the data appeared will be deleted. Data and cells below deleted rows or parts of rows move up to fill the gap created by the deletion. Data and cells to the right of deleted columns or parts of columns move left to fill the newly created gap.

Summary

To	Do This
Edit cell contents	Double-click the cell and then make corrections
Make a cell reference absolute	Press F4 while writing the formula
Copy data	Select data; then use **E**dit, **C**opy and **E**dit, **P**aste
Move data	Select data; then use **E**dit, **C**ut and **E**dit, **P**aste
Replace data with other data	Use **E**dit, **F**ind & Replace
Check spelling	Use **T**ools, **S**pell Check

On Your Own

Estimated time: 30 minutes

1. Enter your last name in a cell. Then edit the cell, adding your first name before your last name.

2. Create a small worksheet, using several formulas that refer to one cell. Make references to that cell absolute.

3. Create and then correct a circular cell reference.

4. Write a formula, using parentheses to change the order of precedence of the calculations.

5. Copy your name to another cell.

6. Move your name to another cell.

7. Quick-copy your name to a range five cells above.

8. Delete your name from the quick-copied range, and then undo the deletion.

9. Replace your first name with your initials wherever it appears in the worksheet.

4

Chapter 5

Changing the Appearance of a Worksheet

Until you take the time to improve the appearance of your worksheet, it is an unfinished product. Improving a worksheet's appearance not only makes the work look more professional, but also can make the data easier to read and interpret.

This chapter covers the techniques used to change the appearance of data and of the cells in which the data is placed.

Specific topics covered are:

- Formatting values
- Aligning cell entries
- Changing the font in cell entries
- Adding borders and shading to cells and ranges
- Adding drawn objects to a worksheet
- Changing the appearance of drawn objects

Formatting Values

Formatting
Changing the way a number is displayed (without changing its value).

When you enter a number or a formula into a cell, the entry may not have quite the appearance you hoped for. You might have entered 5, for example, but wanted it to look like $5.00. When you want to change the appearance of a number, you *format* it.

Note: *You cannot format labels except with Hidden format, which hides the contents of any selected cells, and with Label format, which makes all new entries in a range labels.*

Applying Formats

You can format numbers in several ways. Regardless of the method you use, the best practice is to select the range of values you want to format and then execute the command.

Note: *Although you can enter values and then format them, if you format a range before you start entering data, it may be easier to ensure that you entered the correct number.*

To format a range:

1. Select the range that includes the values you want to format.

2. Choose **S**tyle, **N**umber Format, or choose Number Format from the quick menu. The Number Format dialog box appears.

Select number of decimal places to display here

The Number Format dialog box.

Selected range

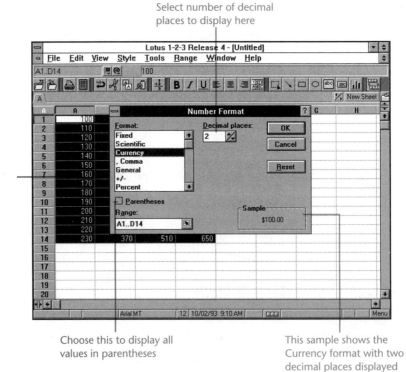

Choose this to display all values in parentheses

This sample shows the Currency format with two decimal places displayed

3. Select a format from the **F**ormat list box.

   You can press the first letter of the format, if you already know which format you want to use, or you can scroll through the list. As you highlight a format name, the Sample box shows the value in the current cell with the highlighted format.

4. Choose OK when you finish.

The formatted range.

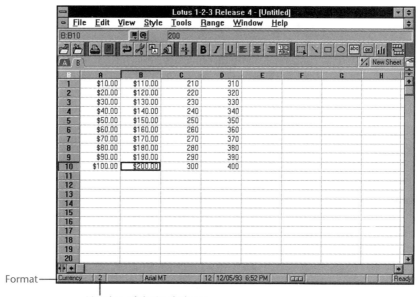

Format — Number of decimal places

In the **D**ecimal Places text box, you indicate how many digits will be displayed after the decimal point. Remember that changing the number of displayed decimal places does not change the actual value of the number; only its displayed value changes. Choosing **P**arentheses puts parentheses around all values in the selected range, not just negative numbers.

Note: *Some formats, such as Comma, automatically use parentheses for negative numbers. If you choose* **P***arentheses in the Number Format dialog box and use the Comma format, the number –123 will be displayed as* ((123)).

The **R**ange box shows the range that you selected in the worksheet. If you need to change the range, type the correct range in the **R**ange text box, or click the arrowhead next to the box and then use the mouse to select a range.

Reset removes any existing formats from values in the selected range and restores the default format. (For instructions on how to change the default format, see "Changing the Default Appearance of the Worksheet" later in this chapter.)

If you have problems...

If you set the number of decimal places rather high, you may see asterisks in cells in which the number of digits exceeds the width of the column. To widen the column, use one of the techniques discussed in Chapter 4, "Modifying Data in a Worksheet."

The following table shows how the number 1,000 would be displayed in the various formats:

Table 5.1 Number Formats		
Format	**Appearance**	**Description**
Fixed	1000.00	Up to 15 decimal places; minus sign if negative; leading zero for decimals.
Scientific	1.00e+.03	Exponential notation; up to 15 decimal places.
Currency	$1,000.00	Currency symbol; thousands separator; up to 15 decimal places.
Comma	1,000.00	Thousands separator; up to 15 decimal places.
General	1000	Minus sign for negative values; no fixed number of decimal places; no trailing zeros.
+/−	*****	Displays plus signs or minus signs equal to integer value of the number (1,000 is too big to be displayed with this format).
Percent	100000%	Multiplies number by 100; adds a percent sign and up to 15 decimal places.
Text	1000	Displays a formula as a formula, not as an answer. The formula @SUM(*X1..X9*) appears as the formula, not the answer.
Hidden		Hides values or labels.
Automatic	1000	Applies format automatically (see the following section, "Using Automatic Formatting").
Label	1000	Displays old entries with General format; displays new values as labels.

Note: *Date and time formats are covered in "Using Date and Time Formats" later in this chapter.*

By far the fastest and easiest way to format numbers is to use the status bar at the bottom of the screen. Follow these steps:

1. Select the range to be formatted.

    At the left end of the status bar is the format selector, showing the name of the format.

You can change the format and number of decimal places by using the two left sections of the status bar.

Format

Number of decimal places

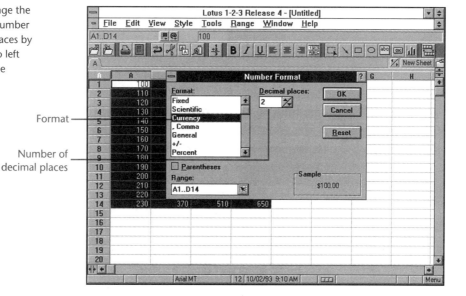

2. Click the format selector.

3. Click the format you want to apply to the selected range.

4. Next to the format box in the status bar is the number of decimal places in the range. Click this box, and then select the number of decimal places you want to be displayed in all cells in the range.

| **If you have problems...** | If you select a range in the worksheet that contains several different formats, no format name appears in the format box of the status bar. By the same token, if the range contains several different decimal-place settings, the decimal-places box in the status bar will be empty. Nevertheless, when you click either box in the status bar, the list of formats or number of decimal places will appear, so you can choose a setting for the whole range. |

Using Automatic Formatting

You can determine the format of a number by typing the proper characters as you enter a value into a cell. For example, if you want to enter the number 1000 into a cell, but want it to look like $1000.00, type the dollar sign, the digits, the decimal point, and the numbers that follow. 1-2-3 for Windows automatically applies the Currency format, including the number of decimal places you typed. Even if you delete or replace the number in that cell, new numbers typed there automatically will have the Currency format with two decimal places. If you enter the first number into a cell without adding extra characters, of course, 1-2-3 for Windows does not give the number a special format.

Enter **5%**, for example, and the program uses the Percent format. Remember that the stored value may not look like the displayed value, even though the values are equal. You see 5% in the cell, for example, but the stored value is .05. Keep this in mind when you enter another number in the cell. Enter **10**, and you see 1000% because 1-2-3 for Windows multiplies the entry by 100 before adding the percent sign. To display 10%, enter **.1** or **10%**, not just **10**.

By default, 1-2-3 for Windows applies the Automatic format to all cells. You can change the format for individual cells or ranges, using one of the techniques described earlier, or change the format for the entire worksheet by changing the worksheet defaults (see "Changing the Default Appearance of the Worksheet" later in this chapter).

You also can turn the automatic formatting feature off, as follows:

1. Choose **T**ools, **U**ser Setup. The User Setup dialog box appears.

2. Deselect Use **A**utomatic Format.

3. Choose OK.

The General format becomes the default format for all worksheets and files you create and retrieve in the future, but it does not affect the files that currently are in memory.

Using Date and Time Formats

Occasionally, you need to do math with dates or times—for example, calculating how long your company has owned a piece of equipment.

Caution
To use dates in math calculations, enter dates as values. If you enter **May 28, 1979**, for example, 1-2-3 for Windows automatically makes that entry a label.

The format selections possible from the status bar.

Subtracting the purchase date from today's date tells you how many days have elapsed since the purchase. You can subtract two numbers representing times to determine the elapsed time.

To make a date or time a value rather than a label, you must enter it with a standard date or time format. One acceptable format is 7/23/93. If you enter a date with that format, 1-2-3 for Windows accepts the date as a value with the mo/da/yr format (displayed in the status bar as 12/31/93.) To see other acceptable formats, click the format box in the status bar.

Remember that the stored value may look different from the displayed value, especially in the case of date and time values. Change the format of a date cell to General, for example, and you see a number. The date 12/25/93, displayed in General format, appears as 34328, because 1-2-3 for Windows assigns a serial number to every date, starting with January 1, 1900.

Note: *If you enter a date using mo/da/yr format, as in 5/28/91, you can enter just the month and day of other dates; 1-2-3 for Windows will add the year you used originally. Enter **11/21**, for example, and the date 11/21/91 appears.*

Note: *You don't have to worry about which serial number goes with which date. Enter a date in the proper format, and 1-2-3 for Windows supplies the number.*

Times, displayed in General format, are decimals. Midnight is 0 or 1; all times in between are expressed as a decimal part of a day. Noon, for example, is .5 because noon is halfway through a day.

If you have problems...	If you write a formula that subtracts two dates, make sure that you don't format the formula cell with a date format. If you subtract two dates that are a week apart, for example, you want the answer to be 7, not January 7, 1900. Use General or Fixed format for the formula cell rather than a date format.

The following table shows the standard date and time formats. If you want to use dates or times in formulas, enter them in one of these formats.

Table 5.2 Date and Time Formats		
Dates	**12-hour Clock**	**24-hour Clock**
2-Oct-93	8:00:00 AM	6:23
2-Oct	8:56:34 PM	6:23:45
10/2/93	8:34 AM	20:56

Aligning Labels

By default, a label is placed on the left side of a cell, and a value or the result of a formula is placed on the right side of a cell. You can, however, change the alignment of all cell entries, labels, and values. In 1-2-3 for Windows Release 4, you can align labels vertically as well as horizontally.

Aligning Cell Entries Horizontally

At times, you will want to realign some labels or values. For example, you may decide that column labels would look better centered. The fastest way to realign both values and labels is:

1. Select the cell or range where you want to realign cell contents. To realign the contents of all cells in a column or row, for example, click the column letter or row number.

2. Click the SmartIcon that represents the alignment you want.

As fast as using the alignment SmartIcons is, you may find an advantage to using the menus, which offer more choices. Follow these steps:

1. Select the range for which you want to change the alignment.

2. Choose **S**tyle, **A**lignment, or choose Alignment from the quick menu. The Alignment dialog box appears.

Using this dialog box, you can change the horizontal and vertical alignment of cell contents, rotate the text, and align text across several columns.

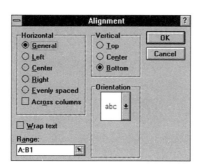

3. Make a selection in the Horizontal box. **G**eneral, the default, aligns labels left and values right; **E**venly Spaced spreads labels across the cell. In the following figure, the word *evenly* is evenly spaced across the cell. **L**eft and **R**ight place the cell entry at the appropriate side of the cell; **C**enter places it in the center of the cell.

5

Some examples of the types of alignments available in 1-2-3 for Windows.

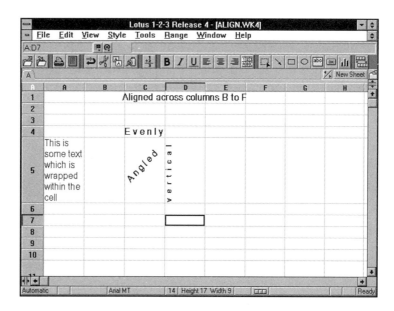

4. Choose OK.

To align a label (but not values) across several columns:

1. Select a horizontal range. You can select more than one row to align several labels. Make sure that all the labels are in the leftmost cells of the selected ranges.

2. Choose **S**tyle, **A**lignment, or choose Alignment from the quick menu. The Alignment dialog box appears.

3. Choose the horizontal placement for the cells: **L**eft, **C**enter, **R**ight, or **E**venly Spaced.

4. Choose Acr**o**ss Columns.

5. Choose OK. The label aligns itself within the horizontal range of cells you selected.

Note: *Evenly Spaced and Across Columns do not work with values.*

Wrapping Text

A cell can accept up to 512 characters, which means that you can enter a long sentence into a single cell. Because such a long sentence would disappear off the screen, you can elect to *wrap* it within the cell.

Wrap
To cause a long line of text to break into separate lines.

To wrap text within a cell:

1. Place the cell pointer in the cell that contains the text to be wrapped.

2. Choose **S**tyle, **A**lignment, or choose Alignment from the quick menu.

3. Choose a horizontal alignment; **L**eft, **C**enter, or **R**ight. Evenly Spaced is not an active choice.

4. Choose **W**rap Text. The long label breaks into smaller lines, each of which fits within the horizontal boundaries of the current cell.

5. If the cell is too narrow, widen the column. The text rewraps to fit the new width.

Aligning Cell Entries Vertically

If a cell entry does not already fill a cell from top to bottom, you can realign the entry vertically by using one of the options in the Vertical list box of the Alignment dialog box. By default, 1-2-3 for Windows places each entry at the bottom of the cell; you may elect to place entries at the top or the center of the cell.

Reorienting Cell Entries

You can not only realign a cell entry vertically, but also determine its *orientation* within the cell. You can display the entry vertically, horizontally, or at an angle that you determine.

For a bit of variety in your worksheets, you can display cell entries at an angle.

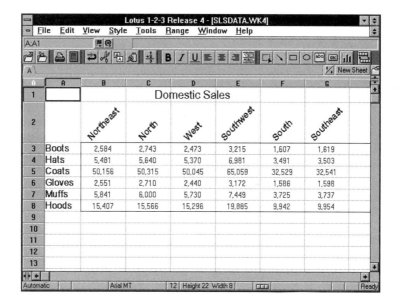

To change the orientation of a cell entry:

1. Select the range in which you want to reorient cell entries.

2. Choose **S**tyle, **A**lignment, or choose Alignment from the quick menu. The Alignment dialog box appears.

3. In the Orientation box, choose the orientation you want.

    Note: *Before choosing an orientation option, make sure that Across Columns is not checked.*

4. If you choose the last orientation option—the one that displays at an angle—a text box appears in which you can specify the exact angle at which you want to display the label. Your choices range from 1 (almost horizontal) to 90 (vertical).

   Note: *Make sure that your printer can support printing at an angle, especially if you have switched to a different font in the reoriented cells.*

5. Choose OK.

Changing Fonts and Attributes

Font

The type style and type size of characters. Type size is expressed in *points* (1 point is 1/72 of an inch) or *pitch* (characters per inch).

Besides moving text around inside the cell, as discussed in the preceding section, you can change the appearance of a cell entry by changing its *font*, text attributes, and text color.

To change the font:

1. Select the range in which you want to change the font.

2. Choose **S**tyle, **F**ont & Attributes, or choose Font & Attributes from the quick menu. The Font & Attributes dialog box appears.

The Font & Attributes dialog box.

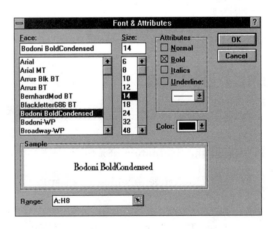

3. Choose a type style in the **F**ace list box. As you highlight a type style's name, an example appears in the Sample window.

4. Choose a point size in the **S**ize list. Remember that 1 point is 1/72 of an inch, so 72 points is 1 inch.

5. Choose OK. All cells in the range display the new font, and the row height automatically adjusts for the new font (assuming that it is the largest font in the row).

In addition to changing the font and size, you can apply bold, italic, and underline attributes. To apply any of these attributes:

1. Select the cell or range in which you want to apply the attributes.

2. Choose **S**tyle, **F**ont & Attributes, or choose Font & Attributes from the quick menu. The Font & Attributes dialog box appears.

3. Choose **B**old, **I**talics, **U**nderline, or **N**ormal.

   Note: *To remove all attributes at once, choose **N**ormal.*

4. If you choose **U**nderline, select an underline style in the drop-down box. The options are regular, wide, and double.

5. Choose OK.

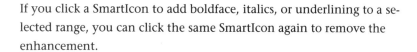

If you click a SmartIcon to add boldface, italics, or underlining to a selected range, you can click the same SmartIcon again to remove the enhancement.

Note: *If you use lines around cells, you should not use underlining in the same cells. The underlining is difficult to see, and the bottom of the cell becomes rather cluttered.*

You can use either of two **S**tyle commands to add or change text color: **F**ont & Attributes or **L**ines & Color.

To change text color:

1. Select the range in which you want to change text color.

2. Choose **S**tyle, **F**ont & Attributes or **S**tyle, **L**ines & Color, or use the quick menu to choose either command.

   Depending on the command you chose, the Font & Attributes or the Lines & Color dialog box appears.

3. In the Font & Attributes dialog box, choose **C**olor. In the Lines & Color dialog box, choose Te**x**t Color.

5

After you make either choice, a grid appears, displaying 256 color options.

The 256-color grid in the Lines & Color dialog box.

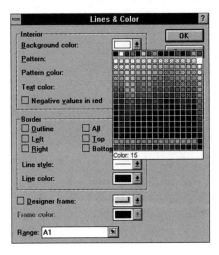

4. Click a color option.

5. Press Enter. 1-2-3 for Windows immediately applies the color you chose to the text in the selected cells.

*Note: To color only negative values red, choose **Style**, **Lines** & Color, and check Negative **Values** in Red.*

If you have problems...

If you can't see the colored text on-screen after you choose a color, either of two things may have happened:

■ The color you chose doesn't stand out from the background. White letters on a white background, for example, are invisible.

■ You chose a pastel color. On-screen characters are invisible in some pastel colors.

Rather than simply click a color option in the grid, use the arrow keys to move from color to color to see how letters appear when the color is applied. When you have highlighted the color you want to use, press Enter.

Working with Cell Borders and Shading

Now that you know how to change the appearance of cell contents, you're ready to explore changing the appearance of the cells themselves.

Adding Shading and Patterns

When you choose **S**tyles, **L**ines & Color, you can make four changes in the interior of a cell: **B**ackground Color, **P**attern, Pattern **C**olor, and Te**x**t Color. Text color is covered in the preceding section, but notice that an extra choice in the Lines & Color dialog box enables you to display Negative **V**alues in Red.

To change the background color of cells:

1. Select the cell, range, or collection of cells.

2. Choose **S**tyle, **L**ines & Color, or choose Lines & Color from the quick menu. The Lines & Color dialog box appears.

3. Choose **B**ackground Color.

4. Choose a color from the grid that appears.

5

Use the Lines & Color dialog box to change the color of a cell's background and any borders you added.

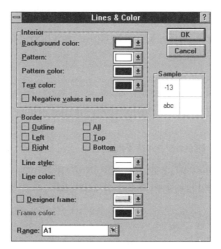

Because the squares in the color grid are rather small, use the arrow keys on the keyboard to move from color to color in the grid. The highlighted color appears in the slightly larger box next to the word *Background Color*. Seeing that color there gives you a better idea of how it will look in the cell.

Pattern is a series of 64 designs that you can place in the cell. The first three choices are solid colors. The box with the *T* is used for drawn shapes when you want the shape to be colored but transparent (hence, the *T*). The second colored box places only the pattern color in the cell or range. The third color box places only the background color in the cell.

To place a pattern in a cell:

1. Select the cell, range, or collection of cells.

2. Choose **S**tyle, **L**ines & Color, or choose Lines & Color from the quick menu.

3. Choose **P**attern.

4. Choose a pattern from the grid that appears.

The default color for cell backgrounds is white; the default pattern is black. The pattern you choose is placed over the background color in black unless you choose a different color for the pattern.

To change the color of the pattern:

1. Select the cell, range, or collection of cells.

2. Choose **S**tyle, **L**ines & Color, or choose Lines & Color from the quick menu.

3. Choose Pattern **C**olor.

4. Choose a color from the grid that appears.

Adding Lines and Frames

Frame
A fancy border that you can place around a cell or range. A frame is different from a simple line border in that it is more elaborate.

To set data apart, you can add lines or a *frame* to the border of a high-lighted range or the border of each cell.

To add lines or a frame:

1. Select the cell or range to which you want to add the lines or frame.

2. Choose **S**tyle, **L**ines & Color, or choose Lines & Color from the quick menu.

3. In the Border section of the Lines & Color dialog box, indicate whether you want to place a line at the **L**eft, **R**ight, **T**op, or Botto**m** of each cell in the range, or choose A**l**l to place lines all the way around each cell. Alternatively, choose **O**utline to put a border around the selected range but not around each cell in that range.

4. Select one of the eight line styles from the Line St**y**le drop-down list.

The Lines & Color dialog box, showing the available line styles.

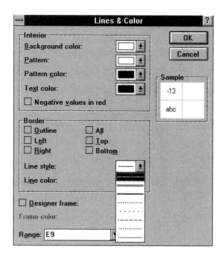

Caution

As you choose patterns and colors, keep in mind whether people will view your work on a color screen or as a black-and-white printout. Colored letters on a colored background may be clear and beautiful on-screen (especially in combination with a lovely pattern) but very hard to read in printed form.

5. Select a color from the Li**n**e Color drop-down list, which contains 16 options. You can use different colors for lines applied to different ranges.

6. If the simple lines around cells or ranges are not the ones you want to use, choose a frame and color from the **D**esigner Frames and **F**rame Color drop-down lists. The 16 frame styles and 256 colors give you quite a bit of latitude in the way you frame a range.

7. When you finish, choose OK.

Note: *Before you apply a new frame, remove the old one if the frame will not be around exactly the same cells; otherwise, pieces of the old frame will be visible. Also, be careful about text in cells that are close to but outside the frame; a thick frame could obscure some text.*

The following figure shows some examples of frames.

Frames, applied carefully, are attractive additions to a worksheet.

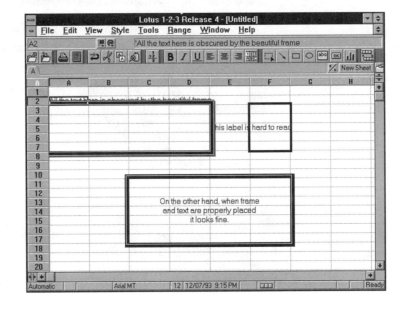

Caution

Be careful how you place frames. As the figure shows, frames can disappear into the worksheet frame or obscure some text.

Named style

The formats and enhancements in a cell or range, grouped together under a single name. After you name a style, you can apply it to other cells or ranges.

Naming and Using Styles

After you apply a series of enhancements to a range or a cell, you may want to take a "snapshot" of those enhancements so that you can apply them to other ranges. Applying the same *named style* to different ranges, for example, is one way to illustrate the relationship of the ranges.

To create a named style:

1. Place the cell pointer in a cell that already has all the enhancements you will use to define the style.

2. Choose **S**tyle, Named **S**tyle. The Named Style dialog box appears.

In this worksheet, the title cells have named enhancements that identify them as title cells.

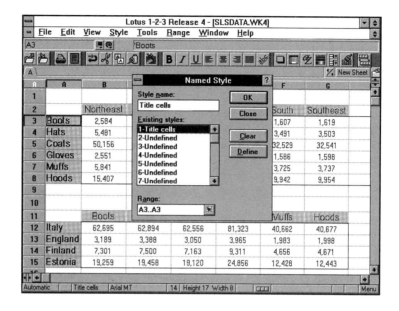

3. Type a name (up to 36 characters) in the Style **N**ame text box.

4. Choose **D**efine. The enhancements applied to the cell or range named in the R**a**nge box at the bottom of the dialog box are combined and identified as a named style.

5. Choose OK.

To apply a named style to a new range:

1. Select the range to which you want to apply the style.

2. Choose **S**tyle, Named **S**tyle. The Named Style dialog box appears.

3. Choose the style you want to apply.

4. Choose OK.

Using the Gallery To Apply Preset Styles

For those who don't want to take the time to do the interior decorating in a cell, or who prefer to leave decorating decisions to the experts, a gallery of styles exist.

The styles in the gallery are a combination of colors, borders, and patterns that you can apply to a range of cells, creating a professional-looking worksheet in a flash.

To apply a style from the gallery:

1. Select the range to which you want to apply the styles.

2. Choose **S**tyle, **G**allery. The Gallery dialog box appears.

The Gallery enables you to pick a series of enhancements for your data.

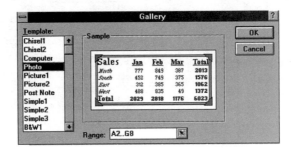

3. Scroll through the **T**emplate list. As each template name is high-lighted, the Sample box shows how that template looks on a sample worksheet.

4. Choose the template you want to use.

5. Choose OK.

Applying a Style Quickly to Another Range

If you have a set of styles in one range and want to apply them to an-other range, you can use the **C**opy and Paste **S**pecial commands, as follows:

1. Select a cell containing the styles you want to copy.

2. Choose **E**dit, **C**opy, or choose Copy from the quick menu.

3. Select the cell or range where you want to place the style.

4. Choose **E**dit, Paste **S**pecial. The Paste Special dialog box appears.

5. Choose **S**tyles Only.

6. Choose OK.

Note: *One other way to apply a series of styles to several ranges is to highlight all ranges as a collection. Highlight the first range to which you want to apply styles, hold down the Ctrl key, and then highlight the other ranges. When all ranges are selected, apply each style to the collection, which remains selected until you move the cell pointer.*

Changing the Default Appearance of the Worksheet

You may want to change the font for all cells in a worksheet or the width of every column. To make these changes (and others), you change the worksheet defaults. Remember that the changes you make in the worksheet defaults affect every cell in the current worksheet. You can change individual cells at any time.

Note: *Changing worksheet defaults has no effect on cells to which you have applied a unique setting. Changing the default column width, for example, will not affect a column whose width you changed earlier.*

To change the defaults for font, column width, alignment, and several other appearance attributes:

1. Choose **S**tyle, **W**orksheet Defaults. The Worksheet Defaults dialog box appears.

The Worksheet Defaults dialog box is used to change the way cells and their contents are displayed. Changes made here affect every cell in the current sheet.

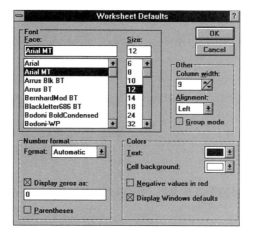

2. Change the default items as desired.

   Note: *If you aren't sure what will happen when you change a setting in this dialog box, review earlier sections of this chapter for details on formatting and appearance options. Two other options are explained later in this chapter.*

3. To apply the format to all cells in all worksheets in the file, make sure that **G**roup Mode is selected; otherwise, only the current worksheet is affected.

Note: *When **G**roup Mode is on, the following changes affect all worksheets in a file: number formats, fonts, text attributes, colors, alignment, row height, column width, protection settings, frozen titles, and page breaks.*

4. When you finish, choose OK.

The two options that were not explained earlier are as follows:

■ *Display **Z**eros As.* This option determines how zeros appear in the current worksheet. They will be displayed as zeros by default, but you can delete the zero from the text box; thereafter, any time a formula returns a zero, the cell containing the formula will appear to be empty. This allows you to copy a formula to cells where you will enter data later without having zeros littering the landscape.

You also can elect to display zeros as labels, such as N/A. Formulas that process cells containing zeros still consider the cell contents to be zero; they do not return ERR even though the label is visible in the cell.

■ *Display Windows Defaults.* When you choose this option, the colors you chose in the Control Panel of Windows' Program Manager take precedence over the color settings you made in the Worksheet Defaults dialog box. If you want your new color settings to take effect, make sure that the Displa**y** Windows Defaults box is unchecked.

Putting Drawings in Your Worksheet

You can use a line to connect two related cells, or an arrow to connect a comment to a specific cell or to an item in a chart. You can use a rectangle as a background for a chart or as a colored area between two sections of a worksheet.

Using **T**ools, **D**raw, you can add 11 graphic objects to a worksheet. Two of them—**B**uttons and **T**ext Boxes—are covered in chapters 11 and 13, respectively.

Drawing Objects

The techniques for drawing the various objects are essentially the same. Follow these steps:

1. Choose **T**ools, **D**raw, and then (from the cascade menu) choose the object you want to draw.

2. Click and drag from the place where you want the drawn object to start to the place where you want the object to end. Specifically, for each object:

The shapes you can create with **T**ools, **D**raw.

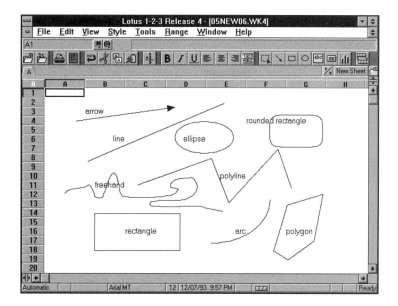

- ■ *Line.* Click and drag from the place where you want the line to begin to the place where you want the line to end.

- ■ *Polyline* (several straight lines connected at the ends). Click at the beginning point of the polyline, release the mouse button, click at each elbow in the line, and then double-click to end the polyline.

- ■ *Arrow.* Click and drag from the object the arrow points from, to the object the arrow points to. The arrowhead is placed when you release the mouse button.

■ *Rectangle.* Click and drag from where you want the top left corner of the rectangle to the place where you want the bottom right corner.

■ *Rounded Rectangle* (a rectangle with rounded corners). Same as rectangle.

■ *Arc.* Like a line, but bends as you click and drag the mouse pointer. Move the end selection handle, and the middle of the line whips from side to side.

■ *Ellipse* (an elongated circle). An ellipse will occupy a rectangular area. Click and drag from the place where you want the top left corner of the rectangle containing the ellipse to the place where you want the bottom right corner.

Note: *To create a square instead of a rectangle, a circle instead of an ellipse, or an arrow at a 45-degree angle, hold down the Shift key while you click and drag the mouse.*

■ *Polygon* (a multisided object). Click the beginning of the polygon, click at each corner, and double-click when you're done. You don't need to draw the last side; double-clicking completes the polygon from the last side you drew.

■ *Freehand* (a free-form object). Click and drag from where you want the drawing to start. The mouse pointer becomes a pencil and draws like a pencil until you release the mouse button.

Note: *To draw another object, you must click the tool or choose the menu command again.*

Selecting Objects

When you finish drawing an object, it will be selected. While an object is selected, it has selection handles.

The rectangle is selected. Notice the selection handles.

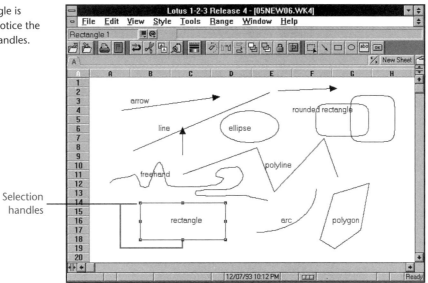

Selection handles

To select an object, click it. Notice that the mouse pointer changes shape when it is on a drawn object.

The rectangle is selected, and the mouse pointer has changed shape.

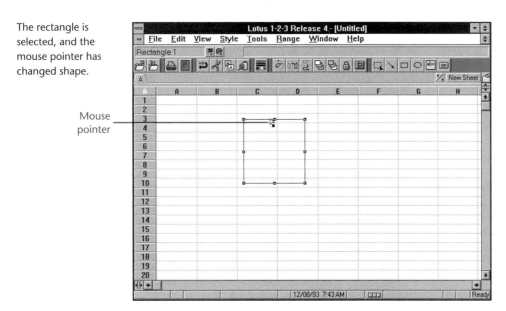

Mouse pointer

To select several drawn objects, Ctrl+click each object to be selected. If you want to select several objects that are close together on-screen, using the selection icon may be easier than Ctrl+clicking.

To use this icon to select objects, click the icon and then drag the mouse pointer around all the objects. Be sure that you enclose each part of each object; if any part of an object is not enclosed in the selection box, the object will not be selected.

Use the Select Several Objects icon to select more than one object.

Mouse pointer

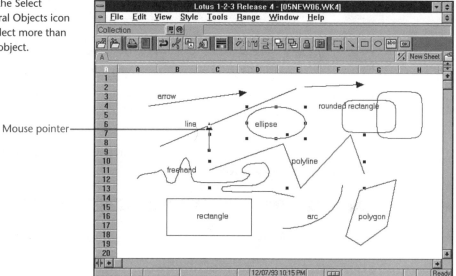

Moving and Resizing Objects

You can click and drag a selection handle to move or resize an object. For example, you can click and drag a rectangle's corner selection handle to move both adjacent sides at once, increasing or decreasing the size of the rectangle. To move only one side of a rectangle, click and drag a selec-tion handle in the middle of that side. To move the entire object, click and drag a side without touching a selection handle. To resize a two-dimensional object without changing its proportions, Shift+click and drag.

A rectangle being resized.

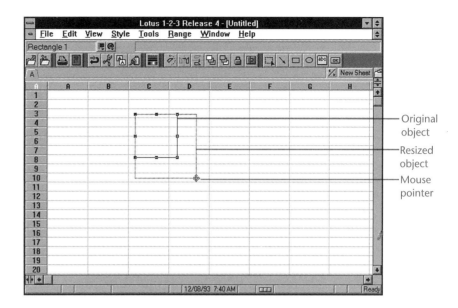

Original object

Resized object

Mouse pointer

An ellipse being moved.

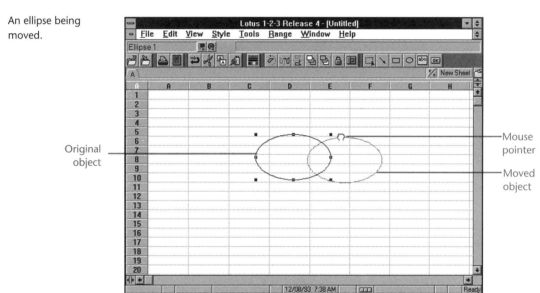

Original object

Mouse pointer

Moved object

To delete a drawn object, select the object and then press Del.

Arranging, Rotating, and Grouping Objects

While an object is selected, the **Edit, Arrange** command is active. Use the commands in the cascade menu associated with **Arrange** to perform the following tasks:

- ***B**ring to Front.* Causes the selected drawn object(s) to cover other objects.

- ***S**end to Back.* Causes the selected drawn object(s) to be covered by other objects.

- *Flip **L**eft–Right.* Turns the selected objects over around the object's Y-axis.

- *Flip **T**op–Bottom.* Turns the selected objects over around the object's X-axis.

In this figure, we selected the ellipse, and then used commands in the **Edit, Arrange** cascade menu to bring the ellipse to the front and rotate it.

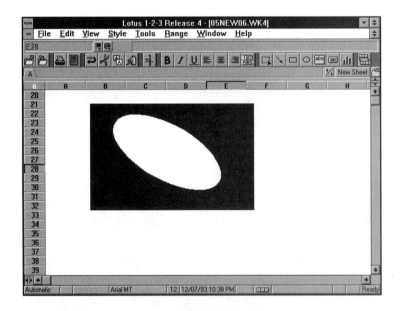

- ***R**otate.* Enables you to tilt the selected object(s).

- ***G**roup.* When several objects are selected, **G**roup causes any changes to affect them all. Moving grouped objects, for example, moves all of them at once, rather than one at a time.

- *Lo**c**k.* Makes it impossible to change or move the selected drawn object(s).

■ *Fasten to Cells.* By default, a drawn object is fastened only to the top left cell of the range it covers. If you insert a row or column, change column width or row height, or hide columns or rows in that range, the object's size will not change. If you choose **E**dit, **A**rrange, **F**asten to Cells, **T**op Left and Bottom Right Cells, the drawn object is anchored in both the top left and bottom right corners. The object's size will change if you insert rows or columns, change row height or column width, or hide rows or columns.

Changing an Object's Color, Shading, and Style

When one or more drawn objects are selected, you can use the **S**tyle, **L**ines & Color command to access the Lines & Color dialog box. The options available in the dialog box depend on the object selected. If a line or arrow is selected, you can change Line St**y**le, Line **W**idth, Line **C**olor, and the arrangement of **A**rrowheads on the line. If a rectangle or another two-dimensional object is selected, the full Lines & Color dialog box is available.

To change the appearance of an object:

1. Select the object or group of objects.

2. Choose **S**tyle, **L**ines & Color, or choose Lines & Color from the quick menu.

3. In the Lines & Color dialog box, choose one of the following options:

   ■ *Line St**y**le* to change the appearance of the line or sides

   ■ *Line **W**idth* to change the thickness of the line or sides

   ■ *Line **C**olor* to change the color of the line or sides

   ■ ***A**rrowheads* to change the placement of arrowheads on the line

   ■ ***B**ackground Color* to change the color of the background of a two-dimensional object

   ■ ***P**attern* to select a pattern to fill a two-dimensional object

   ■ *Pattern **C**olor* to select the color for the pattern of a two-dimensional object

■ *Designer Frame* to put a frame around a two-dimensional object

■ *Frame Color* to color the frame of a two-dimensional object

4. Choose OK.

Note: *Arcs and freehand drawings occupy a two-dimensional range, so when you choose **S**tyle, **L**ines & Color, you see the full Lines & Color dialog box. Because arcs and freehand drawings really are only lines, making pattern and background-color choices has no effect.*

The following figure contains two colors, one blending into the other. This effect is one that you can use in closed drawn objects and chart elements.

This rectangle has two colors blending into each other.

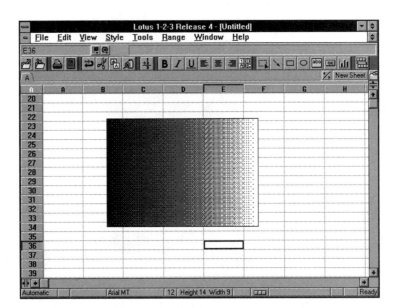

To blend one color into another:

1. Create the object.

2. Choose **S**tyle, **L**ines & Color, or choose Lines & Color from the quick menu.

3. Choose a color for the background and another for the pattern.

4. Choose one of the last four patterns in the pattern-selection box, showing the two colors on opposite sides of the box.

The pattern selections in the Lines & Color dialog box.

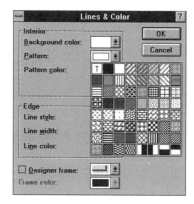

5. Choose OK.

Summary

To	Do This
Format a value	Select the cell or range; choose a format in the status bar
Automatically format a value	Type the digits and necessary other symbols (such as **$**)
Align text in a cell	Choose **S**tyle, **A**lignment
Change font	Choose **S**tyle, **F**ont & Attributes
Add lines, color, pattern, or frame	Choose **S**tyle, **L**ines & Color

On Your Own
Estimated time: 30 minutes

1. Enter **1000** in a cell, and then change the format to Currency with two decimal places.

2. Enter **1000** in another cell, and then automatically format the cell as Currency with no decimal places.

3. Enter today's date in one cell and your birthdate in another. Write a formula that calculates the number of days that have elapsed since your birth.

4. Align the 1000 that you entered in the first exercise in the center of the cell.

5. Raise the height of the cell, and then align the 1000 in the middle of the cell.

6. Change the font in the cell to a larger typeface.

7. Boldface and italicize the cell contents, and then remove the italics.

8. Color a selected range's background red.

9. Place a frame around the same selected range.

10. Name the style in that range and apply it elsewhere.

11. Draw a circle around a group of cells.

Chapter 6

Using Basic Functions

A special type of formula in 1-2-3 for Windows is a function. In Release 4 of 1-2-3 for Windows, more than 220 different functions are available. This chapter provides a overview of functions, describes the steps used to create functions, and explains a few of the functions in each category.

Specific topics covered in this chapter are:

- An overview of functions

- Categories of functions

- Functions in cells

- Incorrectly entered functions

- Commonly used functions

- A customized function list

Understanding Functions

Functions
Preprogrammed series of substitutes for custom formulas.

Argument
The information included in a function that specifies the data or location of data to be processed.

Several differences exist between standard formulas and *functions*. One difference is that you can customize standard formulas to a greater extent than you can functions. The reason is simple: you can specify a large number of individual cells and any combination of mathematical operations in the custom formula. Functions require specific *arguments* and perform one operation at a time.

In a custom formula, you must specify every operation to be performed. In a function, however, the operations are programmed in, so you need only supply needed information in the form of arguments.

Whether you should write a formula or a function is determined by the degree of flexibility you need in processing data or the complexity of the calculations to be performed.

Writing Correct Functions

Syntax
The exact and correct way to type commands and functions. In general, computer programs are rather inflexible about even one wrong keystroke, such as a missing comma.

When the time comes to add arguments to a function, you must use the proper *syntax*. Forgetting the argument separators (usually commas or semicolons), entering spaces where none are allowed, and typing invalid cell references are examples of incorrect syntax that will activate Edit mode. You have to eliminate the syntax errors before 1-2-3 for Windows accepts the formula into the cell.

When the argument placeholder says "list", it usually means that a cell or range of cells is required. Using the name of a named range rather than cell addresses is not only acceptable, but often preferable. Using range names is faster than typing range addresses, and it gives greater assurance that certain actions—such as moving or copying data, or insertion or deletion of rows and columns—will not corrupt the results of the function. (Naming ranges is covered in Chapter 9, "Working with Multiple Worksheets and Multiple Documents.")

Types of Function Arguments

Arguments must be separated by an *argument separator*: a comma, a period, or a semicolon. Be sure that you use only one type of separator in a function. For example, you cannot use both a comma and a semicolon in one function. Use **T**ools, **U**ser Setup, **I**nternational, **P**unctuation to change the argument separator.

Functions include four types of arguments:

■ *Location.* A location argument could be the address or name of a cell or range, or a formula that returns a range address or name. The function assumes that a cell address is in the current worksheet unless you precede the address with a worksheet letter (for example, C:A5).

- *String.* A string argument is text (as opposed to a value) that consists of any sequence of letters, numbers, and/or symbols, or a reference to a cell or range that contains a string. The argument must be enclosed in double quotes (for example, "string").

- *Value.* A value argument is a number or a reference to a cell or range that contains a number, or a formula or function that returns a number.

- *Condition.* A condition argument is an expression that uses a logical or relational operator (for example, < > = <> >= <= #NOT# #OR# #AND#), a cell or range that contains a conditional expression, or a formula or function that returns a conditional expression.

The parenthesized argument of a function often is the range of cells whose data the function processes. When you include a range as an argument, be sure that you type the cell address of one corner cell, followed by two periods, and then the address of the opposite corner cell. If you want the sum of cells A1 through B10, for example, you could use A1..B10, A10..B1, B10..A1, or B1..A10 as an argument.

Note: *Using two periods between the corner-cell addresses in a range argument is only a convention; actually, you can use any number of periods. Don't bother editing the number of periods if you type too many; you have more important things to do.*

6

Entering a Function into a Cell

The @SUM function in the following figure contains all the requisite parts. A correctly written function includes the at symbol (@), the name of the specific function, and the arguments in parentheses.

The formula in cell
A11 is a typical
@SUM function.

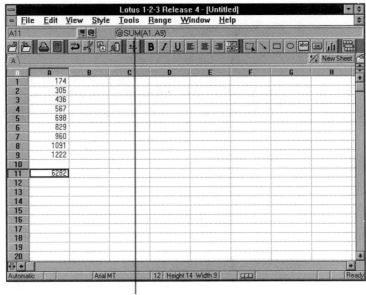

This formula results in the value shown in A11

You can use either of two methods to enter a function into a cell. The
first method is to type every keystroke. This method is useful and probably fast if you are familiar with the function and the use of its arguments. Type the entire function, including arguments, and then press
Enter; the result of the function appears in the cell.

**If you have
problems...**

Functions cannot contain spaces. If you try to enter a function with a space
into a cell, 1-2-3 for Windows goes into Edit mode, with the insertion point
blinking at the place where you typed the space.

The other method is to use the Function List dialog box, which lists all
the functions and briefly describes how to use them. This method is
useful if you are not familiar with the function you need to use.

To enter a function by using the Function List dialog box:

  1. Position the cell pointer in the cell where you want to create the
      function.

2. Type an at symbol (**@**). Then press the F3 (Names) key or click the function icon in the edit line, and choose List All. The Function List dialog box appears.

The Function List dialog box displays an alphabetized list of all possible function names.

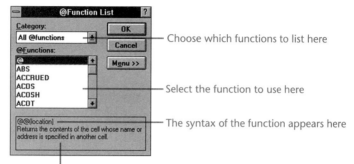

Choose which functions to list here

Select the function to use here

The syntax of the function appears here

A brief description of the use of the function appears here

3. If you want to narrow down the list of functions shown and know the category of the function you are looking for, choose that category in the **C**ategory drop-down list. Otherwise, leave All Functions selected to display the complete list.

4. Scroll through the **F**unctions list until you find the function you want to use.

Alternatively, you can locate the function you want by typing the first letter of its name. The highlight jumps to the first function name that starts with that letter. Scroll from there to the specific function you want to use, or press the same letter again to jump to the next function beginning with that letter.

5. When the function you want to use is highlighted, choose OK.

1-2-3 for Windows places the @ symbol and function name in the current cell, along with the necessary parentheses and a brief description of the required arguments. If more than one argument is required, the arguments are separated by argument separators as they should be when the function is complete. The insertion point is placed after the opening parenthesis.

6

After you choose a
function from the
dialog box, it
appears like this
in a cell.

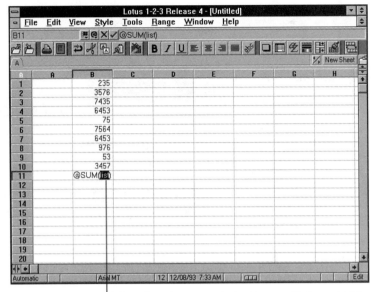

You replace this with the location of the cells to be summed—in this case, B1 through B10

6. Enter the necessary arguments by typing them.

Alternatively, if the argument is a range, you can use the mouse to
select the range. 1-2-3 for Windows enters the address in the function as you drag the mouse.

Clicking and
dragging to enter a
range in a function.

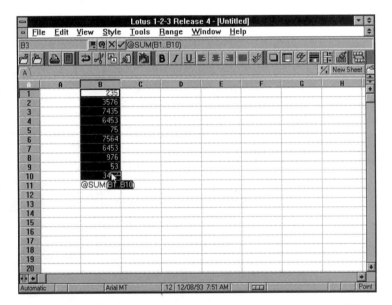

7. When you finish, press Enter or click the checkmark icon.

The finished @SUM function.

The formula actually entered in the cell

	Lotus 1-2-3 Release 4 - [Untitled]	
	File Edit View Style Tools Range Window Help	

B11   @SUM(B1..B10)

	A	B	C	D	E	F	G	H
1		235						
2		3576						
3		7435						
4		6453						
5		75						
6		7564						
7		6453						
8		976						
9		53						
10		3457						
11		36277						
12								
13								
14								
15								
16								
17								
18								
19								
20								

Automatic   Arial MT   12   12/08/93 7:52 AM   Ready

The result of the @SUM function

If you have problems...

If you press Enter after you make a mistake in a function, ERR appears in a cell, or 1-2-3 for Windows refuses to enter the formula into the cell and goes into Edit mode, where you can fix the mistake. In the best of circumstances, the insertion point jumps to the place where you made the mistake, but this doesn't always happen, so plan to study the entire formula to find the mistake. For details on how to correct mistakes, see "Fixing Incorrect Functions" later in this chapter.

6

Caution
Do not click another cell in the worksheet to finish writing the function. If you do, the cell you click will be included as an argument, replacing the range you selected.

Understanding How To Use Ranges in Functions

You can include several separate ranges in many functions. If you want one @SUM function that adds the data in A1 through A10, C1 through C10, and E1 through E5, type the formula with commas between the ranges. The correct syntax is visible in the edit line of the following figure.

A function that adds several ranges. In such a case, you cannot use the mouse to select multiple ranges.

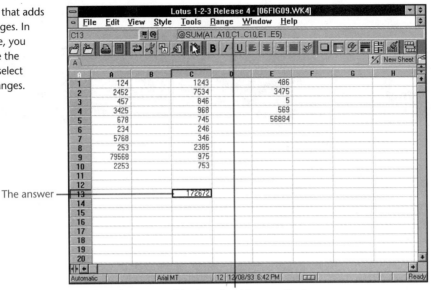

The answer

The formula as entered in the cell, adding a collection

Some functions require you to select only the cells that will be used in the formula (for example, @VLOOKUP or @HLOOKUP). @SUM, on the other hand, allows you to include empty cells or cells that contain labels; these cells do not cause the function to return an inaccurate result.

If you have problems...   Users commonly select more cells than the ones containing the data to be processed by the function. Sometimes, this is a good idea; you might plan to fill the extra cells later and want the formula in place now. Sometimes, however, it's a bad idea; you might include extraneous data. Worst of all, you might accidentally include in a range argument the cell in which the formula was written, thus creating a circular argument. (Circular arguments are covered in Chapter 4, "Modifying Data in a Worksheet.") In general, make it a rule to select only the cells whose contents you want to include in the formula.

If you have problems...   If a function that uses a range is not returning the right answer, make sure that the range is correctly entered. Ensure that all cells are included and that no extraneous cells containing data are included.

Fixing Incorrect Functions

The time will come when you are trying to enter a complicated function into a cell, but no matter what you do, 1-2-3 for Windows beeps and goes into Edit mode or displays ERR in the formula cell. To enter into the cell whatever you typed, so that you can go on to something else, put an apostrophe in front of the function. An apostrophe at the beginning of a formula makes the formula a label; it won't return an answer, but you can enter it into the cell.

When you are ready to fix the function:

1. Go to the cell and enter Edit mode (press F2 or double-click the cell).

2. Remove the apostrophe, and then place the insertion point in the name of the function right after the @ symbol.

3. Press F1 (Help). A screen of information about that function appears, including details on the required arguments, which is where most people make mistakes.

If you have problems...   A common mistake in complicated functions involves parentheses. Be sure that for every open parenthesis, there is a corresponding closed parenthesis. All parentheses must be placed in the right location to honor the program's demand for perfect syntax.

If you have problems...   A fairly common mistake among new users is substituting a plus sign for the periods in an @SUM formula. @SUM(A1..A10) is much different from @SUM(A1+A10); in the latter formula, only the first and last cells are added.

Entering Commonly Used Functions

You can write several common kinds of functions solely with the mouse, never touching the keyboard. Initially, the Function List dialog box contains six functions that you can use this way; you can add or delete functions to fit your needs.

Because these six functions are so commonly used, the next several sections provide step-by-step directions.

Summing a Range of Cells

@SUM adds the values in a range. Follow these steps to write an @SUM function quickly:

1. Click the cell in which you want the answer to appear.

2. Click the @function selector icon, and then choose SUM.

3. Click and drag across the cells that contain the numbers to be summed.

An @SUM function being written without use of the keyboard.

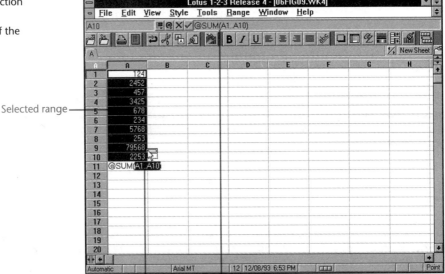

Selected range

The range address in the formula   The formula

4. Finish the process by clicking the checkmark icon in the edit line.

Calculating the Average of Cell Values

To write an @AVG formula:

1. Click the cell in which you want the answer to appear.

2. Click the @function selector icon, and then choose AVG.

3. Click and drag across the numbers to be averaged.

4. Click the checkmark icon to finish the formula.

If you have problems...

If the average does not appear to be correct, make sure that the range doesn't include any extra cells with values or labels. When writing an @AVG formula, you should be sure to highlight only the specific cells whose contents you want to average.

An @AVG formula.

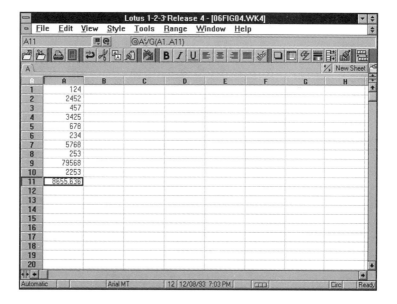

Rounding Values

If you need to round a monetary amount to the nearest dollar or to the nearest cent, you would use the @ROUND function. You can round to decimals or to whole numbers.

To use @ROUND:

1. Click the cell in which you want the answer to appear.

2. Click the @function selector icon, and then choose ROUND.

3. Replace the first argument, x, with the number you want to round or with a cell address for the cell that contains the value you want to round.

Note: *You can enter the address of only a single cell for @ROUND.*

4. Replace the second argument, *n*, with a number that tells the function how precisely to round the number. Use positive precision values to specify places to the right of the decimal point and negative precision values to specify values to the left. The function uses the number as a power of 10. For example, an entry of 3 rounds the number to the nearest thousandth, –3 rounds to the nearest thousand, and 0 rounds to the nearest whole number.

A series of @ROUND formulas showing the effect of substituting different values for *n*.

@ROUND(A3,2)

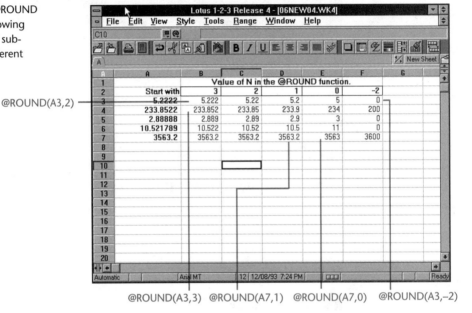

@ROUND(A3,3)   @ROUND(A7,1)   @ROUND(A7,0)   @ROUND(A3,–2)

 5. Finish the process by clicking the checkmark icon in the edit line.

Using Conditional Statements

Conditional statements are used to implement different actions depending on whether the condition is true or false. The simplest conditional function in 1-2-3 is @IF. Use this function to get one answer if the condition is true and another if it is false.

An example of an @IF function is @IF(*condition,x,y*), which checks the condition to see whether it is met. If the condition is met, the function takes the action specified in the *x* argument. If the condition is not met, the function takes the action specified in the *y* argument.

To enter an @IF function:

1. Click the cell in which you want the answer to appear.

2. Click the @function selector icon, and then choose IF.

3. Replace the first argument, *condition*, with the condition on which your statement is based.

A condition argument usually is a logical argument, one that returns 0 or 1. The logical common operators are:

$$= < > >= <=$$

The following figure shows some common examples.

An example of an @IF formula.

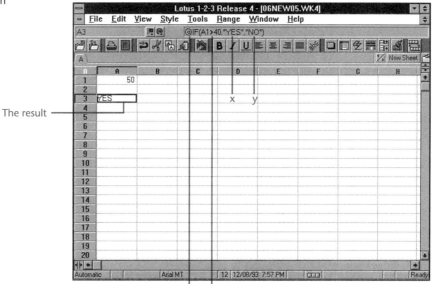

The result

The formula   The condition

4. Replace the second argument, *x*, with the value you want the cell to have if the condition is true.

5. Replace the final argument, *y*, with the value you want the cell to have if the condition is false.

6. Finish the process by clicking the checkmark icon in the edit line.

Entering Today's Date

Entering the current date is useful for a variety of reasons—for example, to include the date in a report or to use the date in calculations.

To enter the current date:

1. Format the cell with a date format.

2. Click the cell in which you want the date to appear.

 3. Click the @function selector icon, and then choose TODAY.

After you enter the date, you should format it in Date format (if you want the date to show) or in a numeric format such as General (if you want to use it in calculations). For details on numeric formats, refer to Chapter 5, "Changing the Appearance of a Worksheet."

Calculating Net Present Value

The final item in the default Function List is NVP, which stands for net present value, a financial function that is used to determine the worth of stream-of-cash flows.

To use the @NVP function:

1. Click the cell in which you want the answer to appear.

 2. Click the @function selector icon, and then choose NPV.

3. Replace the first argument, *interest*, with the interest rate by which you want to discount the cash flows.

4. Replace the second argument, *range*, with the range that contains the series of cash flows.

 5. Finish the process by clicking the checkmark icon in the edit line.

An example of an
@NPV function.

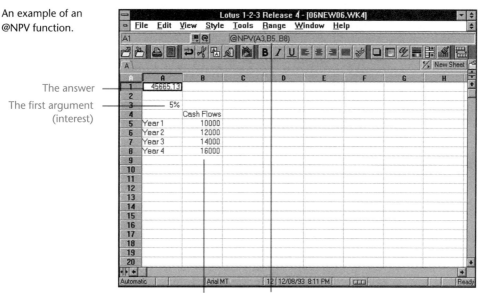

The answer

The first argument
(interest)

The second argument (range)   The formula

Customizing the Function List

The functions initially included in the Function List are those that the
manufacturer assumes are the ones most users will choose most often. You
may need to add some functions to the list and may never use others.

To remove functions from the list:

1. Call the Function List to the screen by typing @ and then pressing F3,
   or by clicking the @function selector icon and then clicking List All.

2. Choose M**e**nu. The Function List expands to include a Current
   Menu section.

6

Clicking M**e**nu in
the Function List
box adds the
Current **M**enu
section to the box.

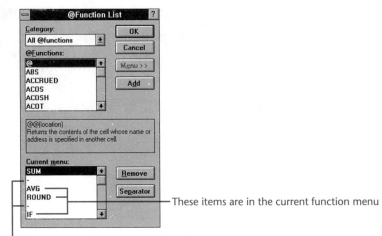

These items are in the current function menu

These lines indicate separators in the current function menu

3. Select the function in the Current **M**enu list.

4. Choose **R**emove.

To add an item to the list:

1. In the Current **M**enu list, select the function below which you want to place the new function.

2. In the @**F**unctions list, choose List All.

3. Select the function you want to add.

4. Choose A**d**d.

5. To add a *separator*—the line across the list of functions in the drop-down list—select the function below which you want to add the separator, and then choose Se**p**arator.

The modified
function list, with the
separator added,
CELLPOINTER added,
and NPV removed.

 — Separator

Separators are not essential. But if you add a large number of new functions to the list, you may want to use separators to group the functions by categories, making them easier to find.

If the list becomes too long for all functions to be visible when you click the @function selector icon, the list appears with a scroll bar.

Summary

To	Do This
Enter a function	Type **@**, the name of the function, and the required arguments
Use the Names key to enter a function	Type **@**; then press F3
Use an icon to enter a function	Click the @ icon; then select the function
Get help on a function	Type the name of a function in a cell, or select it from the @function selector icon list; then press F1
Add or delete functions from the Function List	Click the @ icon; choose List All; choose Me**n**u;, select a function; choose A**d**d or **R**emove

On Your Own

Estimated time: 20 minutes

1. Enter 10 numbers in a column, and then use the @ icon to write an @SUM function.

2. Write an @SUM function without touching the keyboard.

3. Write an @SUM function to add the first three and the last three numbers.

4. Calculate the average of the 10 numbers.

5. Add a function to the drop-down list associated with the @ icon, and then delete the function.

6. Calculate the number of days that have elapsed since your last birthday.

7. Calculate the net present value of a series of five annual cash flows with an interest rate of 3.75 percent.

8. Write an @IF function that refers to the column of numbers you entered for the first exercise. If the first number in the list is greater than 100, have the function return the label YES; if that number is less than 100, have the function return NO.

6

Part III
Getting the Most from 1-2-3 for Windows

Chapter 7

Printing a Worksheet

Unless you plan to walk around the office carrying your monitor so that people can see your work, you have to print your documents. In this chapter, you learn the steps you must take to make your document ready to print, to add enhancements, and to cause a piece of paper to come out of your printer with legible data on it.

This chapter covers the following topics:

- Arranging data for printing
- Changing the page setup
- Saving page settings for use in other documents
- Setting page settings as defaults
- Specifying what to print
- Previewing your work
- Setting up the printer
- Printing your work

Arranging the Data for Printing

Before you print, you must ensure that the printed page is well-organized and appealing. You might perform the following tasks:

- Move data so that it is logically arranged for inclusion in the range of cells being printed.
- Arrange data in accordance with the shape of the printed page.
- Reduce white space between blocks of text so that the data fits on one page, or add some white space to separate blocks of data.

■ Position charts near the data they represent to prevent confusion.

■ Display titles in large fonts so that they stand out.

■ Hide rows or columns that contain sensitive data. (For details on hiding and changing the size of columns and rows, refer to Chapter 4, "Modifying Data in a Worksheet.")

Changing the Page Setup

Portrait
Printing a page of data so that the long sides of the page are the left and right.

In addition to arranging data, you can change the page setup before printing your document. If the printed pages must be wider than they are long, you can change the direction in which the worksheet is printed on the page. If you have a multiple-page document, you probably want to add headers or footers that include the page number and titles, so that readers know what the data on the pages after the first page refer to. These changes and others are covered in the next several sections.

Changing the Page Orientation

Landscape
Printing a page of data so that the long sides of the page are the top and bottom.

Depending on the arrangement of data on-screen, you can switch from the default *portrait* orientation to *landscape* orientation. Use landscape orientation when the data is too wide to fit on a page in portrait orientation.

Using a landscape page in a report means that readers have to rotate the report to study your data, but that probably is better than breaking the data over two pages.

This data looks better printed in landscape orientation. The data is not crowded between the margins, so the printout is easier to read.

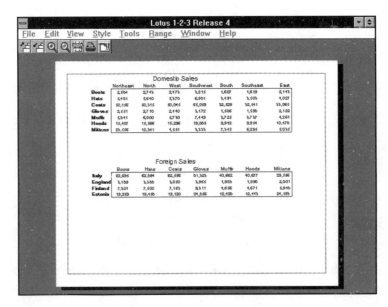

Note: *The preceding figure shows the Print Preview view of a worksheet. To learn how to use Print Preview, see "Previewing Your Work" later in this chapter.*

To change page orientation:

The Orientation section of the Page Setup dialog box determines the direction in which the page is printed.

1. Choose **F**ile, Pa**g**e Setup. The Page Setup dialog box appears.

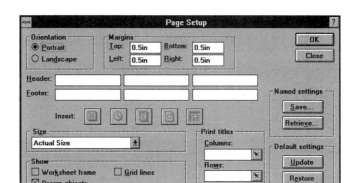

Note: *Other portions of the Page Setup dialog box are discussed later in this chapter.*

2. In the Orientation section, choose **P**ortrait or Lan**d**scape.

3. Choose OK.

Making the Data Fit the Page

You can take several steps to get data to fit within a single page. Moving the data closer together and narrowing columns or rows, especially empty ones, is certainly one obvious step. A second step is to change the fonts you use for the data. Smaller font sizes take up less space. For information on changing fonts, refer to Chapter 5, "Changing the Appearance of a Worksheet."

You also can use several options in the Pa**g**e Setup dialog box to fit data to the page. To use any of these options:

1. Choose **F**ile, Pa**g**e Setup. The Page Setup dialog box appears.

2. Choose an option in the Si**z**e drop-down box. The five choices are:

■ *Actual Size.* This option prints data without making any effort to fit it onto a single sheet. Use this selection to cancel another size selection.

- *Fit All to Page.* This option adjusts the size of the displayed data so that it fits on a single page. 1-2-3 for Windows compresses the data as small as one-seventh its original size in an attempt to make it fit one page.

- *Fit Columns to Page.* This option adjusts column width (but not row height) to make the data fit one page.

- *Fit Rows to Page.* This option adjusts row height (but not column width) to make the data fit one page.

- *Manually Scale.* This option enables you to enter a number between 15 and 1,000 to specify the percentage of compression or expansion of the data. Setting the scale at 1,000 increases the size of the display to 10 times its original size; setting it at 15 shrinks the display to about one-seventh its original size.

3. Choose OK.

This Print Preview page, set manually, is 125 percent normal size. Compare it with the first figure in the preceding section, which is actual size.

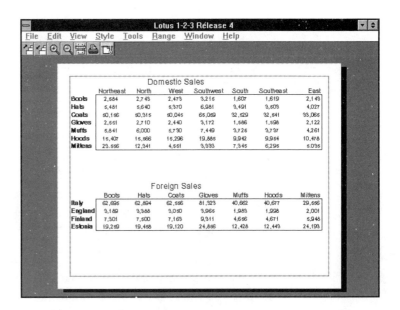

If you have problems...

Using one of the fit-to-page options can shrink the display so much that you can't read it. To avoid too much compression, insert a manual page break so that less data fits on a single page. (For details, see "Inserting a Page Break" later in this chapter.)

If you select a drawn object, such as a chart, and then choose Page Setup, a different set of choices is available:

- *Actual Size.* This option shows the drawn object at its actual size compared with other items in the worksheet.

- *Fill Page.* This option changes the shape of the selected drawn object so that it fills the entire page.

- *Fill Page but Keep Proportions.* This option makes the selected drawn object fill as much of the page as possible without changing the object's shape.

For details on selecting objects to print, see "Specifying What To Print" later in this chapter.

Adding Headers and Footers

Header/footer
A single line of text that appears automatically at the top (header) or bottom (footer) of each printed page.

When you are printing several pages, consider using a *header* or *footer*. Headers and footers remind the reader of the name of the entire document and enable you to add page numbers or other useful information without having to type it on every page.

Headers and footers are the first or last line of text, respectively, and are separated from the main text by two blank lines. They are printed in the worksheet's default font.

To add a header or a footer:

1. Choose **F**ile, Pa**g**e Setup.

2. In the Page Setup dialog box, place the cursor in one of the three text boxes for **H**eader or **F**ooter.

   Entries in the left text box align at the left margin; entries in the center box are centered; and entries in the right box align with the right margin.

   Note: *You can use as many of the header and footer boxes as you want, but using more than one of each might result in a cluttered worksheet that would distract the reader. Also, if you use two long headers or two long footers, the text could overlap when you print the file.*

3. Type the text for the header or footer. Click any of the icons to add features, as described after these steps. Type a space between text and elements added with icons.

7

Caution

If you create three headers or footers, make sure that they aren't too long. If any of the three is too long, it will overlap the adjacent text. Unless you want overlap for a decorative effect, make sure that all header and footer text is legible.

These are the icons you can use to include extra information in headers and footers.

Note: You can combine the date, time, page number, and file name with text you type in a header or footer, but you cannot combine cell contents with typed text or other features.

4. Choose OK.

You can include certain kinds of information in headers or footers by clicking the icons in the Page Setup dialog box below the footer line. The icons are inactive until you place the cursor in one of the text boxes.

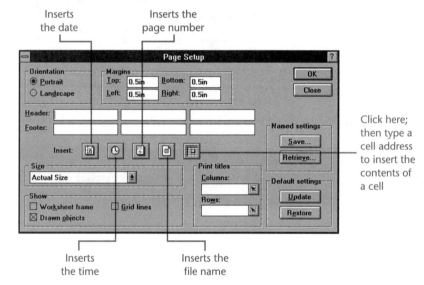

Inserts the date

Inserts the page number

Click here; then type a cell address to insert the contents of a cell

Inserts the time

Inserts the file name

One reason for using the date or time in a header is to let readers know what version of a report they have if you are continually updating and printing the report. You could create a header that says, "Printed on @ at +". When you print the report, 1-2-3 for Windows replaces the symbols with the date and the current time, respectively.

Note: If the printed date and time aren't correct, fix the computer's date and time, using the Date/Time setting in the Windows Control Panel. (For instructions on setting the date and time, see Que's Using Windows 3.1, Special Edition *or your Windows documentation.)*

The Page Number icon prints only the number, so if you want the word *Page* to appear with the number, type it in one of the text boxes before you click the icon.

If you have problems...	The header and footer boxes accept a range address rather than a single cell, but only the first cell in the range is printed, so there is no point in entering a range address.

Also, text in the cell is printed in the worksheet's default font and size, even if you changed those settings for that cell.

Including the Frame, Grid, or Drawn Objects in the Printout

The options in the Show area of the Page Setup dialog box enable you to include the Wor**k**sheet Frame, **G**rid Lines, and Drawn **O**bjects in the printout. The *frame* is the row-number, column-letter part of the worksheet, visible above and to the left of the work area. The *grid lines* are the dotted lines that are visible between rows and columns. When you include a frame and grid lines, readers can easily see the row and column locations of data.

To include any or all of these elements in the printout:

1. Choose **F**ile, Pa**g**e Setup.

2. In the Show section of the Page Setup dialog box, choose Wor**k**sheet Frame, **G**rid Lines, and/or Drawn **O**bjects.

This is how your print job looks if you choose to display a worksheet grid and frame but not drawn objects.

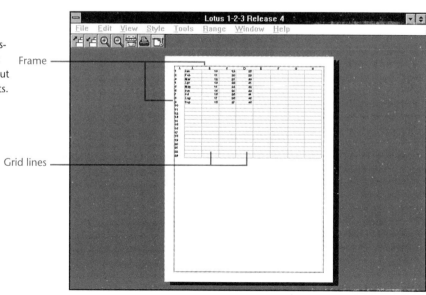

Frame

Grid lines

7

Drawn objects include charts and objects that you create with the **T**ools, **D**raw command.

This is the same worksheet with drawn and chart objects displayed, but without the frame or grid lines displayed.

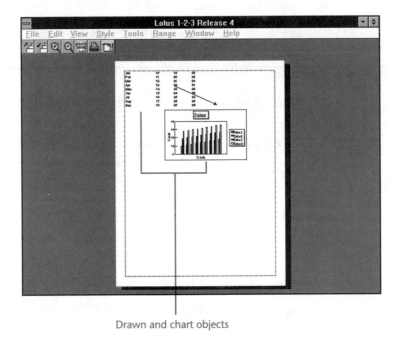

Drawn and chart objects

Changing the Margins

By default, margins are set around the page at one-half inch, measured from the nearest side of the page. You can change any or all of the margins.

To change the margins:

1. Choose **F**ile, Pa**g**e Setup.

2. In the Margins section of the Page Setup dialog box, choose the margin you want to change—**T**op, **L**eft, **B**ottom, or **R**ight—and then type the new margin measurement in the adjacent text box.

   You can type metric measurements in millimeters or centimeters and abbreviate them mm or cm. A space is optional. The maximum margin you can use is 32 inches or 812 mm; the minimum margin is zero.

   Note: *When you change one measurement from English to metric units, all four margin measurements change to the new units. If you use centimeters, 1-2-3 for Windows automatically converts the other margins' measurements to millimeters.*

If you have problems...

If you set the margins so that the total left and right margins are greater than the width of the paper, or the total top and bottom margins are greater than the length, you get an error message when you try to print or preview. Check your paper size to make sure that the margins fit on the page; then try again.

3. Choose OK.

If you have problems...

Some printers cannot print exactly to the edge of the paper, so setting margins to zero may cause data at the edges to be lost.

Using Print Titles

The term *titles* here is misleading, because it does not refer to a title for a worksheet. To give a worksheet a title, you have to type the text in a row near the top and then change the font if you want the title to stand out.

Titles
Rows or columns designated to print on every page of a printout.

In this context, *titles* refers to certain rows or columns designated to print on every page. When a table of data is so large that it appears on several pages, the data on later pages appears in rows and columns, but without benefit of the column or row titles that appear only on page one. Titles ensure that your column or row heads appear on each page in which your table of data appears, so that the reader can tell which column or row each data item is in.

This is page two of a list of cars in a used-car lot; print titles were used in the worksheet. The frame shows the actual row numbers.

The print title

Data in rows well below title row

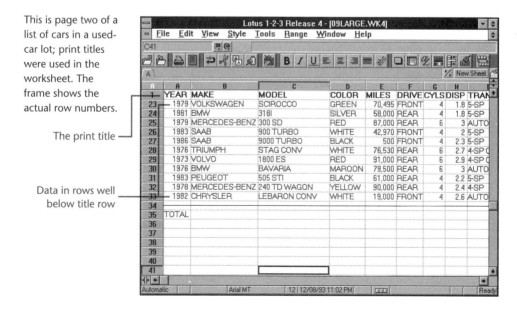

7

To designate a column or a row as a title:

1. Choose **F**ile, Pa**g**e Setup.

2. Click the **C**olumns or **R**ows text box, and then type the address of at least one cell in the column or row that you want to designate as a title.

If you use the SmartIcons to designate the current row or column as a print title, make sure that you first place the cell pointer in the proper row or column.

or

Click the arrowhead next to the **C**olumn or **R**ow text box. The worksheet appears on-screen. Drag the selection indicator to highlight the column or row you want to designate as a title. When you release the mouse button, you return to the Page Setup dialog box, where the range is filled in.

3. Choose OK. Only the column or row you selected becomes a print title.

Note: *Selecting one cell in a row or column causes the entire row or column to become a print title, so you don't have to select every cell.*

If you have problems...   If the print titles appear twice in the printed page, make sure that you did *not* include in the print range the rows or columns that you designated as print titles. For information on printing only a selected range, see "Specifying What To Print" later in this chapter.

Reusing Your Page Settings

At the right side of the Page Setup dialog box are sections titled Named Settings and Default Settings. Each setting enables you to save the changes you made in the page setup so that you can apply those changes to future print jobs. The Named Settings options enable you to save a variety of settings; the Default Settings options make the current settings the defaults for all future print jobs.

Naming and Saving Page Setups

If you routinely print several types of files with identical page setups, save the settings for each type of file so you don't have to change them for each file before you print.

To save the settings in the current document:

1. Choose **F**ile, Pa**g**e Setup.

2. Choose **S**ave. A dialog box appears that enables you to specify the file name and, if necessary, to change the drive or directory in which the settings are saved. Unless you specify otherwise, the settings file is saved to the same directory as the current file.

The Save Named Settings dialog box enables you to save the current page settings so you can apply them to another document.

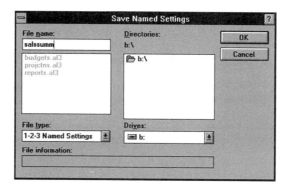

3. Type a file name in the File **N**ame text box. The settings are saved—with the file name you choose and with the extension AL3—to the same drive and directory as the current file.

4. Choose OK to save the settings and return to the Page Setup dialog box.

To apply the saved settings to another document:

1. Choose **F**ile, Pa**g**e Setup.

2. In the Named Settings section of the Page Setup dialog box, choose Retrie**v**e. The Retrieve Named Settings dialog box appears.

7

The Retrieve Named
Settings dialog box
enables you to
apply a specific
group of page
settings to the
current document
when you print it.

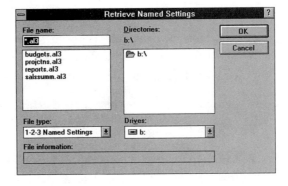

3. Specify the drive and directory (if the file you want to use is not in the current drive or directory), and then choose the proper file name.

4. Choose OK to return to the Page Setup dialog box.

The Page Setup dialog box reflects the settings you saved earlier, in case you want to make changes. At this point, you can make any necessary changes specific to printing the current worksheet.

If you have problems...   After you apply a named setting and then print or preview the file, the header or footer may look strange if the named setting refers to a cell as a source for the header or footer. Choose **F**ile, Pa**g**e Setup to open the Page Setup dialog box, and then examine the **H**eader and **F**ooter text boxes. If one box includes a cell reference, the cell in the current file might contain information that you don't want to use as a header or footer. Delete the reference or replace it.

Working with Page Setup Defaults

You can specify that whenever you choose **F**ile, Pa**g**e Setup, settings different from program defaults should appear automatically. You might, for example, prefer always to have 1-inch margins all around the page. Or you might have a standard header and prefer not to enter it every time you start a new document.

To change the page-setup defaults:

1. Choose **F**ile, Pa**g**e Setup.

2. Make all the changes you want.

3. Choose **U**pdate in the Default Settings section.

4. Choose OK. From now on, whenever you see the Page Setup dialog box, the new settings will be the defaults.

   Note: *Undo does not reverse changes saved as the default. Make sure that you really want to change the default before you choose **U**pdate; otherwise, you have to manually change the settings if you decide to return to the original program default. That task may be difficult if you don't know all the original settings and have made many changes.*

Caution

Don't update the default with changes that are appropriate for only a few files. Use **U**pdate only for settings that you want to use for most of your files.

If you start to make many changes in the Page Setup dialog box, or if you retrieve a saved settings file and then decide to use the default settings rather than the changed ones, choose R**e**store to remove all the changed settings and return to the default page settings.

Note: *R**e**store returns the default settings. If you used **U**pdate to change the default, the new defaults will be the ones restored in the Page Setup dialog box—not the original program defaults.*

Specifying What To Print

By default, when you print, every cell that contains information is included in the printed document. You might not want to include every cell in the printout, however. If your file contains macros off to one side, data that you don't want everyone to see, columns or rows designated as print titles, or large amounts of white space, you have to specify the range or ranges you want to print. In general, the best technique is to select the range or ranges you want printed before you use the **P**rint command.

To select a print range, use any of the following techniques (the first three essentially are the same mouse methods used to select a range for any purpose):

- Click and drag across all cells you want to print.

- Place the cell pointer in one corner of the print range, and then use the scroll bars to bring the opposite corner of the range into view (don't move the cell pointer from the original cell). Shift+click the opposite corner of the print range. Every cell between the two corner cells is selected. This technique is especially useful for selecting a large range.

7

- When you want to print several ranges, select them as a collection. (Press the Ctrl key while you select all the ranges after the first range.) You can either preselect the collection or choose **F**ile, **P**rint and then type all range addresses (separated by commas) in the **S**elected Range text box of the Print dialog box. To print A:A1 through B:F10 and B:H1 through C:J10, for example, you would type **A:A1..B:F10,B:H1..C:J10**.

- Select a range, and then click the Print Range SmartIcon to set the range. This technique is useful if you plan to print later. (This SmartIcon does not recognize collections.)

After using any of the first three methods, choose **F**ile, **P**rint to open the Print dialog box. Then choose Selected **R**ange to designate the selected range as the portion of the worksheet to be printed. (For details on printing a selected range, see "Printing Your Work" later in this chapter.)

If you have problems...

If you designate a print range, dotted gray lines appear around the print range. If these lines clutter your display, choose **V**iew, Set View **P**references, and then deselect **P**age Breaks in the Set View Preferences dialog box. Although the print range and page breaks remain in place, they are not visible.

Note: *No print-range lines appear if you preview or print the entire worksheet; they appear only when you designate a specific range or collection.*

Inserting a Page Break

If the amount of data you are printing is too much to fit on one page, 1-2-3 for Windows will start a new page when necessary. You may want to change the place where these default page breaks occur so that data is not separated in the wrong place.

To insert a page break:

1. Place the cell pointer in a cell above where you want a horizontal page break. The current row is the first row on the new page.

   or

Place the cell pointer in a cell to the right of the column in which you want to place a vertical page break. The current column is the first column on the new page.

2. Choose **S**tyle, Page **B**reak. The Page Break dialog box appears.

3. Choose **R**ow or **C**olumn. If you want both a horizontal and vertical page break above and to the left of the current column, choose both **R**ow and **C**olumn.

4. Choose OK.

A page break was inserted between the two tables to force 1-2-3 for Windows to print each table on a separate page.

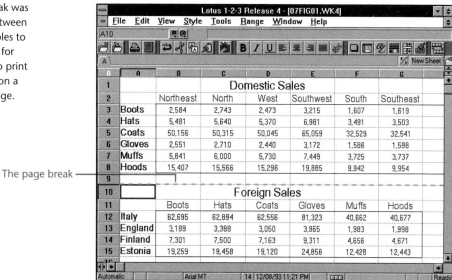

When a region with page breaks is printed, page one is the top left section of the print range, the second page is the section below the first page, and so on. The pages are sent to the printer from the top left corner downward, so the last page is the bottom right section of the print range.

To remove a page break:

1. Place the cell pointer in the cell to the left of or below the existing page break that you want to remove.

2. Choose **S**tyle, Page **B**reak.

7

3. In the Page Break dialog box, deselect **R**ow or **C**olumn, or both. Removing the x from the **R**ow check box, for example, removes the horizontal page break.

4. Choose OK.

Previewing Your Work

When you use 1-2-3 for Windows' Print Preview feature, you can see a representation of the worksheet as it will look when you print it. You should preview your work to ensure that it looks the way you want, rather than send multiple experiments to a printer, tying up the print queue at the office and wasting paper, toner, or ink.

To preview your print job:

1. Select the range, if you don't want to preview all cells.

2. Choose **F**ile, Print Pre**v**iew. Whether or not you selected a range, the Print Preview dialog box appears. In this dialog box, you can specify whether you want to preview the Current **W**orksheet, **A**ll Worksheets, or the Selected **R**ange.

The Print Preview dialog box.

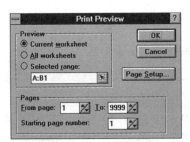

Note: *You also can choose the **P**review button in the Print dialog box to get to this point.*

3. If you don't want to preview the current worksheet, change the selected range or select which pages to preview.

4. Choose OK. The document (or the first page of a multipage document) appears, displaying any enhancements you added, such as headers or changed margins.

The Print Preview screen also features a new set of icons that you can use to work with the document.

The initial Print Preview screen.

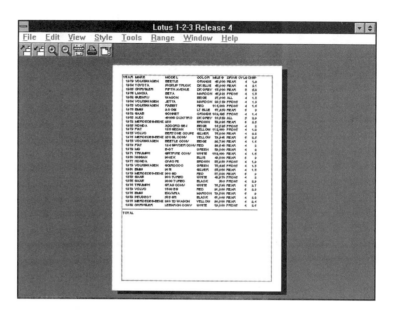

  You can preview other pages in the file while you are in the Print Preview screen. Press PgDn or Enter to see later pages; press PgUp to see previous pages. Data in later worksheets is placed on the same page as data from earlier worksheets, if space permits. If you want some data on a separate page, put a page break at the end of the data on one worksheet to force a new page to start at the new worksheet.

  The two magnifying-glass icons increase or decrease by 10 percent the size of the document being displayed each time you click them. Data is not easy to read in the default Print Preview display, but you can see how the page is composed. When you increase the display size, you can read the text but cannot see the entire page.

7

This is a Print Preview screen. Only the upper part of the document is visible because the Zoom In icon was clicked.

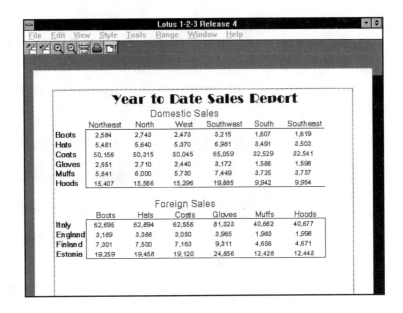

Press the asterisk key (*) to return to the default magnification setting.

If you have problems...

When you magnify a preview screen, you focus on the center of the page. If you don't see anything, press the up-arrow key to move the focus to the top of the page.

 You can open the Page Setup dialog box to make changes by clicking the Page Setup SmartIcon. Make any changes you want, as described in earlier sections. When you choose OK, you return to the Print Preview screen, where you see the results of your changes.

 To print the job, click the Print SmartIcon, which opens the Print dialog box. Then follow the directions in "Printing Your Work" later in this chapter.

 To close the Print Preview screen and return to the work area, click the Close SmartIcon.

Setting up the Printer

If your computer can access more than one printer, or if you must change the available font cartridges or paper size, you can change those settings in 1-2-3 for Windows. To make these changes:

1. Choose **F**ile, Prin**t**er Setup. The Printer Setup dialog box appears.

2. Choose the printer you want to use for the current print job (assuming that you can choose more than one printer). A dialog box pertaining to the printer you chose appears.

3. Choose **S**etup to make such changes as paper source, font cartridges, number of copies printed, or paper size.

The dialog box for setting up the printer is specific to the type of printer you have installed.

Select print orientation here

Specify which cartridges are installed in your printer here

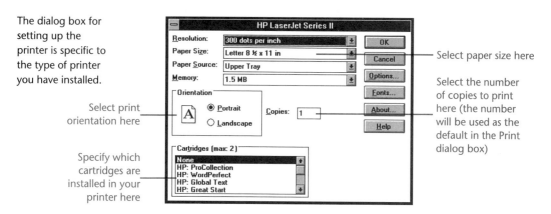

Select paper size here

Select the number of copies to print here (the number will be used as the default in the Print dialog box)

4. Choose OK to close the printer-specific dialog box.

5. Choose OK to close the Printer Setup dialog box.

Some options, such as number of copies and page orientation, also are available in the Print and Page Setup dialog boxes.

Note: *It makes no difference where you select such options as copies and page orientation; it's just a convenience that these options appear in two separate dialog boxes.*

Printing Your Work

After selecting the printer and the print range, setting up the page and the printer, and previewing your work, you are finally ready to print.

To print your work:

1. Choose **F**ile, **P**rint. The Print dialog box appears.

7

In the Print dialog box, you can specify how many copies you want as well as the pages to be printed.

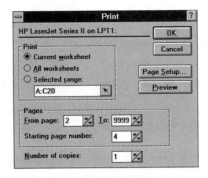

2. Specify what you want to print: the Current **W**orksheet, **A**ll Worksheets, or the Selected **R**ange.

   Note: *You can select a drawn object, such as a chart, and then choose* **P***rint to print only that object. The Print dialog box that appears will include Selected* **C***hart, rather than Selected* **R***ange, as an option.*

3. If you have not already selected a print range, you can choose Selected **R**ange and then enter a range.

4. In the Pages section of the dialog box, indicate which pages are to print and the page number of each one. You might want to print only the second and third pages of a multipage report, for example, and include them in a different report in which they will be pages 18 and 19. In this case, you would type **2** in the **F**rom Page text box, **3** in the **T**o text box, and **18** in the Starting Pa**g**e number text box to specify the page number to appear in a header or footer.

5. Use the Page **S**etup command button to make any last-minute changes, and use the **P**review command button if you want to take one final look at the file before you print.

6. Choose OK to send the work to the printer.

While the work is printing, a message box appears on-screen, telling you that the work is printing. If you discover a mistake or decide that you don't want to print after all, choose Cancel in the message box to stop the print job. (It can take a moment before your printer stops printing after you choose Cancel, because much of the job has already been sent to the printer.)

Summary

To	Do This
Insert a page break	Position cell pointer, and then click Page Break icon
Print in landscape orientation	Choose **F**ile, Pa**g**e Setup; choose Lan**d**scape
Make data fit printed page	Choose **F**ile, Pa**g**e Setup; choose Si**z**e
Create a header or footer	Choose **F**ile, Pa**g**e Setup; type text in header or footer text box
Set print titles	Choose **F**ile, Pa**g**e Setup; designate a cell in the appropriate row or column
Preview the print job	Choose **F**ile, Print Pre**v**iew
Print your work	Choose **F**ile, **P**rint
Print several copies	Choose **F**ile, **P**rint; specify **N**umber of Copies

On Your Own

Estimated time: 40 minutes

1. Create a large table of data, and then insert a horizontal and a vertical page break.

2. Remove the vertical page break.

3. Change the print orientation to landscape, and fit all text to page.

4. Use manual settings to fit print to page.

5. Add a header that shows the page number as *Page* followed by the number, and add a footer that shows the current date. Center both elements.

6. Add a grid and frame.

7. Designate row 1 and column A as print titles.

8. Preview the print job, and zoom in to see the top of the page more clearly.

9. Print only the first five rows and columns.

10. Print only the last page of the document.

7

Chapter 8

Charting Data

A *chart* (sometimes called a graph) is a pictorial representation of data. Making a point about data often is much easier when the reader sees pictures rather than columns and rows of numbers. This chapter discusses creating charts, choosing the proper type for the point you want to make, and adding features to the chart.

Specific topics covered in this chapter are:

- Learning the parts of a chart
- Creating a chart automatically
- Changing chart types
- Changing the default chart type
- Adding, moving, deleting, and resizing charts and chart elements

Learning the Parts of a Chart

The first step in mastering charts is knowing the parts of the typical chart.

This bar chart represents the sales figures of five items in several geographic regions.

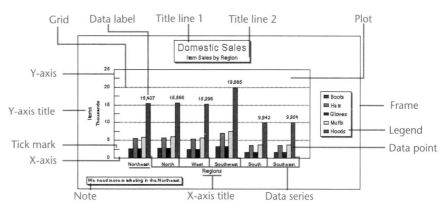

Data point

A place in a chart where an individual value is displayed.

Normally, a chart is rectangular, with the vertical left side called the *Y-axis*. The numbers on the Y-axis range from zero at the bottom to a value at the top slightly higher than the highest value in the data represented by the chart. The *X-axis* is the bottom of the rectangular area. Along this axis are the names of the groups in which the items are placed. In the data represented by this chart, the groups are the regions. The axes and the *data points* appear in the main part of the chart, called the *plot*.

In this chart, the data points are the tops of the individual bars. In other types of charts, the data points may be pie slices or points on a line. The *legend* shows what color or pattern is associated with which item. The *titles* and *notes* help explain the chart. Adding a *grid* helps the reader see where each data point falls relative to an axis. *Data labels* are added to show the exact amount represented by each of the longest bars.

This is the worksheet on which the chart in the preceding figure is based.

Lotus 1-2-3 Release 4 - [08SS01.WK4]

	A	B	C	D	E	F	G	H	I
1				Domestic Sales					
2		Northeast	North	West	Southwest	South	Southeast	East	
3	Boots	$2,584	$2,743	$2,473	$3,215	$1,607	$1,619	$2,143	
4	Hats	$5,481	$5,640	$5,370	$6,981	$3,491	$3,503	$4,027	
5	Gloves	$2,551	$2,710	$2,440	$3,172	$1,586	$1,598	$2,122	
6	Muffs	$5,841	$6,000	$5,730	$7,449	$3,725	$3,737	$4,261	
7	Hoods	$15,407	$15,566	$15,296	$19,885	$9,942	$9,954	$10,478	

Series

Numbers whose data points are grouped in a chart. A bar chart uses one bar for each series in each group.

In the preceding worksheet, the rows of figures next to the items including hats and boots are called *series*. The groups of data points represent the series. The first is Series A, the second is Series B, and so on. Each number in the series is represented by a bar in a group of bars. If the chart were a line chart, each series would be represented by a line.

Creating an Automatic Chart from Worksheet Data

You can create a chart in a worksheet simply by clicking an icon and selecting two ranges. Follow these guidelines in selecting the ranges:

- The main title of the chart must be in the top row of the range you will select for the chart.

- A title in the second row will become the subtitle of the chart.

- If the worksheet has more columns than rows, the chart will display the data by rows. This means that the first *row* of data will appear as X-axis labels and that each row of numerical data below that will be a data series. Make sure that series are arranged in rows.

- If the worksheet has more rows than columns, the chart will display the data by columns. The first *column* of data will be the labels on the X-axis, and each column of numerical data to the right will be a data series. Make sure that series are arranged in columns.

- If the worksheet has an equal number of columns and rows, the chart will be arranged by columns.

- 1-2-3 for Windows will ignore any blank rows.

To create a chart automatically:

1. Select the entire range of data you want the chart to represent. This range can include titles at the top and should include any labels at the top and to the left of numerical data.

2. Choose **T**ools, **C**hart. The mouse pointer becomes a small chart.

3. Click and drag across the range where you want to display the chart. (To create a square chart, hold down the Shift key while you click and drag.)

8

Selecting the range
where the chart will
be placed.

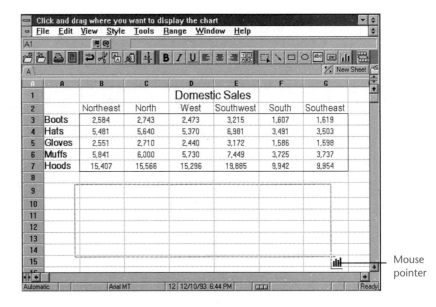

Mouse
pointer

4. Release the mouse button. 1-2-3 for Windows creates the chart in
   the range you selected.

   By default, the chart you create is a bar chart. Later in this chapter,
   you learn how to change the default chart type.

   Note: *Your chart region is not limited to full cells only. You can begin and
   end a chart region in any part of the screen, whether or not that location is
   a cell edge.*

Caution

Placing a chart over
data does not delete
the data underneath,
but it makes the data
impossible to read.

Notice that the new chart has selection handles, that **C**hart is included in
the main menu, and that a new set of chart-related SmartIcons is available. As long as the chart is selected, the **C**hart menu item and the special
SmartIcons remain visible. If the chart is not selected, **C**hart disappears
from the menu, and the standard SmartIcon palette returns.

The chart is selected. Notice the selection handles.

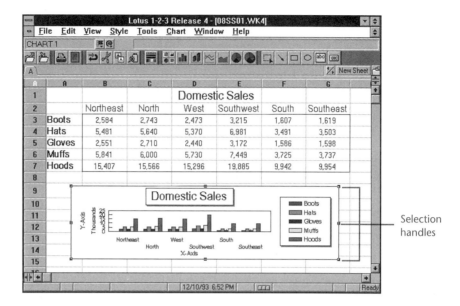

Selection handles

When you want to work with a chart, select it by clicking anywhere on its frame. The selection handles reappear, as do the **C**hart menu item and the charting SmartIcons.

Creating a Chart Manually

If you did not enter data according to the guidelines in the preceding section, or if you want to control the way data is displayed in the chart, you will have to create a chart manually. Suppose that you want to create a chart for the data in the worksheet shown earlier in this chapter, but you want to exclude the data for hats. You cannot select the entire worksheet, because the Hats row would be included, so you must designate each series separately.

When you create a chart manually, you do not start by selecting a range of data. Follow these steps:

1. Choose **T**ools, **C**hart.

2. As described in the preceding section, select the range where you want to place the chart.

3. Choose **C**hart, **R**anges. The Ranges dialog box appears.

8

The Ranges dialog
box, which you use
to assign a specific
range to each
series.

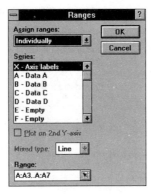

4. Use the Assign Ranges drop-down menu to specify how ranges will
be assigned to the chart: by row, by column, or individually.

In the following figure, the By Column option is selected, and a
Sample box appears, showing how the data will be used in the
chart. The vertical arrows mean that data points representing the
data in the column will be grouped in a series.

When you choose
By Columns in the
Ranges dialog box,
this dialog box
appears.

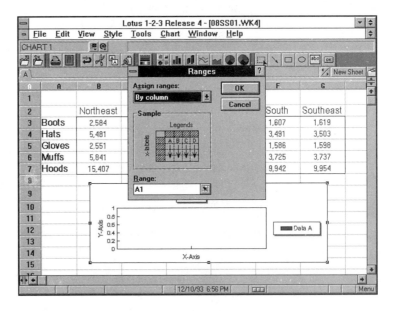

Caution
Be consistent when you choose rows or columns for series. If the X-axis series is a row, it is extremely likely that all other series will be rows of data. Make sure that you have one piece of data for every label on the X-axis.

5. Enter the ranges of data for each series. Click the button next to the Range box, and then click and drag to create a selection. When you release the mouse button, you return to the Ranges dialog box.

When you choose to assign series by row or by column, you can select the entire range of data at once. When you choose to assign series individually, however, you need to select one **S**eries at a time and then select the **R**ange for that series.

6. Choose OK when you finish. The chart, with data points, appears in what was an empty frame.

Naming Charts

The charts you create are automatically named Chart 1, Chart 2, and so forth. You can, however, change a chart's name to something more descriptive.

To rename a chart:

1. Select the chart you want to rename.

2. Choose **C**hart, **N**ame. The Name dialog box appears.

Use this dialog box to give charts descriptive names.

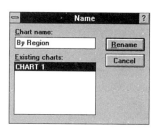

3. The name of the selected chart is highlighted in the **E**xisting Charts list box. Type the new name in the **C**hart Name text box, and then choose **R**ename.

New names will make it easier for you to go to charts when you have created several in a document. You can use the F5 key or the **E**dit, **G**o To command, and then specify Chart in the **T**ype of Item list box. All chart names appear in the list box of names. The choice is much clearer if the names are descriptive.

8

Changing the Chart Type

While a chart is selected, you can use the SmartIcon palette and the Chart menu to make many changes. The first major change you may want to consider is changing the *type* of chart.

You can change chart types by clicking any of six SmartIcons, which immediately change the selected chart to a bar, 3-D bar, line, area, pie, or 3-D pie chart, respectively.

To have more control over the appearance of the chart:

1. Select the chart.

2. Choose **Chart, Type,** or choose Chart Type from the quick menu. The Type dialog box appears.

The Type dialog box.

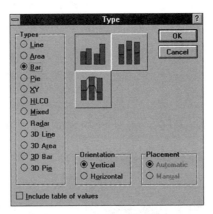

3. Choose a chart type from the Types section. The middle section of the dialog box will display several sample charts showing the different varieties of that chart type.

4. Choose OK.

The major types of charts are bar, line, HLCO (high, low, close, open), X-Y, area, mixed, radar, and pie. These chart types—and some variations—are described in the following sections.

Bar Charts

Bar charts have one bar for each number in the worksheet. These charts compare related data or show trends in groups of related data. Use bar charts only when small amounts of data are involved; too many bars in a chart make for a confusing display.

You can make several variations on bar charts, including making them 3-D or horizontal. You also can change the way the bars are displayed. The horizontal option, as the name implies, rotates the chart 90 degrees so that the bars start at the left and extend to the right. Three-dimensional bar charts give the whole chart and each bar thickness as well as length and width.

If a bar chart is 3-D, you can display the bars for each group side by side or front to back. When you use a 2-D bar chart, you can show the bars side by side. In either 2-D or 3-D bar charts, you can stack the bars to make the contribution of each group to the whole more obvious. One extra variation in 2-D stacked bar charts is the dotted-line bar chart, which connects corresponding parts of the stack to make comparison easier.

This is a 3-D stacked bar chart, using the data from the first bar chart.

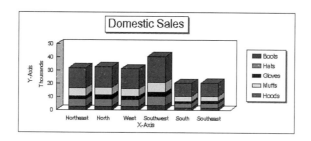

Line Charts

Line charts, which are used to show trends, plot a point for each number in a series, often using a line to connect the points. The variations in line charts depend on whether you use a 2-D or 3-D chart.

You have two options for 3-D line charts: all lines displayed in one plane, or all lines displayed in separate planes. You have six choices for 2-D charts: with or without lines, with or without symbols for data points, and stacked or unstacked. If you choose stacked, series A is closest to the X-axis, the line for series B is shown as a total of series A and series B, and so on.

Caution

In an unstacked 3-D chart, some data points may be lost behind larger data points that appear to be closer to the front. When data points are hidden, use either unstacked or 2-D charts.

8

HLCO Charts

HLCO (high, low, close, open) charts are used primarily for stock-market figures, although they can be used to track other items whose prices fluctuate over time. HLCO charts also can track such data as daily temperature spreads.

Each series in an HLCO chart represents four numbers: the opening value, the closing value, the highest value during the period, and the lowest value during the period.

This is an HLCO chart. The four numbers must be entered in the same order as they are in the cells above the chart.

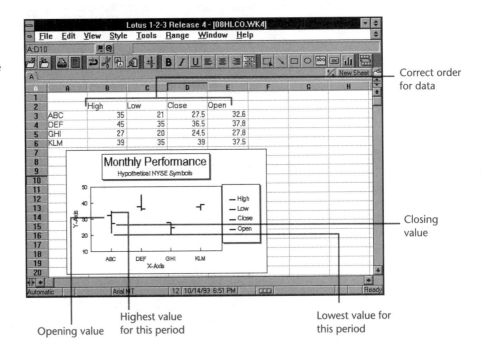

Correct order for data

Closing value

Opening value   Highest value for this period   Lowest value for this period

The only variation on the HLCO chart is the candlestick, in which a box represents the difference between close and open. In the following figure, the empty box for KLM shows that the stock's closing price was lower than its opening price.

This is an HLCO
candlestick chart.

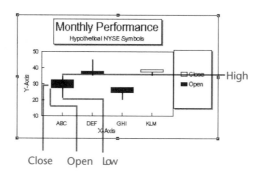

Close   Open Low

X-Y Charts

X-Y charts are different from the other charts in that they plot one value against another. The X-axis labels are numbers rather than words, and the data points are plotted against the values on both the X- and the Y-axis.

These charts are used to show the relationship between an independent variable and a dependent variable. The values for the independent variable are shown on the Y-axis; the values for the dependent variable appear on the X-axis.

You should create an X-Y chart manually, because 1-2-3 for Windows otherwise will treat the values intended for the X-axis as a data series.

To create an X-Y chart:

1. Create a blank chart.

2. Use **C**hart, **R**anges to define the ranges individually.

   Note: *For specific directions for steps 1 and 2, refer to "Creating a Chart Manually" earlier in this chapter.*

3. Choose **C**hart, **T**ype, or choose Chart Type from the quick menu. The Type dialog box appears.

4. Choose **X**Y, and then choose OK.

The X-Y chart in the following figure compares the weight of boxes of candy with sales. The line in the chart slopes up at first, showing that sales increase as the weight of each type of box increases. It then slopes down because sales are lower for the heavier boxes of candy.

8

An X-Y chart shows the relationship between two values.

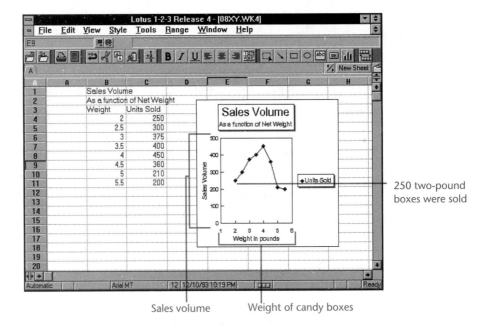

250 two-pound boxes were sold

Sales volume   Weight of candy boxes

Variations on X-Y charts enable you to use only lines, only data points, or a combination of data points and lines.

Area Charts

Area charts are like line charts, but with the areas below the lines colored in, and generally are used to show broad trends. The only variation possible in area charts is stacking them.

This area chart is 3-D and unstacked. All 2-D area charts are stacked.

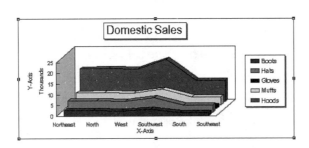

Mixed Charts

Mixed charts are combinations of chart types. One data range may deserve more attention or may represent a different type of data from the other ranges. Displaying that range as another type of chart makes it stand out.

The following figure shows an example of a mixed chart. The line above the bars gives added emphasis to one range—in this case, the values associated with hoods.

A mixed chart emphasizes one data range.

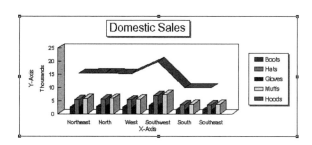

To create a mixed chart and change a series to another chart type:

1. Select the chart.

2. Choose **C**hart, **T**ype, or choose Chart Type from the quick menu. The Type dialog box appears.

3. Choose **M**ixed, and then choose OK.

4. Click one data point for the series you want to change.

5. Choose **C**hart, **R**anges, or choose Chart Ranges from the quick menu. The Ranges dialog box appears. Make sure that the series you want to change is highlighted.

6. Choose Line, Area, or Bar from the **M**ixed Type drop-down list.

7. Choose OK.

Radar Charts

Radar charts plot data on radiating lines, with the distance from the center reflecting the value of each data group. The Y-axis is the length of each line radiating from 0 at the center (unless you changed the minimum value of the Y-axis). The end of each line is an X-axis label.

8

A radar chart.

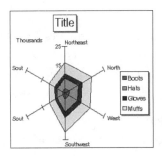

The radar chart in the preceding figure shows the sales of four items: boots, hats, gloves, and muffs. (Hoods are not included in the chart; their sales figures are so high that the lines for the other items would have been too close to the center.) The stacking makes the chart easier to read.

Pie Charts

A pie chart, which represents only one set of data, is used to show the contribution of each value to the total (the entire pie).

This pie chart shows sales for five items sold in the Northeast. The piece representing muffs is "exploded."

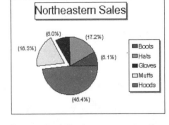

Explode

To move a piece of a pie chart some distance from the pie itself. Exploding a piece calls attention to the data that the piece represents.

Several variations on pie charts are available. You can, for example, make these charts 2-D or 3-D. You also can *explode* pieces of the pie (as described in "Modifying Pie Charts" later in this chapter).

Changing the Default Chart Type

When you create a chart, a bar chart appears by default. To change the default chart type:

1. Select and activate a chart of the type you want to make the default, or change a chart to the preferred type and be sure it is selected.

2. Choose **C**hart, **S**et Preferred. The selected chart type becomes the new default. From now on, every chart you create will be the new default type.

Any time you want to convert another chart in the worksheet to the default type, select the chart and choose **C**hart, **U**se Preferred. The selected chart is changed to the default type.

Changing the Appearance of Charts

You can make many changes in the charts you create. Many changes can be made in any type of chart; others are specific to certain charts.

The following sections describe various techniques you can use to alter the appearance of the charts you create.

Moving, Resizing, and Deleting Charts and Chart Objects

If the placement of a chart interferes with the display of important data, you may move it or resize it. If elements in the chart interfere with the display of other elements, you can move or resize them individually. You may also delete charts and chart elements.

If you want to place the chart somewhere else in the worksheet, select it, position the mouse pointer on an empty place inside the chart, and then click and drag the chart to the new location. To move an object in the chart, click and drag the object.

When you need to move a chart a long distance, a better procedure is to select the chart; choose **E**dit, Cu**t**; click the new location; and then choose **E**dit, **P**aste.

8

When the chart or an object in the chart is selected, you can use the quick menu for operations appropriate to the selected object. When an entire chart is selected, for example, you can cut, copy, paste, or clear the object. You also can use the quick menu to change the chart type, to change series ranges, and to alter lines and colors.

Note: *The mouse pointer changes to show you what it is pointing at in a chart. If you are pointing at text, for example, a capital A appears under the arrowhead.*

To change an object's size, select it, and then click and drag one of its selection handles. To change the size of an entire chart, select the chart, and then click and drag a selection handle. You cannot resize an object in a chart to a size larger than the current chart frame.

A chart being resized.

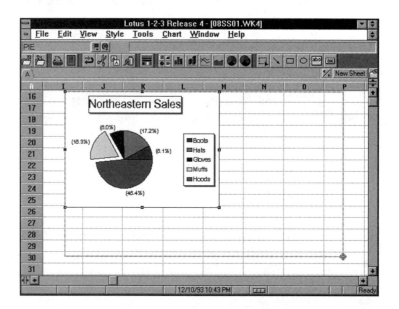

Note: *Charts have eight selection handles. (Objects in charts have only corner handles.) Drag the corners to resize horizontally and vertically at the same time; drag the sides to resize in only one direction at a time. To keep the changes in horizontal and vertical size the same while you drag a corner handle, hold down the Shift key.*

To delete an object, select it and then press Del. You cannot delete a frame without also deleting the contents of the frame. You cannot delete the frame around the title, for example, without losing the title in the process. In addition, you cannot delete the plot, the X-axis labels, or the Y-axis scale.

Adding and Changing Text

To change a chart's main title, subtitle, or note:

1. Double-click the title, subtitle, or note, or select the chart.

2. Choose **C**hart, **H**eadings, or choose Headings from the quick menu. The Headings dialog box appears.

3. In the appropriate text boxes, enter the text for both lines of the title (the title and the subtitle) and for a two-line note.

   Alternatively, you can select title and note text from cells in the worksheet. Select a cell whose contents you want to use for one of the four lines of text, and then click the adjacent Cell box. In the appropriate text box, type the cell address. The contents of the cell become the title or note.

This dialog box uses text from a cell for the main title and typed-in text for the note.

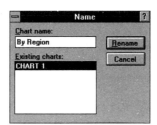

8

4. Place the title or note by choosing **Le**ft, Cen**t**er, or Ri**g**ht.

In addition to determining horizontal placement, you can place the label in the cell vertically. By default, 1-2-3 for Windows places titles at the top of charts and notes at the bottom, but you can move either simply by clicking and dragging.

5. When you finish, choose OK.

You also can change the legend's text—the words that identify each color or pattern in the chart. Follow these steps:

1. Double-click the legend or select the chart.

2. Choose **C**hart, **L**egend, or choose Legend from the quick menu. The Legend dialog box appears.

3. Select the series in the Series box whose text you want to change.

4. Type identifying text or enter a cell address in the **L**egend entry box as the source of the text. If you use a cell's contents as the source for a legend, make sure that the Cell box is checked.

5. Choose OK.

In addition, you can change the font and attributes of text in the legend, the title, and the X-axis labels. Follow these steps:

1. Select the item whose text you want to change.

2. Choose **S**tyle, **F**ont & Attributes, or choose Font & Attributes from the quick menu. The Font & Attributes dialog box appears.

   Note: *The Font & Attributes dialog box described here is the same one you use to format text in worksheet cells. For details on choosing options in this dialog box, refer to Chapter 5, "Changing the Appearance of a Worksheet."*

3. Select the font and font size you want; add boldface, italics, or underlining, if you like. Click **C**olor to change the color of the selected text.

4. Choose OK.

Changing the Axes

You can make several changes in both axes. If you have long X-axis labels that overlap or crowd one another, for example, you can change the interval for labels. You also can edit the X-axis title, as follows:

1. Choose **C**hart, **A**xis, and then choose **X**-Axis; choose Axis from the quick menu and then choose **X**-Axis; or double-click a label on the X-axis. The X-Axis dialog box appears.

2. Type the new title in the **A**xis Title text box.

   Alternatively, you can designate a cell's contents as the new title (see the preceding section for directions).

The X-Axis dialog box, with a new title for the X-axis entered in the text box.

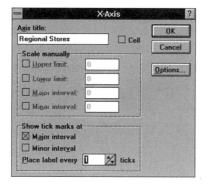

Tick marks
The small lines on the X- and Y-axes that mark the intervals in values or labels.

3. If the labels along the axis are crowded, you can choose to place labels at wider intervals than every *tick mark*.

4. Choose OK.

8

Generally, you can make more changes in the Y-axis, because this axis uses numeric values as labels. You change the Y-axis label the way you changed the X-axis label as follows:

1. Choose **C**hart, **A**xis, and then choose **Y**-Axis; choose Axis from the quick menu, and then choose **Y**-Axis; or double-click a label on the X-axis. The Y-Axis dialog box appears.

2. Type the new title in the **A**xis Title text box.

   Alternatively, you can designate a cell's contents as the new title.

In the main Y-Axis dialog box, you can set the limits of the axis and changes the display of tick marks.

Caution

Resetting the limits may cause some data points to be displayed inaccurately. If the upper limit is set at 500 but the largest value represented is 1,000, for example, the data point for the 1,000 value will stop at the 500 mark.

You can modify the default settings for the display of numbers on the Y-axis. For example, you may want to change the upper or lower limit. If all data points are far above the floor of the plot, changing the Lo**w**er Limit option to a number higher than zero spreads the data points vertically over a wider area. Changing the upper limit may reduce the amount of empty space at the top of the plot.

You can reduce the number of labels on the Y-axis in several ways. Increasing the value of the **M**ajor Interval option reduces the number of values displayed between the upper and lower limit. Choosing to place labels at every second or third tick mark also reduces the number of labels.

Note: *Any time you want to return to the default setting, deselect the check box next to the item. The default will be restored when you close the dialog box.*

You can control the display of tick marks by selecting or deselecting Ma-jor Interval and Minor Inter**v**al. Tick marks at major intervals are slightly larger than minor-interval tick marks. By default, major tick marks are displayed and minor ones are not.

You can use the Y-Axis dialog box to change the axis title and the way values are plotted.

To make further choices in the Y-axis, choose **O**ptions in the Y-Axis dialog box to display the Options dialog box.

The Y-Axis Options dialog box.

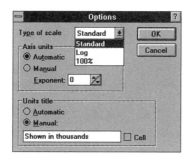

In this dialog box, you can change the Ty**p**e of Scale from Standard (the default) to Log (logarithmic) or 100%. The Log option changes the Y-axis labels so that each one is 10 times larger than the one below it. Use logarithmic scale when there is a large spread between the smallest and largest values represented in the chart, but include a note or change the axis title so that the reader knows that the axis uses logarithmic scale.

A simple logarithmic chart, showing the altitudes at which three objects might be found.

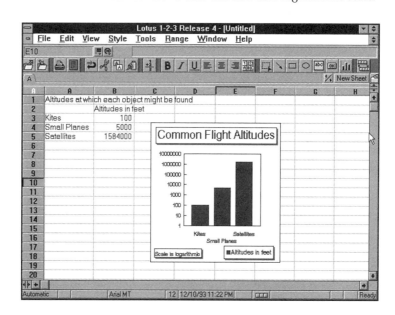

8

The 100% scale changes the values to percentages. The bottom of the scale becomes 0 percent, and the top becomes 100 percent.

You also can change the axis units from Automatic to Manual. After choosing Manual, you must choose an Exponent to be used in the display of the values. If you choose 2 as the Exponent, for example, each value is shown as a factor that must be multiplied by 10 to the power you chose to derive the true value. Using exponential Y-axis units is useful when the numbers are expressed in thousands but rise to a rather high value. If values are in thousands and the Y-axis number is 3,000, some readers may have trouble remembering the true value of 3,000 thousands.

Adding a Grid and Data Labels

If you have a line zigging and zagging around the chart, or bars of differing lengths spreading across the plot, a reader might have trouble understanding exactly what value a data point represents. By placing a grid on the chart, you make it easier for the reader to see how the data points line up with an axis.

To place a grid:

1. Choose Chart, Grids, or choose Grids from the quick menu. The Grids dialog box appears.

2. Choose Y-Axis to specify a horizontal grid or X-Axis to specify a vertical grid. You also can use both horizontal and vertical grids by selecting each one.

3. Select to place grid lines at Major Intervals Only, at Minor Intervals Only, or at Both kinds of tick marks.

4. Choose OK.

To make it perfectly clear what values the data points represent, you can place data labels near them. To place data labels near data points for a series:

1. Choose Chart, Data Labels. The Data Labels dialog box appears.

2. In the Data Labels dialog box, select the series near which you want to place the data labels.

3. In the R**a**nge of Labels text box, enter the range where the values to be used as data labels appear.

4. Choose **P**lacement, then Center, Right, Below, Left or Above to place the data relative to the data points. Depending on the type of chart, the placement command may have no effect.

5. Choose OK.

If you have problems...

Although you can choose All Ranges in the Data Labels dialog box to place data labels at every data point in the chart, the result may be a cluttered chart. As an alternative, consider including in the chart a table of the values on which the chart is based. Choose **C**hart, **T**ype, **I**nclude Table of Values.

This chart uses data labels for the Boots data points, includes a table of values, and places major and minor intervals on the Y-axis.

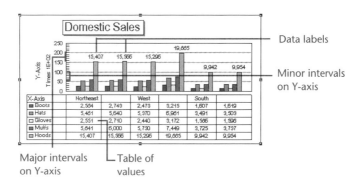

Adding Drawn Objects

Using the techniques described in Chapter 5, "Changing the Appearance of a Worksheet," you can add drawn objects such as lines, arcs, arrows, and geometric shapes. The object need not be confined inside the chart. For example, you could draw an arrow from one value in the worksheet to the data point in the chart that represents that value to show their relationship.

To connect a value in the worksheet with a data point in the chart, choose **T**ools, **D**raw, **A**rrow. Click and drag from the value to the chart to place the arrow.

8

Varying Colors and Lines

Every color and almost every line in a chart can be changed to suit your whim, taste, or preference. Make sure that you select the item for which you want the changes to take effect. If you select the entire chart, for example, and then change lines, the only line that changes will be the frame of the chart.

To change the colors:

1. Select the item for which you want the changes to take effect.

2. Choose **S**tyle, **L**ines & Color, or choose Lines & Color from the quick menu. The Lines & Color dialog box appears.

   Note: *The Lines & Colors dialog box described here is the same one you use to format text in worksheet cells. For details on choosing options in this dialog box, refer to Chapter 5, "Changing the Appearance of a Worksheet."*

Use the Lines & Color dialog box to specify the line style and color, pattern, pattern color, and background color for the selected chart object.

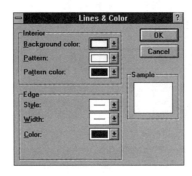

3. Make any changes you want.

4. Choose OK.

Modifying Pie Charts

Caution

Adding colors and patterns to a chart could make any black-and-white printed copy of your chart more difficult to read.

In addition to exploding pie slices, mentioned earlier in the chapter, you can make several other changes in a pie chart. To change the data labels:

1. Select the pie chart.

2. Choose **C**hart, **D**ata Labels, or choose Data Labels from the quick menu. The Data Labels dialog box that appears is different from that of any other chart type.

The Data Labels dialog box for a pie chart enables you to change the appearance of data labels and explode pie slices.

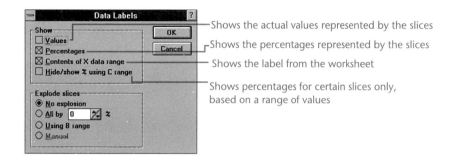

Shows the actual values represented by the slices

Shows the percentages represented by the slices

Shows the label from the worksheet

Shows percentages for certain slices only, based on a range of values

3. Choose a Show option: **V**alues, **P**ercentages, or **C**ontents of X Data Range. If you choose both **V**alues and **P**ercentages, both values appear.

   To show percentages only for certain slices, choose **H**ide/Show % Using C Range. In the C range, enter a **1** (yes) or a **0** (no) in the cell corresponding to a slice to determine whether the percentage value will be displayed in the data label for that slice.

   Note: *To define the C range, choose **Chart**, **R**anges; choose C in the **Se**ries list; and highlight the range of 1s and 0s you entered. For more information on defining ranges, refer to "Creating a Chart Manually" earlier in this chapter.*

4. Choose OK.

To explode a piece of pie, click it and drag it away from the pie.

Caution

Exploding a pie slice can make the entire pie smaller, and also may cause the data labels to be represented by asterisks. If either situation occurs, increase the size of the entire chart.

To explode all slices of the pie:

1. Select the chart.

2. Choose **C**hart, **D**ata Labels, or choose Data Labels from the quick menu. The Data Labels dialog box appears.

3. In the Explode Slices section, choose **A**ll By, and enter a percentage number for the distance from the pie you want to explode all pieces.

4. Choose OK.

8

To explode some pieces of the pie and change their colors at the same time:

1. Select the chart.

2. Choose **C**hart, **D**ata Labels, or choose Data Labels from the quick menu. The Data Labels dialog box appears.

3. In the Explode Slices section, choose **U**sing B Range.

   Note: *A B range needs to be defined the way a C range was defined earlier in this section. In the B range, enter values between 1 and 14. The color of a pie slice is determined by the number in the cell corresponding to that slice. If the monitor is monochrome, colors are replaced by patterns. Add 100 to the number in the cell corresponding to a slice to explode it; make the number 0 or negative to hide the slice.*

If you have problems...

If the numbers you enter in the B range have no effect on the color or explosion of pie pieces, choose **C**hart, **D**ata Labels, and make sure that **U**sing B Range is selected.

---

4. Choose OK.

Summary

To	Do This
Create a chart from a range of data	Select the range of data; choose **T**ools, **C**hart
Create a chart manually	Choose **T**ools, **C**hart; select the range for the chart; use **C**hart, **R**anges to assign ranges
Change a chart's type	Select the chart; then choose **C**hart, **T**ype
Use a different chart Choose type for series	**C**hart, **T**ype; choose one **M**ixed; select the type
Make a chart larger or smaller corner	Select the chart; then click and drag one side or
Move a chart	Select the chart; then click and drag the entire chart

To	Do This
Add or change title text	Choose **C**hart, **H**eadings
Add or change lines or color	Select item to be changed; choose **S**tyle, **L**ines & Color
Explode a pie slice	Click and drag the slice away from the pie

On Your Own
Estimated time: 40 minutes

1. Create a table of data.

2. Create a chart from that data automatically.

3. Create a chart manually, and then cause the series to be displayed by columns and by rows.

4. Change the chart type from the default to line.

5. Change the chart from 2-D to 3-D, and vice versa.

6. Add a note and a main title. Base the main title on a cell's contents, and type text for the note.

7. Move the chart to the right. Move the legend to the bottom of the chart.

8. Change one data series to a different chart type.

9. Change the Y-axis to logarithmic, and add minor tick marks.

10. Change the color of one data series.

11. Widen the chart frame, and change its color.

8

Working with Multiple Worksheets and Multiple Documents

You may need to have several different files open at the same time so that you can copy data among them or simply refer to them as you work. By the same token, you may need to have multiple programs open at the same time so you can switch back and forth among them and copy data from one to another.

This chapter covers the following topics:

- Adding worksheets to a file

- Working with several files

- Navigating among multiple worksheets and files

- Viewing several files on-screen

- Writing formulas that cross worksheet and file boundaries

- Managing large worksheets

Opening Additional Worksheets

Active

A file is *active* (or open) when it has been retrieved from disk and is in the computer's RAM. The file in focus is the *current* file. In Windows, *active* means the window or program currently in use.

Within one file, adding another worksheet is easy. You can have a maximum 256 worksheets *active*, either all in one file or in several open files. The number of active worksheets you can add may be further limited by the amount of memory you have in your computer and the amount of data that the worksheets contain.

To create a new worksheet or worksheets:

1. Choose **E**dit, **I**nsert. The Insert dialog box appears.

2. Choose the **S**heet option.

3. If you want the new worksheet to be inserted before the current worksheet, choose **B**efore. If you want it to be inserted after the current worksheet, choose A**f**ter.

4. If you want to insert more than one worksheet, change the value in the **Q**uantity box.

5. Choose OK.

 You also can insert a new worksheet by clicking the New Sheet box at the right end of the line where worksheet tabs are displayed or by clicking the Add Sheet SmartIcon. Both methods insert a new worksheet after the current worksheet.

Note: *To display the worksheet tabs, click the Tab Display button (an icon showing three files with tabs), located at the top of the vertical scroll bar.*

If you have problems...

If you want to insert a worksheet between worksheets A and B but the new worksheet appears somewhere else, the cell pointer is not in the proper place. Make sure that the cell pointer is located in the worksheet before the position where you want to insert the new worksheet.

Naming Worksheets

1-2-3 for Windows automatically assigns a letter (A, B, C, and so on) to each worksheet. If these letters are not descriptive enough for you, double-click the tab and type a new name. You can use up to 255 characters, but keeping the names much shorter than that is a good idea, because short names enable you to view more than one tab on-screen at a time.

Names also are easier to remember than letters, making it a bit easier to navigate worksheets and write formulas.

Deleting Worksheets

You can delete a worksheet in several ways:

- Select the entire worksheet, and then press Ctrl+– (the Ctrl key and the keypad minus sign).

- Click the Delete Selected Sheet icon, if it is visible.

- Choose **E**dit, **D**elete. If the worksheet is already selected, it is immediately deleted; otherwise, you must choose **S**heet in the Delete dialog box.

If you have problems...   Deleting a worksheet also can delete needed data. To make sure that a worksheet you want to delete contains no data, press Home to move to cell A1 of the current worksheet, and then press End, Home. If the cell pointer does not move from A1, the worksheet contains no data. If the cell pointer does move, the worksheet contains data somewhere above and to the left of the cell pointer.

Opening Additional Files

Files are separate groups of data saved to disk with unique names. Each file can have one or more worksheets. You can open several files at once, as long as the total number of active worksheets does not exceed 256. Open another file the way you opened the first file: choose **F**ile, **O**pen, and then select the file. The newest file appears in a window in front of other open files. (You cannot open a second copy of a file that is already open.)

The number of files you can open, like the number of worksheets you can insert, is limited by your computer's memory and the amount of data contained in the files.

Note: *Opening one file does not automatically close files that are currently open. When you finish using a file, you have to save it and close it.*

9

Navigating among Worksheets and Files

You can use several methods to move the cell pointer among worksheets in a file and among files. Although 1-2-3 for Windows considers each file to be separate from the others, moving from the end of one file to the beginning of the next is a simple procedure.

Moving from Worksheet to Worksheet

The fastest way to move from worksheet to worksheet is to click the tab of the destination sheet.

Another way to move from worksheet to worksheet is to press Ctrl+PgUp or Ctrl+PgDn. Ctrl+PgDn moves to the preceding worksheet; Ctrl+PgUp moves to the following worksheet. If the cell pointer currently is in worksheet C, the preceding worksheet is B and the next one is D.

If you use either of these methods, when you return to a worksheet that you have already visited, you will find that the cell pointer is in the same cell as it was when you left the worksheet.

Yet another way to move from worksheet to worksheet and to arrive in a new cell is to use the Go To feature, accessible with the F5 key or **E**dit, **G**o To. Be sure to specify the worksheet letter or name in addition to the cell address. Specifying only the cell address moves the cell pointer to the specified cell in the current worksheet. If you gave worksheet C the name CHARTS, you can specify either the worksheet name or the letter of the worksheet; CHARTS:A5 is the same thing as C:A5. Worksheet and range names, like cell addresses, are not case-sensitive.

The keystrokes listed in the following table move the cell pointer to the specified destination when more than one worksheet in a file is open. (Remember that a comma means "press one key and then the other"; the plus sign means "press both keys together.")

Table 9.1 Keystrokes for Moving among Worksheets	
Keystroke	**Destination**
Ctrl+PgUp	Following worksheet
Ctrl+PgDn	Preceding worksheet
Ctrl+Home	First cell of first worksheet in file
End, Ctrl+Home	Bottom-right active cell of preceding worksheet*
End, Ctrl+PgDn	Backward through worksheets in current file, staying in same row and column; stops at the first cell with data that is above or below a blank cell in an adjacent worksheet
End, Ctrl+PgUp	Forward through worksheets in current file, staying in same row and column; stops at the first cell with data that is above or below a blank cell in an adjacent worksheet

The cell pointer moves to the bottom row, far-right column, last worksheet of any row, column, and worksheet used. If the bottom row in any worksheet is row 200, the far-right column is AA, and the last worksheet with data is E, the cell pointer moves to E:AA200.

Moving between Files

To move from file to file, choose **W**indow from the main menu. At the bottom of the drop-down menu is a list of all active files, preceded by a number. Click the file you want to go to, or type its number. The cell pointer goes to the cell you last used when you were in that file.

If more than one active file is visible on-screen, click anywhere in that file's window to move the focus and cell pointer to that file.

Viewing Several Files

When you open several files, you might want to see some or all of the files at the same time. You may not be able to see all the cells in all the files, however, because the files must share the available real estate on the screen. If you want the active file to fill the screen, click the Maximize button in the top right corner of the active window. To restore the file from the maximized view to a view in which it partially fills the window, click the Restore button in the top right corner of the maximized window.

9

The **W**indow menu contains two options for displaying all open files on-screen. The first option, **T**ile, displays files with available screen space divided equally.

The **W**indow, **T**ile command displays files with available screen space divided equally.

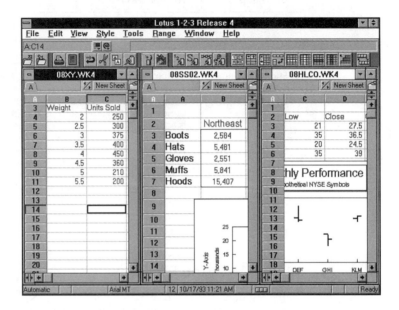

The other option is **C**ascade. In this view, only one file is completely visible; the title bars of the other files are visible behind the one in front. To bring another file to the front, click any visible part of its window.

Window, **C**ascade shows only the title bars of all but one file.

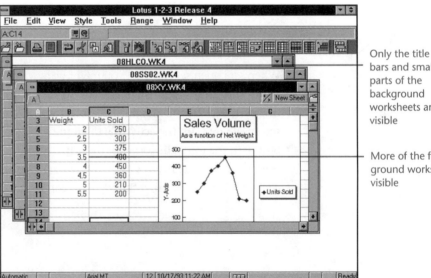

Only the title bars and small parts of the background worksheets are visible

More of the foreground worksheet i visible

When more than one file is visible, you can click and drag the edge or corner of a window to resize it. You can overlap windows or increase one and decrease another to suit your needs.

When you are in one file, you can cascade three worksheets by choosing **V**iew, **S**plit, **P**erspective. To move from worksheet to worksheet, click the destination cell in the destination worksheet. When you want to return to displaying one worksheet in a file at a time, use **V**iew, Clear **S**plit. Other uses for **V**iew, **S**plit are discussed in "Managing Large Files" later in this chapter.

View, **S**plit, **P**erspective shows three worksheets in one file.

Worksheet names are displayed here

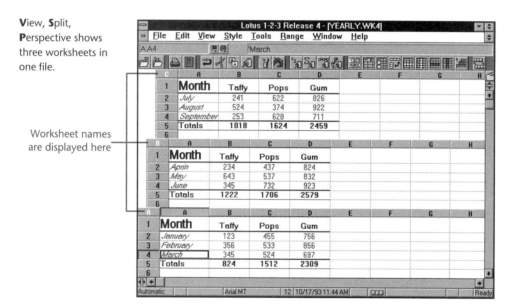

Writing Formulas That Cross Worksheet and File Boundaries

A formula takes data from a cell in another worksheet or file and processes that data if it finds the cell you specify. You have to add to the formula the location of the cell. If the data is in the current worksheet, you simply name the cell or range. To add all values in A1 through E5 in the current worksheet, for example, @SUM(A1..E5) is enough. When A1 is in one worksheet and E5 is in another, however, you have to tell the formula specifically where those cells are.

9

Referring to Other Worksheets

To write a formula that refers to cells or ranges in other worksheets, observe all the standard requirements for writing formulas, and include worksheet references before cell addresses. A typical formula could be +A:A5+B:J10 to add two cells in different worksheets.

If a worksheet has a name, you can substitute the name of the worksheet for the worksheet letter. Thus, a formula could be written +FIRSTQTR:A1+FOURTHQTR:E5.

Referring to Other Files

Path

The drive and directory in which a file is located. You must include the path in a formula that refers to another file.

A formula written in one file can refer to another file as long as you specify needed information in the proper format. You have to specify not only the worksheet and cell address, but also the *path* and file name of the source of the data.

If you want to refer to a cell in another file without opening the file, you have to type every character of the formula that refers to that cell. For example, if the file is named BUDGET.WK4 and saved to the FISCDATA directory on your E drive, and if you want a formula to refer to cell B:A5 in that file, you must type **+<<E:\FISCDATA\BUDGET.WK4>>B:A5**. Following is an @SUM formula that refers to the range A1 to E5 in a file with a worksheet for each quarter:

@SUM(<<E:\FISCDATA\BUDGET.WK4>>FIRSTQTR:A1..FOURTHQTR:E5)

Note: *The concept of relative cell references works in formulas that refer to other files. If you copy to the next cell down a formula that refers to B:A5 in another file, the copied formula refers to B:A6 in the other file.*

To write a formula that refers to an open file without typing all the characters in the formula:

1. Make sure that the file containing the formula is open.

2. Place the cell pointer in the file and cell where you want the result of the formula to appear.

3. Type the formula up to the point at which you have to supply the range or cell argument.

4. If you are using only one cell, move the cell pointer to the cell in the source file; type a closing parenthesis, if necessary; and press Enter.

If you are using a range, highlight the range; Shift+click additional worksheets, if necessary; type a closing parenthesis, if necessary; and press Enter.

Following is an even faster way to link a cell or range from one file to the current file:

1. Highlight the cell or range in the source file, and copy it to the Clipboard.

2. Move the cell pointer to the cell in which you want to enter the linked formula.

3. Choose **E**dit, Paste Lin**k** to create a formula link between the current cell and the source file.

Note: *Paste Lin**k** enables you to paste a reference to a cell in one worksheet (the source) as a formula in another worksheet (the destination) so that when you change the cell in the source, the cell in the destination updates immediately.*

If you have problems...

A formula that returns ERR may be referring to a file on a floppy disk that is not in the disk drive. Insert the disk; choose **E**dit, **L**inks; choose File Links under **L**ink Type; and finally choose Update **A**ll.
An erroneous formula also may be referring to a file that has been moved or renamed. Make sure that the name and path are correct.

Managing Large Files

A file whose data sprawls over distant ranges in several worksheets can be difficult to keep under control. 1-2-3 for Windows offers several tools that make formula writing, navigating, and simply viewing data easier. These techniques are as useful in a single worksheet as they are in several worksheets.

9

Naming Ranges

This chapter has referred several times to named ranges. You can give a name to a cell or a range. A name can be up to 15 characters long and should indicate the contents or use of the range or cell.

Suppose that you have a large file that contains several separate lists of data. Each separate range of data can be given names.

To name a range:

1. Select the cell or range.

2. Choose **R**ange, **N**ame. The Name dialog box appears.

3. Type the name, using 15 or fewer characters and no spaces. Names like TAX RATE are not acceptable because of the space, but you can use TAX_RATE. Range names are not case-sensitive.

The **R**ange, **N**ame
dialog box.

4. Choose OK.

An alternative way to name ranges is to use a label entered into an adjacent cell. To use a label in one cell as a name for the cell to the right:

1. Place the cell pointer in the cell that contains the label.

2. Choose **R**ange, **N**ame. The Name dialog box appears.

3. Choose **F**or Cells and select To the Right in the drop-down box.

4. Choose **U**se Labels.

5. Choose OK. The label in the current cell now is the name of the cell to the right.

The first benefit of naming ranges is ease of navigation. When you have to move to separate ranges around a worksheet, you may have trouble remembering where each group of data is. If you give the entire range a name that reminds you of the data stored there, you will have a better idea where you're going. You can go to a named range in either of two ways:

- Choose **E**dit, **G**o To, and then double-click the name of the range you want to go to.

- Click the navigator icon to display a list of range names. Then click the name of the destination range.

Click the navigator icon to display a list of range names.

Navigator icon

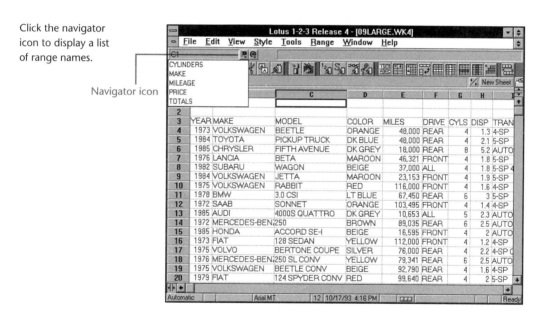

A second advantage of using range names is the ease of writing formulas. Instead of highlighting a range of numbers you want to add, you could type **@SUM(salary)**. All numbers included in the named range are added. If you later increase the size of the named range to include additional values, the formula automatically includes the new values.

In general, any command that requires range input accepts a range name as that input. If you want to change the background color or print a range named PRICE, for example, enter the range name in the range text box of the dialog box for the command you are using; then execute the command.

9

Splitting the Window

Sometimes you have to see two distant parts of a worksheet at the same time. Because you cannot stretch the edges of your screen, the number of cells you can display at any given time is limited. The solution is to split the screen.

At the top of the vertical scroll bar is a small symbol with two parallel lines and two arrowheads. At the left end of the horizontal scroll bar is a similar symbol with two arrowheads. To split the screen, click and drag the symbol at the top of the vertical scroll bar downward. When the split is where you want it, release the mouse button.

The screen is being split into panes. Notice that the mouse pointer changes shape.

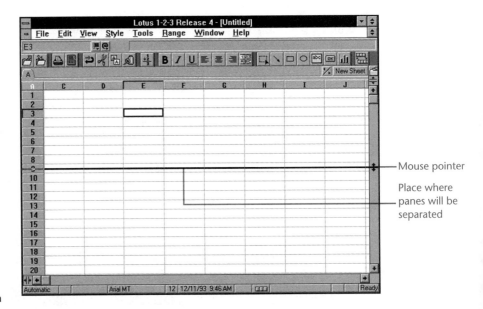

Mouse pointer

Place where panes will be separated

Pane

A separate view of the same window, created by placing a dividing line across the active window.

Caution

The cell pointer does not move until you click a new cell. As you use the scroll bars to move focus, the cell pointer can disappear from the screen. Click a visible cell to bring the cell pointer back into view.

Now you have two views of the same area of the worksheet, but each view, or *pane*, has its own set of scroll bars. You can use the scroll bars in either pane to move around that pane.

The active pane is the one with the outlined cell pointer. You can move the cell pointer around the active window by using any of the cell-pointer-movement keystrokes. Switch the active pane by clicking the other pane.

Depending on your needs, you may prefer to split the window into panes vertically by sliding the split symbol at the left end of the scroll bar to the right.

Synchronized
When two panes are synchronized, moving to an off-screen cell in one pane causes the other pane to scroll, bringing the same area of the other pane into view. When panes are not in synch, you can view different areas of the worksheet at the same time.

Although using the mouse to create panes is fast, there is an advantage to using the menu. You may have noticed that if you create a horizontal pane and move the cell pointer to the right, the focus in both panes moves. This movement occurs because the panes are *synchronized*. Creating panes with the menu enables you to unsynchronize the panes so that you can move in one pane without the other following along.

To create an unsynchronized pane:

1. Place the cell pointer in the row in which you want a horizontal pane or in the column in which you want a vertical pane.

2. Choose **V**iew, **S**plit; then choose **H**orizontal or **V**ertical.

3. To unsynchronize, choose **S**ynchronize. If no X appears in the check box, the panes are not synchronized; each pane moves independently of the other.

Two separate regions of one worksheet displayed in unsynchronized horizontal panes.

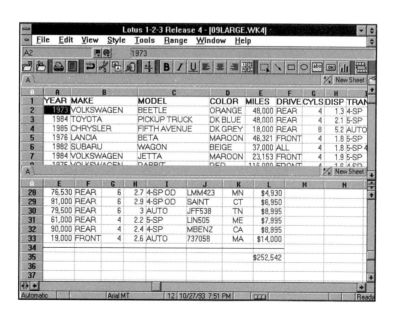

9

To clear the panes and restore the screen to a single-pane view, choose **V**iew, Clear **S**plit, or click and drag the split symbol back to the end of the scroll bar.

Creating Titles

In Chapter 7, "Printing a Worksheet," you learned how to create *print titles*: rows and/or columns of data that print on every page of a printed report. Print titles make it easier to see the row and column location of a given piece of data, even when that data is not on the first page.

You can *freeze* titles on-screen so that rows or columns containing labels are always visible, even when focus shifts far from the edge of the worksheet.

Using row 3 and column A as frozen titles in this large worksheet enables you to see the column and row locations of data items.

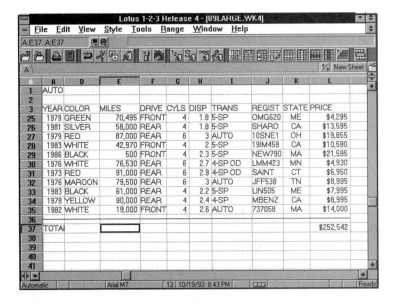

	A	D	E	F	G	H	I	J	K	L
1	AUTO									
2										
3	YEAR	COLOR	MILES	DRIVE	CYLS	DISP	TRANS	REGIST	STATE	PRICE
25	1979	GREEN	70,495	FRONT	4	1.8	5-SP	OMG620	ME	$4,295
26	1981	SILVER	58,000	REAR	4	1.8	5-SP	SHARO	CA	$13,595
27	1979	RED	87,000	REAR	6	3	AUTO	10SNE1	OH	$19,855
28	1983	WHITE	42,970	FRONT	4	2	5-SP	19IM458	CA	$10,590
29	1986	BLACK	500	FRONT	4	2.3	5-SP	NEW790	MA	$21,595
30	1976	WHITE	76,530	REAR	6	2.7	4-SP OD	LMM423	MN	$4,930
31	1973	RED	91,000	REAR	6	2.9	4-SP OD	SAINT	CT	$6,950
32	1976	MAROON	79,500	REAR	6	3	AUTO	JFF538	TN	$8,995
33	1983	BLACK	61,000	REAR	4	2.2	5-SP	LIN505	ME	$7,995
34	1978	YELLOW	90,000	REAR	4	2.4	4-SP	MBENZ	CA	$8,995
35	1982	WHITE	19,000	FRONT	4	2.6	AUTO	737058	MA	$14,000
36										
37	TOTAl									$252,542
38										
39										
40										
41										

Caution

You cannot use the mouse or the normal cell-pointer-move-ment keystrokes to move into the titles area. If you have to place the cell pointer in this area, you must choose **E**dit, **G**o To or press F5. This action brings the titles area into the scrollable area, which means that you can see the same cells in two different places on-screen.

To freeze titles on-screen:

1. Place the cell pointer in the row below the row you want to designate as a title or in the column to the right of the column you want to designate as a title.

   If you want to designate both a column and a row as titles, place the cell pointer in a cell below the row and to the right of the column you want to designate as titles.

2. Choose **V**iew, Freeze **T**itles.

3. Choose **R**ows, **C**olumns, or **B**oth, depending on whether you want vertical or horizontal titles, or both.

4. Choose OK.

Note: *When you designate a certain row or column as a title, all columns to the left or all rows above the title are automatically frozen as titles too.*

To clear the titles from the screen, choose **V**iew, Clear **T**itles.

Summary

To	Do This
Create additional worksheets in a file	Choose **E**dit, **I**nsert, **S**heet
Open additional files	Choose **F**ile, **O**pen
Move to the next worksheet	Press Ctrl+PgUp
View several worksheets at the same time	Choose **W**indows, **T**ile or **W**indows, **C**ascade
Name a range	Choose **R**ange, **N**ame
Split a file window	Slide the split symbol along the scroll bar
Freeze titles on-screen	Choose **V**iew, Freeze **T**itles

On Your Own
Estimated time: 20 minutes

1. Open a one-page worksheet; then add three more worksheets.

2. Insert a worksheet after worksheet A, and name it SECOND.

3. Delete the worksheet named SECOND.

4. Move the cell pointer to the first cell in the first worksheet. Move the cell pointer to the last active cell in the last active worksheet. (*Active* here means a worksheet, row, or column containing data.)

9

5. Move the cell pointer from worksheet to worksheet.

6. Open a second file.

7. In worksheet A of the first file you opened, write two formulas: one that refers to another worksheet in the same file, and one that refers to a cell in the other file.

8. Enter eight numbers in a column, name the range, and write an @SUM formula that sums the numbers in that range.

9. Move to a distant cell, and then use the navigator icon to move to the named range.

10. Color the background of the named range red, using the range name.

11. Split the two windows horizontally, and then unsynchronize the panes so you can see cells C14 and AI200 at the same time.

12. Fill a large range with data (use **R**ange, **F**ill to do it quickly). Then freeze everything above row 3 and everything to the left of column C as a title.

13. Move to the bottom right corner of the data range, making sure that rows 1, 2, and 3 and columns A, B, and C remain visible.

Chapter 10

Managing Data

This release of 1-2-3 for Windows offers redesigned, powerful, and easy-to-use database features. After you create a database, you can *sort* it (put the data in alphabetical or numeric order). Querying the database means finding, extracting, or deleting records that match criteria you set.

This chapter covers the following topics:

- Understanding database concepts

- Setting up a database in 1-2-3 for Windows

- Modifying the database

- Sorting the database

- Using query tables to sort, find, extract, and delete records

Understanding Database Concepts

Database
An organized collection of information.

In 1-2-3 for Windows, *databases* are special worksheets. You must follow certain rules to treat worksheet data as a database, as discussed in "Creating a Database" later in this chapter.

The purpose of creating a database is to organize the data it contains and to view selected portions of the data. A good example of a database is a phone book, in which data is organized by city and then by name. To see only a portion of a phone book, you turn pages. To see only part of a database on disk, you issue commands.

Field
A field is a labeled
piece of information.

Two important concepts in databases are *fields* and *records*.

In 1-2-3 for Windows, column heads are fields. In a phone book, one field is last name, another is first name, another is address, and so on. Records are entered in rows, one row for each record, one cell for each field. A line in the phone book is a record.

The database
featured in this
chapter.

Field names ———

Record ———

Field ———

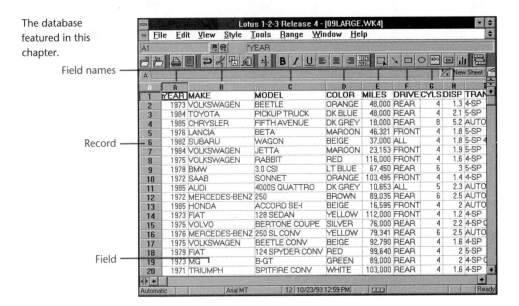

YEAR	MAKE	MODEL	COLOR	MILES	DRIVE	CYLS	DISP	TRAN
1973	VOLKSWAGEN	BEETLE	ORANGE	48,000	REAR	4	1.3	4-SP
1984	TOYOTA	PICKUP TRUCK	DK BLUE	48,000	REAR	4	2.1	5-SP
1985	CHRYSLER	FIFTH AVENUE	DK GREY	18,000	REAR	8	5.2	AUTO
1976	LANCIA	BETA	MAROON	46,321	FRONT	4	1.8	5-SP
1982	SUBARU	WAGON	BEIGE	37,000	ALL	4	1.8	5-SP 4
1984	VOLKSWAGEN	JETTA	MAROON	23,153	FRONT	4	1.9	5-SP
1975	VOLKSWAGEN	RABBIT	RED	116,000	FRONT	4	1.6	4-SP
1978	BMW	3.0 CSI	LT BLUE	67,450	REAR	6	3	5-SP
1972	SAAB	SONNET	ORANGE	103,495	FRONT	4	1.4	4-SP
1985	AUDI	4000S QUATTRO	DK GREY	10,653	ALL	5	2.3	AUTO
1972	MERCEDES-BENZ	250	BROWN	89,035	REAR	6	2.5	AUTO
1985	HONDA	ACCORD SE-I	BEIGE	16,595	FRONT	4	2	AUTO
1973	FIAT	128 SEDAN	YELLOW	112,000	FRONT	4	1.2	4-SP
1975	VOLVO	BERTONE COUPE	SILVER	76,000	REAR	4	2.2	4-SP C
1976	MERCEDES-BENZ	250 SL CONV	YELLOW	79,341	REAR	6	2.5	AUTO
1975	VOLKSWAGEN	BEETLE CONV	BEIGE	92,790	REAR	4	1.6	4-SP
1979	FIAT	124 SPYDER CONV	RED	99,640	REAR	4	2	5-SP
1973	MG	B-GT	GREEN	89,000	REAR	4	2	4-SP C
1971	TRIUMPH	SPITFIRE CONV	WHITE	103,000	REAR	4	1.6	4-SP

Record
A record contains
one piece of infor-
mation for each
field and represents
one entry in the
database.

A file can contain as many databases as you need, or you can create one file for each database. Each database can be on a separate worksheet or in separate ranges in a single worksheet. Leaving the area below a database empty is a good idea; you can use that space to add records or create a query table.

In describing the procedures for using databases, this chapter refers to the database shown in the first figure in the chapter. This database—a list of cars in a used-car lot—extends from cell A1 to cell L33.

Creating a Database

Before you start to create a database, give some thought to the structure you want; advance planning can keep you from having to move and insert columns later. Decide what fields you want to include, and in what order. If you plan to include data from an external database program (such as Paradox or dBASE) or from another 1-2-3 for Window database, check those existing databases first, and be sure to use the same fields, field order, and field types (label or value).

Keeping in mind the preceding definitions and statements, follow these rules to create a database in 1-2-3 for Windows:

■ The field names must be in a single row.

Labels
Cell entries with any combination of letters and numbers that cannot be used in formulas.

■ The field names must be *labels.* Even if a name looks like a number, make it a label.

■ The field names must be unique.

■ A database should not contain blank columns. (It's best not to have blank rows, either.) If you need more space to view data, widen a column rather than leave blank columns between data columns. You can leave a cell empty, but if you delete the contents of a cell, do it properly by pressing Del or choosing **E**dit, Cle**a**r. Don't press the space bar and then press Enter; the cell looks empty, but it's not.

Note: *If you need to change column widths in a file with several worksheets, you might want to choose* **S***tyle,* **W***orksheet Defaults to make sure that* **G***roup mode is off. Otherwise, the change will affect every worksheet.*

Values
Numeric cell entries.

■ All data in a given field should be the same type: either values or labels. In most cases, the choice is obvious. A word such as *Allentown,* for example, is always a label; but department numbers, dates, and area codes can be either labels or *values.*

If you have problems...

If you have trouble remembering to enter a value as a label because it's a pain to type a label prefix, format the column for Labels. Any value you enter from then on automatically is a label. The format does not affect existing numbers, so format before you start entering data. (Formatting data is covered in Chapter 5, "Changing the Appearance of a Worksheet.")

Note: *Don't turn numbers that really are values into labels; you won't be able to perform calculations on those numbers if you do. Area codes can easily be labels, for example, but salaries are another story.*

After you make the necessary decisions, follow these steps to create a database:

1. Enter the field names in the top row of the database.

2. Enter data in the rows and columns immediately below the field names.

   You can enter up to 8,191 records, which is the number of rows left in a worksheet after you enter field names in the top row. The memory in your computer might limit you to fewer records, however.

   Note: *You don't have to add the records in order, because you can sort them at any time in any order you like.*

3. Name the range occupied by the database. Include the field names in the named range, and highlight only the rows and columns that contain data; don't include extra empty rows or columns.

   As the database grows, referring to the collection of data by name will be much easier than trying to remember the first and last cells of the database. (Naming ranges is covered in Chapter 9, "Working with Multiple Worksheets and Multiple Documents.")

Making Changes in a Database

Updating a database can be time-consuming. Your work is a valuable tool, and you need to protect it from corruption or data loss.

Following are several ways you can protect yourself against database corruption:

- Save your work frequently as you add data, but remember that saving a file overwrites the preceding version on disk. If you think that you made a serious mistake since the last save, don't save the file again until you find the error. Alternatively, choose **F**ile, Save **A**s to change the name of the file so that you have both the old version and the new version on disk.

- Consider saving a separate copy of the database on another disk, or under a different name on the same disk, so that you have one backup copy.

- Be ready to use **U**ndo immediately if you realize that you made a mistake. Remember that **U**ndo reverses only the most recent command or procedure.

  Note: *If **U**ndo is not working, choose **T**ools, **U**ser Setup, and make sure that **U**ndo is selected.*

- If you make a mistake that you can't undo, close the file without saving it, retrieve the file again, and then repeat the procedure.

- Create a query table with all data and use it instead of the original database for the sort, find, and query commands so that the original database is untouched. (For more information, see "Creating a Query Table" later in this chapter.)

- Use record numbers as an extra field in each record so that you have a fallback sort order. The easiest way to create record numbers is to type a field name at the top of one column and then choose **R**ange, **F**ill or **R**ange, Fill by **E**xample to enter the record numbers next to each record. If you sort a database and find that the sort is incorrect, you can re-sort on record numbers to restore the original order.

Adding New Records

You can continue to add records to the database after you name the database range, but you have to remember to extend the name to the larger range. If you forget and then perform a query or a sort on the named database, 1-2-3 for Windows ignores the new records.

A better way to add records to your database is to choose **T**ools, Data-**b**ase, **A**ppend Records, as follows:

1. Name the range in which you entered the database, if you haven't already done so. For this example, call the range CARS.

2. Add another worksheet to the file. Name the worksheet tab ENTRY FORM or something similar, or use a range away from the database as a place to enter data. Copy and paste the labels from the first row of the database to the top row of the entry area.

3. Enter as many records as you want in the entry area.

4. When you finish entering records, select all those records, and then choose **T**ools, Data**b**ase, **A**ppend Records. The Append Records dialog box appears.

5. In the **T**o Database Table text box, enter the name of the database to which you want to append the records. Alternatively, press F3 to list the names of all databases, and then select the database you want to use.

The Append Records dialog box, which is easiest to use when you use a named database range.

6. Choose OK.

The records you typed in the entry area are appended to the bottom of the database, and the named range is extended to include the new data.

Changing Data

As you can with any other cell in a worksheet, you can change data simply by entering new data in the cell. To make the same change in many cells at one time, choose **E**dit, **F**ind & Replace. (The **F**ind & Replace command is covered in Chapter 4, "Modifying Data in a Worksheet.") Remember that if you change the column heads—the field names in the database—you must make a similar change in the entry table you used for appending records and anywhere else the title appears.

Establishing Search Criteria and Finding Records

Search criteria
A designation of fields, and of values for those fields, that enables you to narrow the number of records that you work with in a database.

One of the most important skills in working with databases is using *search criteria* to find specific records. Choose **T**ools, Data**b**ase, **F**ind Records or **D**elete Records. **F**ind Records selects all records in the database that match the search criteria you establish. **D**elete Records deletes from the database all records that match the search criteria. If you didn't specify search criteria, you would find or delete every record.

To establish search criteria and then find records:

1. Choose **T**ools, Data**b**ase, **F**ind Records. The Find Records dialog box appears.

2. In the Find Records in **D**atabase Table text box, type the name or range address of the database, or select its range.

Caution
Don't choose OK at this point. If you do, 1-2-3 for Windows will close the dialog box and find only records that match the criteria that the program enters automatically in the Criteria box.

3. In the **F**ield drop-down list, select a field for the first criterion. (By default, the field in which the cell pointer is located is selected.)

Note: *If you know which field will be a criterion, put the cell pointer in that column before using the command to find or delete records.*

4. Specify an operator. The possibilities are:

=	Equal to
<	Less than
>	Greater than
<=	Less than or equal to
>=	Greater than or equal to
<>	Not equal to

You can use operators with a label field. In the following figure, we "found" all records with Year > 1980. In this case, "greater than" means later in the alphabet.

5. Pick a value against which the field value in each record will be compared.

The field and operator have been selected, and the comparison value is being selected.

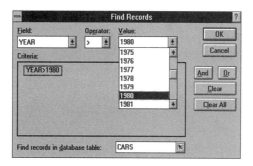

6. Choose OK. 1-2-3 for Windows highlights each record that meets the criterion.

The result of **T**ools,
Database, **F**ind
Records with Year
> 1980.

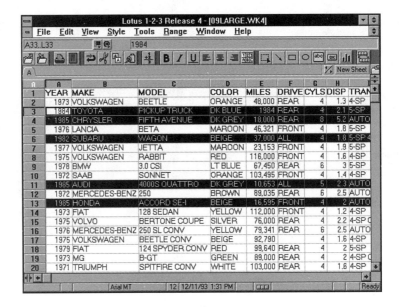

You can use the scroll bars to view all highlighted records. You also can choose to change the appearance of the cells, or the contents of cells in the selected records, to set them apart.

The **A**nd and **O**r command buttons in the Find Records dialog box make it possible for you to set more precise criteria. The difference between **A**nd and **O**r is very important. Connecting two criteria with **A**nd requires 1-2-3 for Windows to include records that must match both criteria, whereas using **O**r tells the program to include records that match one criterion or the other.

To use **A**nd or **O**r in establishing criteria:

1. Choose **T**ools, **D**atabase, **F**ind Records. The Find Records dialog box appears.

2. Choose a field, an operator, and a value for the first criterion.

3. Choose **A**nd if you want a record selected only if it meets both search criteria. Choose **O**r if you want records selected that match either search criterion.

4. Choose a field, an operator, and a value for the second criterion.

5. Choose OK.

The following figures show the results of using **A**nd and **O**r between search criteria.

These search
criteria, connected
by **A**nd, restrict the
search.

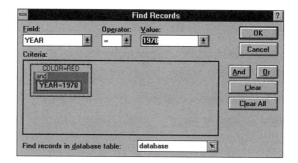

Only two records in
the database match
the search criteria.

Using **O**r to com-
bine the same
search criteria
results in a less
restricted search.

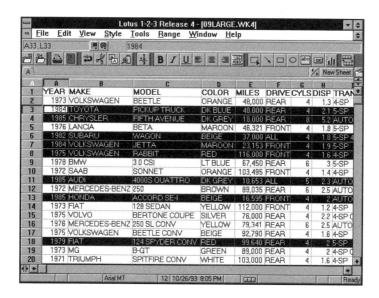

10

*Note: Criteria listed beside each other in the Criteria box of the Find Records dialog box are **Or** criteria. When one criterion is listed above another, those criteria are **And** criteria. Click and drag a criterion from below to beside the other, or vice versa, to change the relationship.*

Click **A**nd or **O**r to set the relationship between search criteria, and then continue to define search criteria. If one criterion is not correct, select it and then choose **C**lear. Choose C**l**ear All to remove all search criteria.

Wild cards
Symbols used in place of other, un-specified characters. Wild cards enable you to expand a search for text by making it unneces-sary to specify every character.

To locate all items in a database that begin with a given letter, you can use *wild cards*: * and ?. The asterisk stands for any number of characters; the question mark stands for one character. Setting a criterion as Make = V*, for example, finds all cars whose names begin with *V*. The criterion Make = V???? finds names that begin with *V* and have four more letters.

Deleting Data, Records, and Fields

Except when you need to add records, you should leave the original data-base alone and make changes, including deletions, in a query table that contains all records. But you may prefer to change the original database to remove unwanted information. To delete a field in a record, go to the cell that contains the data you want to delete and then press Del.

The standard **E**dit, **D**elete command enables you to remove a column that contains a field you no longer need or a row that contains a record you want to remove from a database.

The best way to delete a group of records is:

1. Choose **T**ools, Data**b**ase, **D**elete Records. The Delete Records dialog box appears.

2. Establish search criteria as you would in the Find Records dialog box.

3. Choose OK. 1-2-3 for Windows immediately removes all records that match the search criteria.

Using Query Tables To Sort, Find, Extract, and Delete Records

A *query table* is a copy of your original database in which you can find and manipulate data. The advantages of using a query table are:

- You preserve and protect the original database.

- You can create a query table that contains only selected records and fields.

- You can perform summary calculations on selected fields.

- You can create calculated fields and add them to the query table.

Creating a Query Table

You can create as many query tables as you like, specifying which fields and records are included in each one. To create a query table:

1. Find an empty range at least as big as the original database where you want to place the query table.

2. Place the cell pointer in the top left corner of that range. (Make sure that the cell pointer is not in the original database.)

3. Choose **T**ools, Data**b**ase, **N**ew Query. The New Query dialog box appears.

Caution

Because a query table overwrites any data in the range it covers, make sure that you don't place a query table in the same range as the original database or in a range that contains any other data you don't want to delete.

The New Query dialog box.

4. Make sure that the Select Location for New **Q**uery Table box contains the address of the cell where you placed the cell pointer.

5. In the Select **D**atabase Table to Query box, type the name or the range address of the database, or highlight its range, including the field names at the top of the columns in the database.

6. Choose OK. The query table appears in the specified range, starting at the cell pointer's current location. All records and fields from the original database are included.

   Notice that 1-2-3 for Windows displays new SmartIcons and a new menu: **Q**uery. These elements are visible whenever the cell pointer is in a query table.

Note: *You can change the fields included in a query table by clicking the Select Fields SmartIcon.*

Naming the Query Table

You can name a query table so that you can retrieve it easily or use its name in a macro. By default, each query table you create is numbered sequentially: Query 1, Query 2, and so on.

To change the name of a query table to something more descriptive:

1. Select the table you want to rename.

2. Choose **Q**uery, **N**ame. The current name of the selected table appears in the **Q**uery Name text box of the Name dialog box.

3. Type the new name (up to 15 characters), and then choose **R**ename.

To go to a query table:

1. Choose **E**dit, **G**o To. The Go To dialog box appears.

2. Choose **T**ype of Item, and then select Query Table.

3. Highlight the name of the query table and then press OK, or double-click the name of the table to select the entire table.

Changing the Way the Query Table and Database Work Together

You may decide to change the way data is exchanged between the original database and the query table by using Set **O**ptions, an item included in the **Q**uery menu. 1-2-3 for Windows offers four **O**ptions items. By default, the first two are not selected, and the second two are.

The first option, **A**llow Updates to Database Table, causes any changes in the query table to be passed along to the original database. Use this option with caution, especially if you like the added insurance of keeping the original database immune from accidents.

To allow changes to the query table to be made in the original database:

1. Place the cell pointer in the query table.

2. Choose **Q**uery, Set **O**ptions. The Set Options dialog box appears.

3. Choose **A**llow Updates to Database Table.

4. Choose OK.

The second option, **S**how Unique Records Only, displays only one record of several possible duplications. In the used-car database, if you chose to display only makes of cars in the query table with no other fields, and then selected **S**how Unique Records Only, each make of car would appear only once in the table, regardless of how many records for each make appear in the original database, as shown in the following figure.

List created by
Show Unique
Records Only.

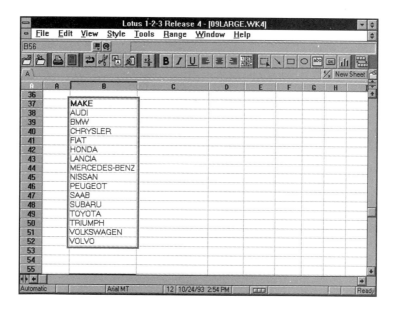

To display only one record of duplicates:

1. Place the cell pointer in the query table.

2. Choose **Q**uery, Set **O**ptions. The Set Options dialog box appears.

3. Choose **S**how Unique Records Only.

4. Choose OK.

Sorting Databases

Sorting means putting the database in order. You can sort a database by choosing **R**ange, **S**ort. Choosing the **Q**uery menu's **S**ort command is faster and easier, however, because you don't run the risk of accidentally sorting field titles along with records. Remember that the **Q**uery menu is visible only when the cell pointer is in the query table; the **R**ange menu is visible when the cell pointer is in a cell outside the query table.

Keys

Fields used to determine the order in which a database is sorted.

Sort order is determined by *keys*: fields and desired order. In the used-car database, you could decide to sort the list of cars on the basis of Make, in ascending order. Cars beginning with *A* are placed before those beginning with *B*, and so on.

What if the database contains several cars of the same make? Use additional keys to break ties. You might prefer to list the cars in each Make field from newest to oldest. Set the second key to Year, descending order, and each make will be listed from the highest year to the lowest, or from newest to oldest.

To sort a database:

1. Place the cell pointer in the query table.

2. Choose **Q**uery, **S**ort. The Sort dialog box appears.

The Sort dialog box.

3. In the **S**ort By text box, specify the field you want to use as the first key.

4. Choose **A**scending or **D**escending to determine the sort order.

5. Choose Add **K**ey.

6. If you want to define more keys, repeat steps 3, 4, and 5 until you define all the keys you want to use.

7. Choose OK. 1-2-3 for Windows sorts the database.

Note: *If you decide to define new keys for a different sort, choose Reset in the Sort dialog box to clear all existing keys.*

The used-car database, sorted on two keys: Make (in ascending order) and Year (in descending order).

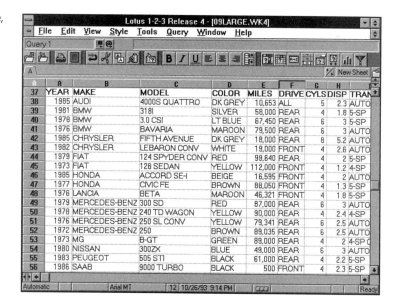

	YEAR	MAKE	MODEL	COLOR	MILES	DRIVE	CYLS	DISP	TRAN
37	YEAR	MAKE	MODEL	COLOR	MILES	DRIVE	CYLS	DISP	TRAN
38	1985	AUDI	4000S QUATTRO	DK GREY	10,653	ALL	5	2.3	AUTO
39	1981	BMW	318I	SILVER	58,000	REAR	4	1.8	5-SP
40	1978	BMW	3.0 CSI	LT BLUE	67,450	REAR	6	3	5-SP
41	1976	BMW	BAVARIA	MAROON	79,500	REAR	6	3	AUTO
42	1985	CHRYSLER	FIFTH AVENUE	DK GREY	18,000	REAR	8	5.2	AUTO
43	1982	CHRYSLER	LEBARON CONV	WHITE	19,000	FRONT	4	2.6	AUTO
44	1979	FIAT	124 SPYDER CONV	RED	99,640	REAR	4	2	5-SP
45	1973	FIAT	128 SEDAN	YELLOW	112,000	FRONT	4	1.2	4-SP
46	1985	HONDA	ACCORD SE-I	BEIGE	16,595	FRONT	4	2	AUTO
47	1977	HONDA	CIVIC FE	BROWN	88,050	FRONT	4	1.3	5-SP
48	1976	LANCIA	BETA	MAROON	46,321	FRONT	4	1.8	5-SP
49	1979	MERCEDES-BENZ	300 SD	RED	87,000	REAR	6	3	AUTO
50	1978	MERCEDES-BENZ	240 TD WAGON	YELLOW	90,000	REAR	4	2.4	4-SP
51	1976	MERCEDES-BENZ	250 SL CONV	YELLOW	79,341	REAR	6	2.5	AUTO
52	1972	MERCEDES-BENZ	250	BROWN	89,035	REAR	6	2.5	AUTO
53	1973	MG	B-GT	GREEN	89,000	REAR	4	2	4-SP
54	1980	NISSAN	300ZX	BLUE	49,000	REAR	6	3	AUTO
55	1983	PEUGEOT	505 STI	BLACK	61,000	REAR	4	2.2	5-SP
56	1986	SAAB	9000 TURBO	BLACK	500	FRONT	4	2.3	5-SP

Making Other Changes in a Query Table

If you need to rename a field in a query table:

1. Place the cell pointer in the query table, in the cell with the field name you want to change.

2. Choose **Query**, Show **F**ield As. The Show Field As dialog box appears.

3. In the Show Field As text box, type the new name for the field.

4. Choose OK.

To redisplay all records after you choose to suppress display of duplicates:

1. Place the cell pointer in the query table.

2. Click the Show All Records icon in the SmartIcon palette that appears when the cell pointer is in the query table.

To determine which fields will be displayed in a query table;

1. Place the cell pointer in the query table.

2. Choose **Q**uery, Choose Fields. The **C**hoose Fields dialog box appears.

3. In the Selected Fields list box, select the fields you want to display.

4. Choose OK.

Summary

To	Do This
Delete records	Choose **T**ools, **D**atabase, **D**elete Records
Find records	Choose **T**ools, **D**atabase, **F**ind Records
Create a query table	Choose **T**ools, **D**atabase, **N**ew Query
To use several search criteria	Define one criterion at a time; choose **A**nd or **O**r before defining the next criterion
Sort a database	Choose **Q**uery, **S**ort

On Your Own
Estimated time: 45 minutes

1. Create a database.

2. Find a group of records that match a single criterion.

3. Define a second criterion, and find records that match one or the other criterion.

4. Create a query table.

5. Reduce the number of fields represented in the query table.

6. Reduce the number of records in the query table by defining a criterion that chooses data in one label field starting with letters before *M*.

7. Sort the database on at least two keys, one ascending and the other descending.

Chapter 11

Using Macros

Simply stated, *macros* are sets of recorded keystrokes. In 1-2-3 for Windows, macros are commands, text, or a combination of text and commands. You can enter a macro into a cell and then play back the macro whenever you want to perform the task that the macro represents.

Macros free you from performing repetitive tasks; they perform complicated tasks quickly; and they help inexperienced users accomplish tasks that those users otherwise could not perform.

This chapter covers the following topics:

- ■ Writing some simple macros
- ■ Naming macros
- ■ Running macros
- ■ Writing a macro with several steps
- ■ Writing command macros
- ■ Recording keystrokes
- ■ Creating a macro library
- ■ Creating a macro button
- ■ Fixing macros

Understanding Macro Basics

To practice writing macros, you probably will use a blank worksheet. When you start to write macros for real work, however, chances are that those macros will be part of a file and will be used for work in that file.

The general steps to follow in creating macros:

1. Decide where to place macros.

   Your first decision must be *where* you will write your macros. One way to place macros is to create a separate worksheet just for macros. Double-click the worksheet tab and name the worksheet MACROS.

   If you choose to keep the macros in the same worksheet as data, make sure that the data and macro sections of the worksheet don't grow and overlap. If your data will spread out to the right, for example, put your macros below the data.

2. Decide what you want the macro to do.

3. List each keystroke necessary to accomplish that task. If the macro is simple, writing down the keystrokes is unnecessary, but a list is helpful for a complicated macro.

4. When you complete your decision-making and research, enter the keystrokes in a cell or range.

   Note: *Important considerations for placing a macro in a cell are covered later in this chapter.*

5. Name the macro.

Writing and Running a Simple Macro

To understand how macros work, it is helpful to create some, run them, and see the effect. You could write a macro that writes your name, for example. Follow these steps:

1. Find a cell in which you can write the macro.

2. Type your name, including the space between the first and last names. After your last name, type a tilde (~), which is the macro symbol for the Enter key.

The cell entry is a macro: the keystrokes required to type your name.

When you run the macro, 1-2-3 for Windows enters your name into a cell. (Make sure that you put the cell pointer in a blank cell so that you don't overwrite the contents of the macro cell.)

You can run a macro in several ways, which will be covered later. For now, use the **T**ools menu.

11

To run the macro:

1. Place the cell pointer in a blank cell.

2. Choose **T**ools, **M**acro, **R**un. The Macro Run dialog box appears.

3. Designate the cell where you placed the macro (your name) by typing its address in the Macro Name text box.

4. Choose OK. 1-2-3 for Windows enters your name in the cell where you placed the cell pointer before you ran the macro. To enter the name into the cell, you need to press Enter.

A macro that enters text into a cell is a text macro. Command macros perform actions but do not enter text. A simple command macro could be the keystroke that moves the cell pointer down one cell. Commands in 1-2-3 for Windows macros must be entered inside curly braces ({ }). Make sure that you type those symbols, not brackets ([]) or parentheses. Commands not enclosed in braces are not interpreted as commands by 1-2-3 for Windows.

The macro command that moves the cell pointer down is {DOWN}. Macros are not case-sensitive, but entering commands in uppercase letters (to distinguish them from text) is a good idea. Alternatively, you could type **{D}** for the same effect. If you want to move the cell pointer down two cells, you could type **{D 2}**.

If you have problems...	If you typed D and 2 inside curly braces and then ran the macro, but nothing happened, you probably forgot the space. You can cause certain commands, such as cursor movement or Esc, to repeat by typing a number in the braces, but you must include a space.

Other command macros execute actions from the menu. Suppose that you enter numbers into cells around your worksheet and want to format those cells as Currency, no decimal places. The macro command is {STYLE-NUMBER-FORMAT "CURRENCY";0}. (Don't worry if you find the macro code a bit daunting. Later in this chapter, you learn ways to make writing commands simple.)

To see how a command macro works:

1. Enter the macro **{STYLE-NUMBER-FORMAT "CURRENCY";0}** in a cell.

2. Enter a number in another cell.

3. Place the cell pointer in the cell that contains the number.

4. Run the macro by choosing **T**ools, **M**acro, **R**un and typing the macro cell's address in the Macro Name text box.

5. Choose OK.

When entering macro code into a range, keep the following rules and guidelines in mind:

- Don't enter non-macro text in the cell immediately below the macro. If possible, 1-2-3 for Windows will run the text in the extra cells as part of the macro.

- Don't put spaces where they don't belong. There is no rule against spaces in macros, but you have to be careful where you place them.

- Watch for incorrect spelling and syntax.

- Enter all lines of macro code as labels. Especially watch lines that begin with numbers or with these characters:

    / + – @ # $, < (\]*

Naming Macros

Running a named macro is easier than running an unnamed macro. The most common names for macros are backslash/letter combinations or range names of up to 15 characters.

So that you don't forget the names of macros, you should place each macro name near its macro. The most common practice is to enter the macro name in the cell to the left of the first cell of the macro.

An additional advantage to placing the name in an adjacent cell is that you can use the special range-naming command to apply that label as a name for the macro cell. Naming a range and naming a macro are the same thing. As you learned in Chapter 9, "Working with Multiple Worksheets and Multiple Documents," you can name a range by applying the label in an adjacent cell.

You can create four types of macros:

- *Unnamed macros.* These macros simply are keystrokes entered into a worksheet.

- *Named macros.* A macro of this type has a name up to 15 characters long. Any text you use as a range name can be used as a macro name. You should use a name that gives you some idea of the function of the macro.

  To distinguish macro names from other range names, you could put M or MAC in front of all macro names. MACPRINT, for example, may sound like a product from a fast-food restaurant, but the name has several advantages. First, when you see a list of range names, you know what is a macro and what is not. Second, you don't run the risk of using unacceptable names, such as the names of keyboard keys. If you name a macro INSERT, for example, the macro will not run, because there is a key named Insert. Starting the macro name with M, M_, or MAC averts the potential difficulty, because no key is named MINSERT or MDELETE.

- *Ctrl+letter macros.* A macro of this type has a backslash and a letter. These macros are the easiest to run; you simply hold down the Ctrl key and press the letter. (Former users of DOS versions of 1-2-3 have to break the habit of pressing the Alt key to run macros, because the Alt key activates the menu in 1-2-3 for Windows.)

Caution

1-2-3 for Windows has designated certain Ctrl+letter combinations as accelerator keys, so using those letters for macros won't work. An example is Ctrl+B, which boldfaces selected text or cells. If you name a macro \B and then run it, 1-2-3 for Windows would boldface text instead of running the macro you wrote.

Avoid using the following letters in macro names: B, C, E, I, L, N, O, P, R, S, U, V, X, and Z.

If you have problems... If a Ctrl+letter macro does not run, make sure that you didn't use the wrong slash in Ctrl+letter macros. The correct slash to use in a Ctrl+letter macro name is \, not /.

11

Auto-execute macro

A macro that runs itself once each time the file containing it is retrieved.

■ *Auto-execute macros.* A macro of this type is named with a backslash and a zero (\0). You can use only one auto-execute macro in a file, because only one range can be named \0 (the name 1-2-3 for Windows uses for auto-execute macros).

You can give a macro any type of name you want, or no name. But named macros are easier to find and remember.

To name a macro:

1. Enter the name in a cell adjacent to the first cell of the macro.

2. Place the cell pointer in the cell that contains the macro name, not the macro itself.

3. Choose **R**ange, **N**ame. The Name dialog box appears.

4. Choose Use Labels, which enables you to use the contents of one cell as the name of an adjacent cell or range.

5. In the For Cells drop-down list, select the direction in which you want to apply the name. (If the name is to the left of the macro, for example, use To the Right.)

6. Choose OK.

If you have problems...

You might enter the backslash and a letter or a zero in a cell and find the cell filled with the character you typed. The reason is that the backslash is a special label prefix that causes any characters you type to repeat enough times to fill the cell. The correct way to enter this type of macro name is to type another label prefix first (', ", or ^), followed by the backslash and letter.

Running Macros

To run any macro, including an unnamed macro:

1. Choose **T**ools, **M**acro, **R**un, or press Alt+F3. The Macro Run dialog box appears.

Use the Macro Run dialog box to designate the macro you want to run.

11

2. Perform one of the following actions:

■ In the Macro Name text box, type the name of the macro or the first cell address of the macro.

■ In the All Named Ranges list box, select the name of the macro. Then choose OK, press Enter, or double-click the name.

■ Point to the first cell in the macro. Then choose OK or press Enter.

When several files are open, each with its own macros, you might need to select the file in which the macro is located.

To run a macro in another file:

1. Press Alt+F3 or choose **T**ools, **M**acro, **R**un to open the Macro Run dialog box.

2. Select the proper file in the **I**n File drop-down list.

3. Highlight the name of the macro you want to run.

4. Choose OK.

If you have problems...

If a macro doesn't run properly, make sure that you didn't move a cell or range to the first cell in the macro. This action removes the macro name, so when you try to run it, you get unintended results.

An auto-execute (\0) macro runs one time when you retrieve the file the macro is in.

If you have problems...

If you want to prevent an auto-execute macro from running in a file because you need to edit the macro first, or if you simply want to suppress execution, choose **T**ools, **U**ser Setup, and then deselect Run Autoexec **M**acros. No \0 macros will run automatically until you select Run Autoexec **M**acros again.

You may find it useful to include an auto-execute macro in a file that is automatically retrieved when you start 1-2-3 for Windows. Name the file AUTO123.WK4, and place it in the default directory (the one named in **T**ools, **U**ser Setup, **W**orksheet Directory). Each time you start 1-2-3 for Windows, the file is retrieved and the macro runs. The file also could contain other macros you frequently use. For information about creating a collection of macros, see "Creating a Macro Library" later in this chapter.

Writing a Macro with Several Steps

Debugging
Removing errors (bugs) that prevent programs and macros from running properly.

Using what you have learned so far, you can write a macro that enters your name and return address. You don't have to enter a macro in only one cell; in fact, there are several reasons why you ought to enter a macro in separate cells. First, *debugging* a macro that is in several cells is easier, because the macro is easier to read. Second, when keystrokes trail far off to the right in a cell, you have to scroll to see the whole macro. Third, large macros may exceed the 512-character limit in a cell.

These macros enter a name and address in three cells. One macro is easier to read than the others.

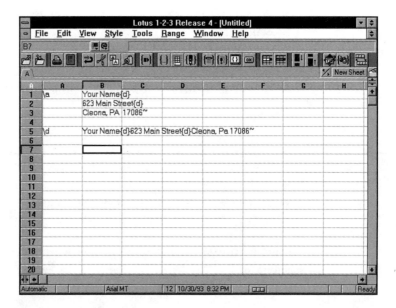

In the preceding figure, macro \A and macro \D do the same thing, but \A is easier to read because it is broken into parts.

If you have problems...	You might have trouble entering a number into a cell in a macro and then trying to run the macro. This problem occurs because you must enter all macro code as a label. Place a label prefix before all values in macros. An easier way to make sure all cell entries in macros are labels is to choose **S**tyle, **N**umber Format, **L**abel to apply the label format to the range where you will enter macros. This action causes all future entries in that range to be labels.

When you designate a cell or a name of a macro to be run, the program continues to execute keystrokes entered in cells below the first cell. This capability is useful when you are entering long macros, but if you inadvertently enter other data in cells immediately below a macro, 1-2-3 for Windows will try to execute those keystrokes, too. Always leave a blank cell below the last cell of a macro.

Writing Command Macros

Each action that you want to perform has a specific macro command. To boldface the contents of a cell, for example, the macro command is

{STYLE-FONT-ATTRIBUTES "BOLD";"ON"}

The command itself is the first, hyphenated part; the arguments follow in quotes. Some arguments in command macros are required, and others are optional; in any case, you must enter arguments in order. Use the help feature to get information on the arguments required in macros and on how to enter those arguments.

Note: *Users of the DOS versions of 1-2-3 will find that many macros written with classic-menu commands work in 1-2-3 for Windows, so it is possible to write slash+key macros.*

You cannot remember the commands and arguments for every action, and you're not expected to. The following sections show you how to use the program to help you write command macros.

Recording Keystrokes

Rather than enter every command into a macro, you can turn on the record feature of 1-2-3 for Windows, as follows:

1. Choose **T**ools, **M**acro, Re**c**ord to start recording your keystrokes. Rec appears at the bottom of the screen to remind you that you are recording all keystrokes.

2. Perform an action. (To write a return-address macro, for example, type the entire series of keystrokes that make up your name and address.)

3. Choose **T**ools, **M**acro, Stop Re**c**ording to stop recording the macro.

Note: *You can stop or pause recording at any time by choosing **T**ools, **M**acro, Stop Recording. To start recording again, choose the command again.*

After you record the macro, you will want to see the recorded keystrokes; choose **T**ools, **M**acro, Show Transcript.

Note: *The transcript where keystrokes are recorded fills quickly. Don't wait to copy the keystrokes into a macro; finding the keystrokes you want for thew macro becomes increasingly difficult as the transcript fills. Eventually, the transcript will eliminate old keystrokes.*

When the transcript is the current window, a new menu appears in the menu bar: Transcript, which replaces the **R**ange menu while the transcript is current. A new SmartIcon palette also appears.

Note: *If the transcript disappears from the screen, choose **W**indow, Transcript to bring it back into view.*

When the transcript is visible, you can select commands in the transcript and play them back to make sure that they run correctly. To play a command back:

1. Place the cell pointer in a blank cell (to avoid overwriting cell contents when you play back the macro).

2. Make the transcript the active window.

3. Select the keystrokes you want to play back by clicking and dragging across them or by holding down the Shift key and using the arrow keys to move across the text.

4. Choose Tra**n**script, **P**layback, or choose Playback from the quick menu.

To create a macro from text in the transcript, copy the keystrokes from the transcript and paste them into the worksheet in a place designated for macros. Follow these steps:

11

1. Choose **W**indows, Transcript to activate the transcript window.

2. Select the keystrokes you want to copy.

3. To paste the keystrokes into the current cell, choose **E**dit, **C**opy, or choose Copy from the quick menu.

You can copy and paste macro code easily when both the transcript and the worksheet menu are visible.

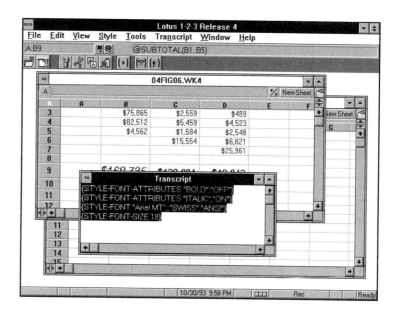

If you have problems...   If you have trouble figuring out where your macro code begins and where other keystrokes end, choose Clear All from the quick menu to clear all text from the transcript before you start recording the keystrokes.

If you record the highlighting of ranges as well as the commands you use on those ranges, you will notice that the macro records the specific range. Every time you run the macro, the same range is affected, because the macro recorded the actual range address. This is because, by default, macros are recorded as *absolute*, meaning that they record the actual cells affected rather than the cells relative to the current cell.

To cause the macro to affect the range relative to the current location of the cell pointer, select the transcript; choose Transcript, **R**ecord Relative; and record the macro again, using the same steps as before. Now when you record the macro, instead of recording the actual cells you highlight, you will record the act of highlighting cells. When you run the macro, the same act of highlighting relative to the current cell will take place. Before you run the macro, place the cell pointer in the proper cell so that the correct range will be affected.

The macro in rows 5 and 6 was recorded absolute; the one in rows 8 and 9 was recorded relative.

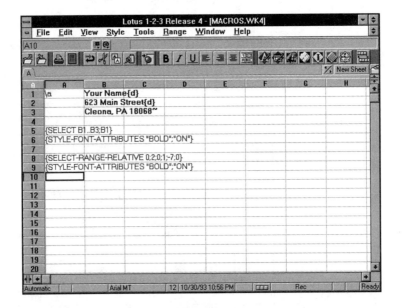

Getting Help with Macro Writing

1-2-3 for Windows can help you enter macro commands. To get this help:

1. Type an open curly brace ({), and then press F3. The Macro Keywords dialog box appears.

2. A list of all possible macro commands appears in the dialog box. Select the command you need by selecting it from the list or by typing it in the **M**acro Name text box.

3. Choose OK to insert the command into the cell.

If you need help with the required arguments in the command you chose, press F1. The help screen that appears contains information specific to the selected macro command.

Note: *Any time you have a cell that begins with an open brace ({), you can press F1 to get macro help. If a command follows the brace, you will get macro help on that specific command.*

11

Creating a Macro Library

A *macro library* is a way to store in one location macros that are useful for many worksheets. 1-2-3 for Windows has no command specifically devoted to creating a macro library, because you can use a file to store macros and retrieve that file along with the files in which you want to use macros. So that you don't forget to retrieve the macros file, name it AUTO123.WK4; as mentioned earlier, files with this name, placed in the default directory, are automatically retrieved when you start the program.

This file should contain macros that are useful for most of your files. (You still can enter into individual files macros that are useful only in those files.) It doesn't matter whether you have macros in several files with the same name. When you run a macro, unless you specify which file the macro is in, 1-2-3 for Windows assumes that the macro is in the current file.

When you want to run a macro from your macro library file while another file is active:

1. Choose **T**ools, **M**acro, **R**un. The Run Macro dialog box appears.

2. In the **In** File drop-down box, select the library file name.

3. Choose OK.

Creating a Macro Button

A *macro button* is a buttonlike graphic that you place in a worksheet. The button remains in one place in the worksheet rather than moving as you scroll around the worksheet. When you click the button with the mouse, you run the macro associated with the button.

To create a button and associate it with a short macro:

1. Choose **T**ools, **D**raw, **B**utton.

2. Move the mouse pointer to the place where you want the top left corner of the button to be.

3. Click and drag across the worksheet to place the button. You also can just click to place a button of the default size.

   When you release the mouse button, the Assign Button dialog box appears.

The Assign to Button dialog box, where you name a button and associate it with a macro.

4. Change the default name from BUTTON by typing a more descriptive name in the **B**utton Text box.

5. Choose Button in the **A**ssign Macro From drop-down list, and then type the macro in the **E**nter Macro Here box.

The Assign to Button dialog box as it appears when you choose to assign a macro to the button.

6. Choose OK.

To assign a long or complex macro to a button:

1. Enter the macro in a range.

2. Create the macro button as described in the preceding steps.

3. In the Assign to Button dialog box, choose Range in the **A**ssign Macro From drop-down list.

4. In the **A**ssign Macro From box, type the name of the macro or the first cell of the macro.

5. Choose OK.

A named macro button.

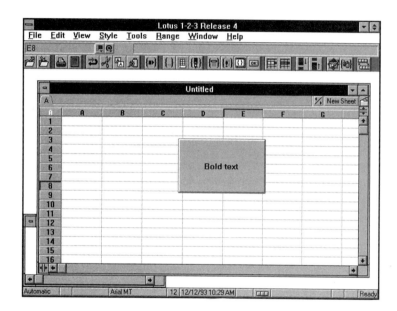

To run the macro, click the button. If you need to make some kind of change in the button, select it by Shift+clicking or Ctrl+clicking; you cannot just click the button to select it, because clicking runs the macro. Alternatively, you can click the macro button with the right mouse button to select it and call up the quick menu.

When the button is selected, you can resize it by clicking and dragging one of the selection handles, and you can move the button by placing the mouse pointer inside the button and clicking and dragging it to a new location. Using the right mouse button, you can copy, cut, or delete the macro button and change the assigned macro. You also can choose **T**ools, **M**acro and select **A**ssign to Button to change the assigned macro.

Fixing Macros

When macros don't run the way you want them to, you need to debug them. Check the macro code. The first step is to read each line and keystroke of the macro.

If the macro code looks fine to you, but the macro still stops and generates an error message, or simply doesn't do what you want it to, you can use either of two tools.

The first tool is Step mode, which enables you to run a macro one command at a time to watch how the commands and keystrokes are executed.

To run a macro in Step mode:

1. Choose **T**ools, **M**acro, **S**ingle Step. The word Step appears at the bottom of the screen.

2. Run a macro. Only one command or keystroke in the macro runs.

3. Press any key to run the next command or keystroke.

4. Continue pressing a key to proceed stepwise through the macro until you see the point at which it stops functioning correctly.

5. Edit the macro to remove the error.

The second tool, Trace mode, helps you see what step is being executed when you are in Step mode. To activate Trace mode, choose **T**ools, **M**acro, **T**race. A window appears, displaying the command that currently is being executed.

This macro is being executed in Trace and Step modes.

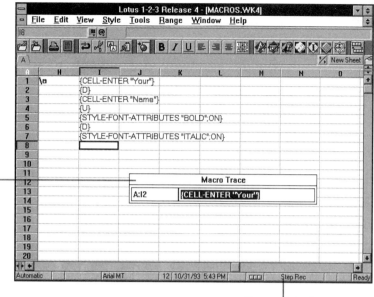

Trace mode window

Step mode indicator

Summary

To	Do This
Write a macro	Write the keystrokes in a cell or range
Write a command macro	Type {, and then press F3
Name a macro	In the first cell of the macro, choose Range, Name
Get help on macros	Type {, select the command, and then press F1
Create a macro button	Choose **T**ools, **D**raw, **B**utton; then enter the macro or range name in the appropriate text box in the Assign to Button dialog box
Debug a macro	Choose **T**ools, **M**acro, **S**ingle Step, **T**race
Create a macro library	Write macros in a separate file; retrieve that file when you need to use the macros in other files

On Your Own

Estimated time: 20 minutes

1. Write a macro that enters your name. Name the macro \A, and run it.

2. Write a macro that colors the background of a range red. Name the macro MAC_REDBACKG, and run it.

3. Create an auto-execute macro that enters Welcome to 1-2-3 for Windows!. Save the macro in a file that will automatically be retrieved when you restart 1-2-3 for Windows. Close and reopen the program to verify that the file and macro work properly.

4. Write a macro that enters your name, street address, and city/state/ZIP in three separate lines.

5. Using Transcript, **R**ecord Relative, record a macro that boldfaces the first line of the address, changes the font for the second line, and italicizes the third line.

6. Turn on Step mode and Trace mode, and run a macro.

7. Create a macro button and associate it with a macro that inserts a blank row at the cell-pointer location.

Chapter 12

Customizing 1-2-3 for Windows

Default

Aspects of a program's appearance or performance that occur automatically. Users can override or change many defaults.

1-2-3 Release 4 for Windows is designed for the preferences of most of its users. However, the *defaults* that determine the way the program looks and works might not be exactly what all users want. In this chapter, you learn how to change some performance characteristics of the program.

This chapter covers the following topics:

- Making performance changes

- Adding, deleting, and creating SmartIcons and palettes

- Creating your own Fill by Example tables

- Creating an icon to launch 1-2-3 for Windows and open a file

Making Performance Changes

You can make many changes in the way 1-2-3 for Windows works. Some changes enhance performance by freeing memory; others simply reflect the way you prefer the program to work. Some changes are effective in the current session or the current worksheet only; others become permanent changes and remain in effect across 1-2-3 for Windows work sessions.

Choose **T**ools, **U**ser Setup to make changes that change the program's performance, even in future sessions. In general, to make performance changes, follow these steps:

1. Choose **T**ools, **U**ser Setup. The User Setup dialog box appears.

The main User
Setup dialog box.

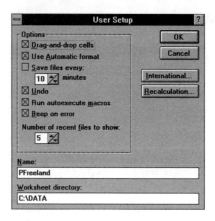

2. Click the check boxes to select and deselect options.

3. Choose OK.

The options in this dialog box are discussed in the next several sections.

Removing Drag-and-Drop Capability

One technique for moving and copying cells is clicking and dragging a cell to another location. This feature, which is enabled by default, is called *drag-and-drop*. Some users find that the way they use the mouse causes them to move cells unintentionally, so they may want to deselect the **D**rag-and-Drop Cells option.

Using Automatic Format

Formatting a number means changing the way it is displayed—for example, changing the number 300 to look like $300.00. When automatic formatting is active, the format of the first number you type in a cell becomes the format for any numbers entered later. If you type **75%** in a cell, for example, 1-2-3 for Windows automatically applies the Percentage format to the cell. Later, if you type **5** in that cell to represent $5.00, 1-2-3 for Windows will display the cell entry as 500%.

Automatic formatting is on by default. If you enter different kinds of numbers into a cell and don't want the new entries to have the format of previous numbers, deselect the Use **A**utomatic Format option to disable the feature. On the other hand, if the first entry you type into a cell includes formatting characteristics such as a dollar sign and two decimal points, and if you want any other number you type into that cell to have the same appearance, be sure that the Use **A**utomatic Format option is selected.

Automatically Saving Files

Ignoring all advice to the contrary, many users persist in not saving their work until they have entered a great deal of data. Naturally, they risk losing all their work if the program terminates unexpectedly.

You can elect to have 1-2-3 for Windows automatically save your work at regular intervals. However, this feature is not on by default. To make the automatic-save feature work, check the **S**ave Files Every box and select an interval in the box below. The default interval is 10 minutes.

When the file is saved, 1-2-3 for Windows saves the updates and new data to disk, using the current file name and the WK4 extension. The earlier version of the file on disk is renamed so that it has the BAK extension with the same file name.

Undoing Errors

Inevitably, a user performs some action and then immediately regrets it. Choosing **E**dit, **U**ndo immediately reverses the mistake.

Undo is available by default. Although **U**ndo is a wonderful feature, its disadvantage is that it occasionally uses large amounts of memory. When available memory is low, the program works slowly, and an Out of Memory error message might appear.

Removing the X from the **U**ndo check box disables this feature, freeing a significant amount of memory—but also eliminating the capability to reverse mistakes.

Preventing the Automatic Running of Auto-Execute Macros

An auto-execute macro—a macro named with a backslash and zero (\0)—executes automatically every time the file that contains the macro is retrieved. Auto-execute macros are used, for example, to call a menu to

Caution
Undo is a useful tool, one that no user should do without. If you need to save memory, consider closing an application that you may be running at the same time as 1-2-3 for Windows rather than turning Undo off.

the screen to get the user started in a particular activity. Macros are covered in Chapter 11.

Auto-execute macros run by default. If an auto-execute macro is not running correctly, or if you want to turn it off for other reasons, remove the x from the Run Autoexecute **M**acros check box. Deselecting this option prevents auto-executing macros from running when the files associated with them are retrieved.

Stopping the Beep

You might not want to be audibly reminded that you made a mistake. If you feel that the noise is superfluous and/or rubbing salt into the wound, remove the x from the **B**eep on Error check box.

Adjusting the Number of Recent Files To Show

At the bottom of the drop-down list that appears when you click **F**ile is a list of as many as five of the files you most recently retrieved in 1-2-3 for Windows, in the current work session and in past sessions. Although you cannot increase the number of file names above five, you can decrease it to zero. To change this option, enter a new number in the Number of Recent **F**iles to Show box.

Changing the Name You Associate with Versions

The name you used when you installed 1-2-3 for Windows, or your network ID, appears in the **N**ame box and is used when you create or update versions and scenarios in the Version Manager. If your network ID appears in the box, the option is grayed and unavailable, so you cannot change it. If the name is the one you used when you installed 1-2-3 for Windows, the option is not grayed, so you can change it. You only see this change, however, when you create versions and scenarios. (For details on Version Manager, see Chapter 13, "Making Use of Advanced Spreadsheet Features.")

Designating a New Worksheet Directory

The **W**orksheet directory text box contains the path for the directory in which 1-2-3 for Windows saves and retrieves files by default. To change this path, type a new drive or directory in the text box. The next time you try to retrieve a file or save a new file, the program will use the new path.

Note: *Changing the worksheet directory will not affect files that have already been saved. They will continue to be saved to the directory to which they were previously saved, unless you choose* **F**ile, Save **A**s *to change the directory.*

Note: *Make sure that you are saving your data files to a different directory from the one in which the 1-2-3 for Windows program files are located. This practice makes backup easier, and you run less risk of overwriting files if you have to reinstall the program.*

Changing International Options

Because different countries use different currency symbols, characters, and punctuation, you can change the default settings for these items. To change these settings, choose **I**nternational in the User Setup dialog box. The International dialog box appears.

The International dialog box enables you to change the appearance of data to conform to the standards of other countries.

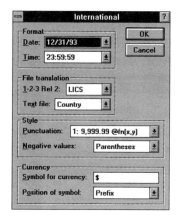

Following are the international settings that you can change:

- Choose **D**ate or **T**ime in the Format box to change the way dates and times are displayed in cells that have a date or time format.

- Change options in the File Translation box to determine the way characters are saved when you save files to Release 2 of 1-2-3 for DOS or text files. (For more information on this topic, choose **H**elp, International Settings.)

- In the Style box, choose **P**unctuation to determine the type of punctuation to be displayed in place of decimal points or as function-argument separators. Choose **N**egative Values to determine whether to display negative numbers with parentheses or minus signs.

■ In the Currency box, choose **S**ymbol for Currency to change the symbol used to denote currency. Choose P**o**sition of Symbol to determine where the symbol is placed: before or after the number.

After making changes in any of these options, choose OK to return to the User Setup dialog box.

Recalculation
The updating of all formulas when data used in those formulas is changed. Recalculation occurs "behind the scenes" so that you can continue working while recalculation occurs.

Recalculating

Normally, a change you make in a cell is immediately reflected in all formulas that refer to that cell. At times, however, you may want to stop the *recalculation* of formulas until you are ready to see the changes. For example, if you have to make several changes in a large worksheet that takes a long time to recalculate, you do not want the worksheet to recalculate after each change. To prevent automatic recalculation of formulas, choose **R**ecalculation in the User Setup dialog box, and when the Recalculation dialog box appears, choose **M**anual.

Use the Recalculation dialog box to change the way 1-2-3 for Windows recalculates formulas or to stop recalculation altogether.

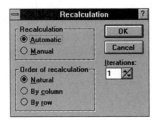

If you save a file with uncalculated formulas, and then retrieve the file later, the formulas remain uncalculated. If formulas have to be recalculated, Calc appears in the status bar. To bring the entire worksheet up to date, press the F9 (Calc) key or click the word Calc.

To find further information about types and order of recalculation, choose **H**elp, Search, and type **recalc** in the Search text box.

Adding, Deleting, and Creating Icons

1-2-3 for Windows offers five sets of SmartIcons. The first set is the group of eight palettes, one of which appears during normal work in a worksheet. The other four sets are individual palettes that represent actions you can perform when you select a chart, a drawn object, a transcript, or a query table.

Caution

When recalculation is set to manual, no formulas are updated after data is changed until you tell 1-2-3 for Windows to do the recalculation. Don't forget to recalculate; if you do forget, formulas could return the wrong answers.

You already know that you can switch among the eight SmartIcon palettes. Each palette contains basic icons, such as those for saving and opening files, copying, moving and pasting, and printing. Each palette also includes icons that are related to a specific task, such as macro building or editing a worksheet.

If you never use some icons in a given palette, you can remove them and replace them with others.

Note: Before you start changing a set of icons, consider saving the set under a different name in case you want to use the original set again. Saving sets is covered later in this chapter.

To remove an icon from a palette:

1. Choose **T**ools, Smart**I**cons. The SmartIcons dialog box appears.

The SmartIcons dialog box.

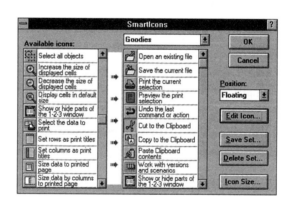

2. Select the palette you want to change.

   The palette that was visible when you chose **T**ools, Smart**I**cons is displayed in the column on the right side of the dialog box. If you want to change a different palette, click the arrow above the list to display the drop-down list of all palettes. If the chart, query, transcript, or drawn-object palette is visible, you have no choice of which palette to change.

3. Click and drag the icon out of the right-hand column. You don't have to drag the icon to any specific location; as long as you drag it out of the column, you have removed it.

4. When you finish, choose OK.

A slight modification of step 3 enables you to add or move SmartIcons. To move a SmartIcon to a new place in the palette, click and drag it on top of another SmartIcon. Other icons move up or down to adjust to the new arrangement.

Note: *You cannot use Undo to reverse actions taken with SmartIcons.*

You can remove the blank areas between some SmartIcons, called *spacers*, by carefully moving an icon into the spacer area.

Note: *The advantage of using spacers is that you can separate SmartIcons into groups. The disadvantage is that you can display more SmartIcons in a palette without spacers.*

Caution

Only 27 SmartIcons are visible in a palette that has no spacers, so be careful about adding too many icons or spacers to a palette; some SmartIcons could disappear off the right side of the screen.

The left-hand column of the dialog box is the complete list of SmartIcons available in 1-2-3 for Windows. To add an icon from this list to a palette, click and drag it from the left to the right column. The left column remains unchanged. You do not remove an icon from the left column when you add it to a palette.

Moving the Entire Palette

SmartIcons don't have to appear at the top of the screen. You can place the palette at the left, right, top, or bottom of the screen; you also can float the palette around the screen.

To relocate the SmartIcon palette:

1. Choose **T**ools, Smart**I**cons. The SmartIcons dialog box appears.

2. Choose an option in the **P**osition drop-down list. The choices are Floating, Top, Left, Bottom, and Right.

   Notice that choosing to display the palette at the left or right side of the screen results in fewer and smaller icons being displayed.

   Choosing Floating puts the palette in the middle of the screen. You can click and drag the entire palette to a new location, and you can resize it by clicking and dragging one side.

A floating
SmartIcon palette.

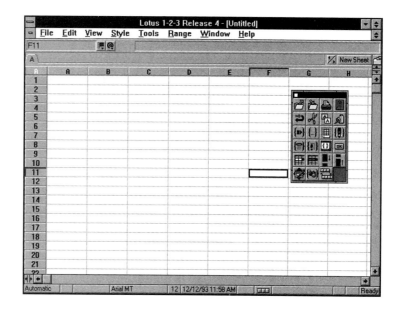

3. When you finish, choose OK.

Note: *If you want a palette with lots of SmartIcons, floating is the best choice, because you can make a floating palette as large as you want.*

When you choose the Floating option, you can remove the palette from the screen by double-clicking the white box in the top left corner of the palette. To bring the palette back into view, click the SmartIcons selector at the bottom of the screen, and then select the palette you want to see.

Redesigning SmartIcons

You can change several features of some SmartIcons. To redesign a SmartIcon:

1. Choose **T**ools, Smart**I**cons. The SmartIcons dialog box appears.

2. Choose **E**dit Icon. The first icon in the left column of available icons appears.

3. If you want to edit another icon, scroll down the list and click the one you want to change.

4. Changing the color of a SmartIcon is like dipping a brush into paint and painting a square. First, click one of the eight color boxes under the icon, or click the down arrow at the end of the colors row to call a second row of eight colors into view.

After you click a color, click inside the icon area. 1-2-3 for Windows applies the new color to the square you clicked. To color more than one square at a time, click and drag across a range of squares.

5. To change the description that is visible when you click a SmartIcon with the right mouse button, enter a new description in the **D**escription text box.

6. To change the function of the SmartIcon, change the macro in the **E**nter Macro Here text box. To associate a macro with the icon, you can:

   ■ Type macro code in the **E**nter Macro Here text box.

   ■ Paste in macro code from the worksheet.

   ■ Paste in macro code from the transcript.

7. When you finish editing the SmartIcon, choose OK.

If you have problems...

If you try to edit some of the SmartIcons, such as Open File or Save File, a message appears, telling you that the icon you chose cannot be edited. You can create a new icon based on the current, uneditable icon by typing a new file name for the icon. You then can "paint" the icon and associate a new macro with it.

Creating a New SmartIcon

Creating a new SmartIcon is very much like editing an existing one. To create a new SmartIcon:

1. Choose **T**ools, SmartIcons. When the SmartIcons dialog box appears, select the palette to which you want to add the new icon.

2. Choose **E**dit Icon. The Edit Icon dialog box appears.

3. Choose **N**ew Icon. The Save as a New Icon dialog box appears.

4. Because each icon is saved to disk as a separate file, you have to name the new icon. Type the new name (up to eight characters, with no spaces) in the Save the New Icon **A**s text box, and then choose OK. The Edit Icon dialog box reappears.

5. Click the colors you want to use, and then click the blank icon to design the new SmartIcon. As you add colors, an actual-size icon appears under Preview to show you how the icon will look.

The Edit Icon dialog box with a blank for a custom-designed SmartIcon.

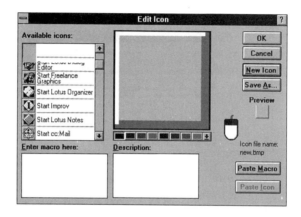

12

6. Associate a macro with the new SmartIcon, using one of the techniques described in the preceding section.

7. Type a brief description of the function of the icon.

8. Choose OK. You return to the SmartIcons dialog box, where the new SmartIcon appears at the bottom of the left column.

9. Click and drag the new icon to the right column to add it to a palette.

10. Choose OK.

The new SmartIcon works like any other SmartIcon. Display the palette and click the icon when you want to run the associated macro.

Creating Custom Palettes

You can not only design your own SmartIcons, but also create custom palettes of icons. To create a custom palette:

1. Choose **T**ools, Smart**I**cons. The SmartIcons dialog box appears.

2. Select a palette.

3. Remove icons from the right column and add new ones from the left column, as desired.

4. Choose **S**ave Set. The Save Set of SmartIcons dialog box appears.

5. In the **N**ame of Set text box, enter a name. (The name should describe the purpose of the palette or of most of the SmartIcons it contains.)

The Save Set of SmartIcons dialog box. Notice that the Directory area shows where the file is saved.

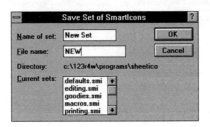

6. Enter a name (up to eight characters, with no spaces) in the **F**ile Name text box.

7. Choose OK.

When you return to the worksheet and click the SmartIcons selector, your new palette is included with the existing palette.

If you want to remove a palette that you never use, choose **T**ools, Smart**I**cons; highlight the palette you want to delete; choose **D**elete Set; then choose OK.

Note: *The SmartIcons and palettes are saved in the 123R4W\PROGRAMS\ directory in one of the subdirectories ending with ICO. You can copy the SmartIcons and the palettes to other computers so that other people can use your creations.*

The last item in the SmartIcons dialog box, **I**con Size, enables you to change the SmartIcons' default size (medium) to large. Fewer SmartIcons are visible when you choose the large option, but they are easier to see. This item changes the size of icons in all palettes.

The printing
SmartIcon palette,
displaying large
icons.

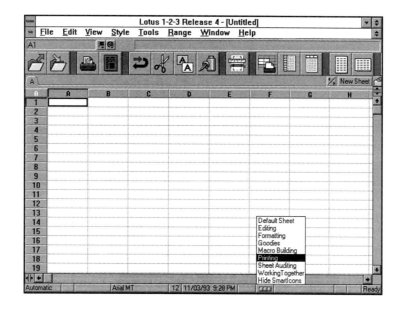

12

Customizing Fill by Example

Chapter 3, "Building a Worksheet," covered the Fill by **E**xample command. If you type **January** in a cell, highlight that cell and others, and
choose **R**ange, Fill by **E**xample, 1-2-3 for Windows fills the rest of the
cells with the names of other months.

You can create unique lists available for Fill by **E**xample, such as corpo-
rate offices, departments, part numbers, products, or employees. You can
include as many as 100 items in a list, and you can create as many as 100
separate sets.

To create your own list:

1. Open the Windows Notepad.

2. Choose **F**ile, **O**pen, and designate the file
   C:\123R4W\PROGRAMS\FILLS.INI, which contains the lists for Fill
   by **E**xample.

3. Type **[SET #]**, substituting for # the number for the next available set, because each set name must be unique. The correct format is [SET 1].

4. Under the set, type **ITEM#=XXX**, replacing # with the number of the item in the series and replacing *XXX* with the item. The first is ITEM1, ITEM2, and so on. (Use uppercase to type the word **ITEM**.)

5. Repeat step 4 for each item.

6. Choose **F**ile, **S**ave, and return to 1-2-3 for Windows.

Note: *All items that you type in the FILLS.INI file are treated as labels.*

FILLS.INI with the
first fill set modified.

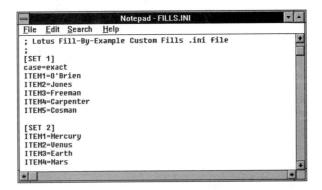

Notice that case=exact appears in the list. This statement causes 1-2-3 for Windows to match the case of the items as you typed them in the list. If that statement is not included, Fill by **E**xample matches the case of the first item you type. If you typed the first item in lowercase letters, the other items also would be lowercase.

The new list, entered with **R**ange, Fill by **E**xample.

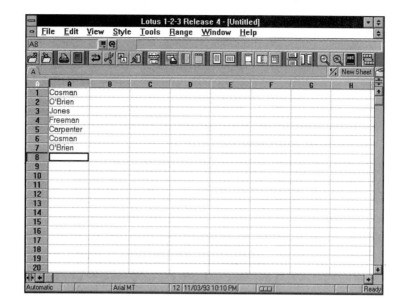

You can type any item from the list in the first cell. Fill by **E**xample finishes the list and then continues with the first item, going on through the list until all highlighted cells are filled. In the preceding figure, the last name in the list is typed to show the effect.

You also can use two items in the list to set an interval. For example, if you want to place every other month in the range, type **January** in the first cell and **March** in the second; then perform Fill by **E**xample.

Creating an Icon To Launch 1-2-3 for Windows and Open a File

There may be one file or several files that you frequently use when you run 1-2-3 for Windows Release 4. You can create an icon for each of these files so that clicking the icon not only starts the program but also retrieves the file you want to use.

Assume that you save your worksheets to the WORK subdirectory of the 123R4W directory on your C drive. If the name of a file that you frequently use is BUDGET.WK4, the command line you use when you create a new icon in Windows is a combination of the command to start the program and the path and name of the worksheet file.

To create a new program icon that starts 1-2-3 for Windows and opens a file:

1. In Program Manager, choose **F**ile, **N**ew to create a program item.

2. Choose Program **I**tem in the New Program Object dialog box and choose OK. The Program Item Properties dialog box appears.

The Program Item
Properties dialog
box.

3. In the **T**itle text box, type a short name that reminds you of the function of the icon.

4. For **C**ommand Line, type something like the following:

   C:\123R4W\PROGRAMS\123W.EXE -w
   C:\123R4W\WORK\BUDGET.WK4

   Use your own directory and file name rather than C:\123R4W\WORK\BUDGET.WK4 in the command line.

5. You can change the icon used to represent the worksheet and make several other changes. For detailed directions, see Que's *Using Windows 3.1, Special Edition* or your Windows documentation.

6. Choose OK.

To start 1-2-3 for Windows and retrieve the named file, double-click the icon.

Summary

To	Do This
Enable or disable **U**ndo	Choose **T**ools, **U**ser Setup; choose **U**ndo
To save files automatically at intervals	Choose **T**ools, **U**ser Setup; choose **S**ave Files Every, and then specify a time interval
Delete a SmartIcon from a palette	Choose **T**ools, **S**martIcons; drag the icon out of the palette
Create a new SmartIcon	Choose **T**ools, **S**martIcons; **E**dit Icon; **N**ew Icon
Customize a Fill by **E**xample list	Edit FILLS.INI, using Windows Notepad; type list name and items
Create a program icon that starts 1-2-3 for Windows and opens a file	In Program Manager, choose **F**ile, **N**ew; in Command Line, type path and name of file

12

On Your Own
Estimated time: 10 minutes

1. Turn on the automatic save feature, and set the save interval to 15 minutes.

2. Change the default directory to a new directory you created.

3. Delete a SmartIcon from the printing palette.

4. Add the same SmartIcon to the printing palette.

5. Create a new SmartIcon that enters your full name in a cell, and then add the icon to the default SmartIcon palette.

6. Display large SmartIcons.

7. Create a new Fill by **E**xample sequence of names of co-workers or neighbors. Use this sequence to fill a range of cells.

8. Create a new icon in Program Manager that starts 1-2-3 for Windows and opens a worksheet file.

Chapter 13

Making Use of Advanced Spreadsheet Features

The features discussed in this chapter are called advanced not because you need a graduate degree to understand them, but because they advance your use of 1-2-3 for Windows to a higher, more sophisticated level.

This chapter coveres the following topics:

- Creating text boxes
- Using the Version Manager
- Ensuring worksheet security
- Using the Audit feature

Creating Text Boxes

A text box is a box that contains text. The box is not part of a cell or a range, but a drawn object that you can move around the worksheet the way you move charts or other drawn objects.

To create a text box:

1. Choose **T**ools, **D**raw, **T**ext.

2. Select the range where you want the text box to appear.

3. An insertion point appears inside the box. Type the text you want.

4. If you want, choose **S**tyle and then **L**ines & Color, **F**ont & Attributes, or **A**lignment to change the appearance of the box and the text it contains.

A text box added to a worksheet.

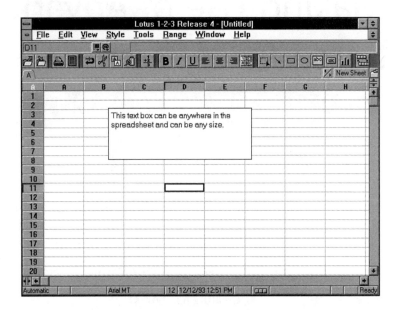

If you have problems...   If the text disappears as you type it because the box is too small, don't worry. Keep typing. When you finish, select the box and resize it until all text is visible.

You return focus to the worksheet by clicking outside the text box. Click once in the box to select it so that you can move it, resize it, or change its attributes. Double-click inside the box to place the insertion point in the box so you can add or delete text. You can change style characteristics whether you single-click or double-click in the box.

Note: *You can apply only one font, attribute, size, or color to the text in the text box. You cannot select different sections of text and apply different attributes to each section.*

Using Version Manager

This powerful, useful new feature enables you to place several cell entries in one cell. Only one cell entry is visible at a time, but answers to formulas that use that cell change as the different values in that cell are displayed.

To understand this feature, you will have to do a bit of imagining. In a range in your worksheet is a table like the one shown in the next figure, which lists expenditures for several items in all four quarters of the current year. Suppose that you are thinking about changing some of those values to see the effects on the totals, but you don't want the original values to be deleted.

The basic worksheet into which you will place versions.

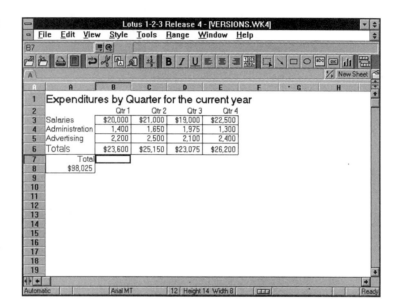

In this kind of situation, you would use the Version Manager, which enables you to place several different entries in the same cell, see those entries one at a time, and judge their effect on formulas. You can create several versions of the worksheet on your own. Alternatively, by saving the worksheet to a network either as a WK4 file or as a database file in Lotus Notes, you can allow co-workers to create and update versions.

Creating Versions

You place *versions* in named ranges. The worksheet in the preceding figure has three named ranges with versions: Salaries, Administration, and Advertising. The specific ranges are the four cells in columns B through E, one for each of the expenditure categories. There are three versions in each range: Minimum, Maximum, and Realistic, which contain three different values in each cell in the ranges (the highest possible amount, the lowest possible amount, and the most realistic figure). These figures represent a guess about how market conditions will affect the company.

Version
One of several entries in a cell. Multiple cell entries are permitted in Version Manager; each entry is a version.

To create a *version* in a range:

1. Name the range or ranges into which you want to place versions, using **R**ange, **N**ame as described in Chapter 9, "Working with Multiple Worksheets and Multiple Documents."

2. Choose **R**ange, **V**ersion. The Version Manager dialog box appears.

3. In the Named **R**ange text box, enter the name of the range in which you want to create a version.

4. Choose **C**reate. The Create Version dialog box appears.

The Version Manager dialog box and the Version Create dialog box.

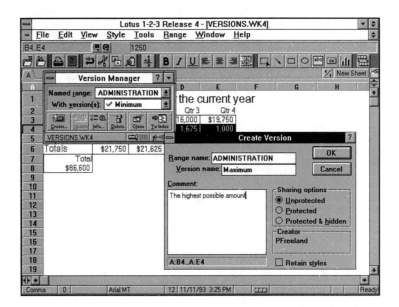

5. Type a more descriptive name for the version, if you like, and add an optional comment for the version.

6. Make changes in any of the sharing options, as desired. These options are **P**rotected, **U**nprotected, and Protected & **H**idden. **P**rotected means that the version will not accept any changes; **H**idden means that the version name and its data will not be visible. More details about the **P**rotected and **H**idden options appear near the end of this section.

7. Choose Retain St**y**les if you want to save cell and text enhancements along with the data in the version.

8. Choose OK.

A single version now exists. Because the whole point of Version Manager is to have several versions in the same range, you will need to create at least one more version. To see a version you have created:

1. Choose **R**ange, **V**ersion. The Version Manager dialog box appears.

2. In the Named **R**ange box, select the range that contains the version you want to see or use.

3. In the With **V**ersion(s) box, select the version you want. The data associated with the version appears in the range.

The same work-
sheet with the
Minimum version in
each range visible.

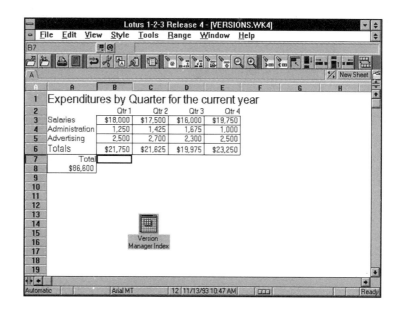

If you have problems...   The Version Manager window remains on-screen even while you are working in the worksheet. If this window is in the way, move it or minimize it. If you have trouble double-clicking the minimized icon to restore the Version Manager, choose **R**ange, **V**ersion again.

When a version is visible, you can enter data in the cells in that range that will become the unique values for that version.

To enter data in a version:

1. In the Version Manager dialog box, choose the version you want to update.

2. Select the cell in the worksheet that you want to update first.

3. Enter the data in all cells that you want to update.

When you enter or change data in a version, notice that the version name becomes italicized, a crossed checkmark appears next to the version name, and the **U**pdate icon in the Version Manager window becomes active.

All these changes occur to remind you that if you don't choose **U**pdate, your changes will be lost when you switch to another version or close the file. If you want your changes to be permanent, always choose **U**pdate after changing data in a version.

You can create as many versions for each range as you like, and you can view any combination of versions.

In addition to creating new versions, the Version Manager dialog box contains the following items:

- *Info*, which enables you to see the range address, the range name, the sharing status, the comment, the name of the creator, and the date of creation or update. You can change the range name by typing a new name in the text box. Sharing options include **U**nprotected, **P**rotected, and Protected & **H**idden. When a version is protected, you cannot make permanent changes to it. You can enter changes into cells in the version, but you cannot **U**pdate it. When you exit that version, you lose your changes. Choosing **H**idden prevents anyone from seeing the data in the hidden version. The comment is text that helps explain the purpose or contents of the version. If you click the Retain S**t**yles box, you save not only data, but also any unique style enhancements that you added to the version.

- *Delete*, which deletes the version from the range.

- *Close*, which dismisses the Version Manager dialog box from the screen.

- *To* Index, which calls to the screen the Version Manager Index, described in the following section.

Using the Version Manager Index

Choosing **T**o Index calls to the screen a more elaborate dialog box: the Version Manager Index, which contains more commands and options.

You will find using the Index preferable to using the Version Manager dialog box because of the larger number of tasks possible. The Index is a bit bigger than the Version Manager dialog box, so more of your worksheet will be covered.

The Version Manager Index.

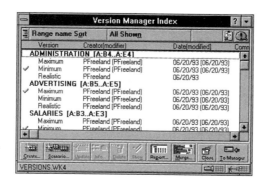

To sort versions and scenarios (described in the next section) by range name, version name, scenario name, date of update, or person who did the updates, choose Range Name So**r**t and choose the means by which versions or scenarios are to be sorted. However you sort the names, you can view a version or scenario by double-clicking its name or by high-lighting it and choosing Sho**w**.

To remove a scenario or version that is no longer useful, highlight the name and choose **D**elete. In the dialog box that appears, confirm your decision to delete the item.

Choosing Re**p**ort enables you to create a separate file that lists the contents of each selected version and the effect of the data in each on formulas.

To create a report based on versions:

To create a report:

1. In the Version Manager Index, choose Re**p**ort. The Version Report dialog box appears.

The Version Report dialog box.

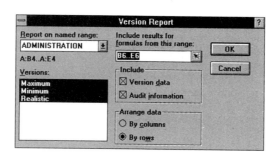

2. Select the named range and the versions to be included in the report.

3. To see the effect of each range on the formulas, enter the range of formulas in the Include Results for **F**ormulas from This Range text box.

4. To eliminate the name and date of creation of the versions, deselect Audit **I**nformation.

5. Select By **C**olumns or By Ro**w**s, depending on how the data is entered in the table.

6. Choose OK. A separate file is created and given the name REPORT01.WK4. If you created other reports earlier, 1-2-3 for Windows gives the new report the next available number.

The report created by the Version Manager.

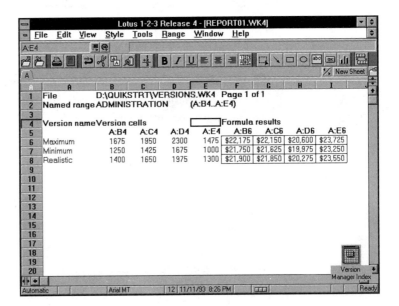

The **M**erge button in the Version Manager Index enables you to combine the versions from another file into the current file. You must have the same range names in the current file before performing the merge.

To merge versions from another file into the current file:

1. Choose **M**erge in the Version Manager Index. The From File dialog box appears.

2. Select the file name.

3. To restrict the versions merged, you can enter a date in the Modified on or after **D**ate text box or choose a name in the **L**ast Modified By list box.

4. Choose OK. A screen appears, displaying the merge results, including the ranges, versions, or scenarios not merged and the reason why they were not merged.

At the bottom of the Version Manager Index are two icons. The flashlight icon determines whether the versioned range will be displayed with an outline. The radar icon to its right causes the cell pointer to be placed in the versioned range when you select the range's name in the Index.

Creating Scenarios

Scenario

A grouping of versions, one for each range. Selecting a scenario causes the versions included in that scenario to be visible in each range. You do not need to select a version in every range.

Rather than select versions in ranges one at a time, you can group versions into named *scenarios*. An example is a scenario in which you want to concentrate on advertising at the expense of other categories, so you would group the Minimum version of Administration and Salaries with the Maximum version of Advertising. The scenario could be called Emphasis on Advertising.

Note: *Version Manager is not case-sensitive for range names, but it* is *case-sensitive for version and scenario names.*

To create a scenario:

1. Switch to the Version Manager Index and choose **S**cenario. The Create Scenario dialog box appears.

The Create Scenario dialog box.

13

2. Highlight a version name in the **A**vailable Versions list box, and then click the <<>> button to add it to the scenario. You also can double-click the version name to include it in the scenario.

3. Repeat step 2 for each version you want to include in the scenario, one version per named range.

4. As you can with versions, you can choose **P**rotected, **U**nprotected, or Protected & **H**idden, and you can add a comment.

5. Choose OK. 1-2-3 for Windows creates the new scenario.

Ensuring Worksheet Security

You can take several steps to prevent unwanted viewing or editing of your work. You can put an invisible protective shield on the worksheet or selected cells, or you can save the entire file in such a way that unauthorized people cannot even retrieve it.

Protecting Cells

Two menu items relate to sealing all cells in a worksheet from data editing, deletion, or addition.

To seal all cells:

1. Choose **F**ile, **Pr**otect. The Protect dialog box appears.

2. Select **S**eal File, and then choose OK.

Caution

Don't forget the password you use to seal the file. If you do forget, you can never remove the seal.

3. A dialog box appears, in which you type a password. Type the same text in the **P**assword text box and the **V**erify text box. (The password is case-sensitive, so be sure to type exactly the same entry in both text boxes.)

4. Choose OK.

In the status bar at the bottom of the window, you see the message Pr as you navigate from cell to cell, indicating that the cells are protected.

When a file is protected, you cannot do the following things:

- Enter, delete, or edit text in cells.

- Change the protection status.

- Use the **S**tyle, **D**raw, **C**hart, or **N**ew Query command.

- Name or rename worksheet tabs.

Regardless of the cell, if you try any of the tasks in the preceding list, a message appears, reminding you that the file is sealed. If you plan to work in some ranges or cells, you need to unprotect those cells.

To unprotect a cell, range, or collection:

1. Unseal the file by choosing **F**ile, **Pr**otect and then deselecting **S**eal File in the Protect dialog box.

2. Choose OK. 1-2-3 for Windows prompts you for the password. Type it, remembering that the **P**assword text box is case-sensitive.

3. Select the cell, range, or collection you want to keep unsealed.

4. Choose **S**tyle, **P**rotection. The Protection dialog box appears.

5. Choose **K**eep Data Unprotected after File is Sealed, and then choose OK. Data in the selected range appears in blue.

6. Choose **F**ile, **P**rotect, and then choose **S**eal File to reseal the file.

7. Choose OK.

Preventing a File from Being Retrieved

The simplest way to keep a file from being retrieved by those who shouldn't see it is to save it to a floppy disk that you keep with you or to a directory other than the default directory.

A better way is to save the file with a password. Only those who know the password will be able to retrieve the file.

To save a file with a password:

1. Choose **F**ile, **S**ave or File, Save **A**s (if the worksheet has already been saved without a password).

2. Choose **W**ith Password in the Save **A**s dialog box.

3. Type the password in the **P**assword and **V**erify text boxes. (The password feature is case-sensitive.)

4. Choose OK.

The next time you attempt to retrieve the file, 1-2-3 for Windows prompts you for the password. If you don't type it exactly, including the proper case, you will be told that the password is incorrect, and you will not be able to retrieve the file.

Using the Audit Feature

Complex worksheets or those created by other people can be hard to figure out. Audit helps you locate formulas and find out which cells are included in a formula. It also locates formulas that use the contents of a given cell.

Note: *You can use a special SmartIcon palette for auditing a worksheet. Using the menu gives you more control of the way the audit report is made, however.*

You can use Audit, first of all, to find all the formulas in a file. To use the menu to find formulas:

1. Choose **T**ools, **A**udit. The Audit dialog box appears.

2. Make sure that **A**ll Formulas is selected.

3. If more than one file is open, you also can decide whether to find formulas in the C**u**rrent File or in All F**i**les.

4. You also can decide how the report will be presented.

   Choosing **S**election causes all cells containing formulas to be high-lighted. You can press Ctrl+ Enter to move to the next highlighted formula or Shift+Ctrl+Enter to move to the preceding highlighted formula.

   If you choose **R**eport at Range, you can designate an empty range where the list of cells with formulas will be placed.

5. Choose OK to complete the process.

The worksheet with an audit report.

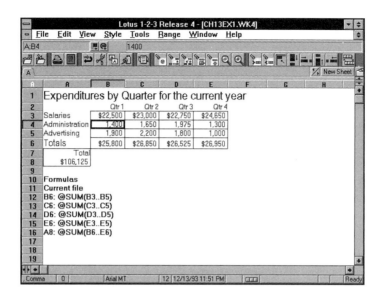

Precedents

Cells whose contents are used in a formula.

To find the *precedents* for a formula:

1. Select the cell or range that contains the formula(s).

2. Choose **T**ools, **A**udit, and then choose Formula **P**recedents in the Audit dialog box.

3. If you used the menu, you can determine whether the precedent cells will be highlighted (choose **S**election) or whether the list will be placed in a range (choose **R**eport at Range).

4. Choose OK.

The result of **T**ools, **A**udit, Formula **P**recedents.

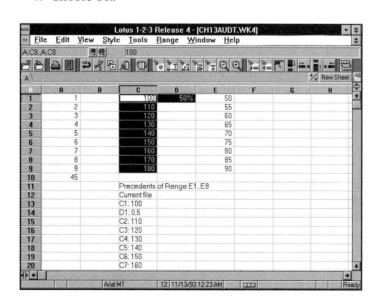

The preceding figure shows the result of choosing **S**election and choosing Report at **R**ange. When you choose **S**election, the cells are highlighted. When you choose **R**eport at Range, the list of formula precedents appears, listing the cell and its contents for each formula cell.

Dependents
Cells containing data is used by a formula. A cell has many dependents if many formulas use its data.

Another use for the Audit feature is finding formulas that process data in selected cells. To find cell *dependents*:

1. Select the cell or range containing data for which you want to find dependents.

2. Choose **T**ools, **A**udit. The Audit dialog box appears.

3. Choose Cell **D**ependents.

4. Choose **S**election or **R**eport at Range.

5. Choose OK. The cells that are highlighted are those containing formulas that depend on the values in the cells you highlighted in step 1.

Summary

To	Do This
Create a text box	Choose **T**ools, **D**raw, **T**ext; then type the text
Create a version	Choose **R**ange, **V**ersion in a named range
See a different version	Maximize the Version Manager; then select the version
Group versions in a scenario	Switch to Version Manager Index; choose **S**cenario
Protect a file from editing	Choose **F**ile, **P**rotect; **S**eal File
Save a file with a password	Choose **F**ile, **S**ave or **F**ile, Save **A**s; choose **W**ith Password
See the precedents of a formula	Choose **T**ools, **A**udit, Formula **P**recedents
See the dependents of a data cell	Choose **T**ools, **A**udit, Cell **D**ependents

On Your Own

Estimated time: 45 minutes

1. Create a text box; then enter some text.

2. Color the text in the box, and change its font to a smaller size.

3. Move the text box to a different location.

4. Create three versions in a named range, naming the versions Minimum, Maximum, and Realistic.

5. Enter different values in each version.

6. Combine the Minimum versions in a scenario called Minimum.

7. Seal the entire file except for the versioned ranges.

8. Save the file with a password.

13

Chapter 14

Advanced Analysis Tools

The subject of this chapter is the use of 1-2-3 for Windows to help you make decisions. The techniques described here are useful when a problem has too many variables or too many possible solutions for you to enter all of them into a worksheet.

This chapter covers the following topics:

- Creating a what-if table
- Using the Solver

Creating What-If Tables

What-if table
A worksheet range containing all possible answers for a formula. The answers in the what-if table change as the formula's input values change.

A *what-if table* is the simplest way to show the results of many permutations of a formula. For example, you could use a what-if table to calculate the monthly payment on a mortgage, entering several different input values, such as principal amounts and interest rates.

There are three types of what-if tables: one-, two-, and three-way tables. Regardless of the type of what-if table you use, you must supply some required information in specific cells.

Creating a One-Way Table

Variable
A formula component that can have several different values.

A one-way table uses only one *variable*, such as various interest rates with one principal amount for a loan. The following figure shows the monthly payments for a principal amount of $100,000.

A one-way table.

Input cell

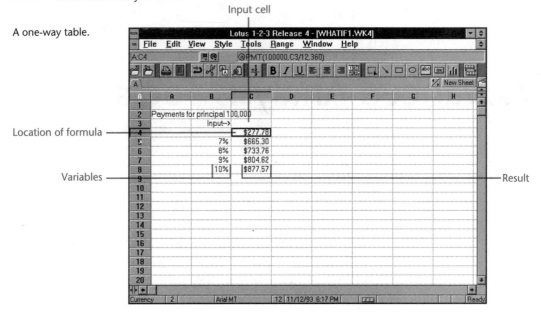

Location of formula

Variables

Result

To create a one-way table:

Input values
The different
amounts used in a
formula. In a mort-
gage table, inputs
could be interest
rates.

1. Enter the *input values* in a column, leaving at least the top two cells
   in the column empty. In the preceding figure, the inputs are the
   interest rates.

2. Enter the formula for the table above the top cell of the column in
   which the answers will appear. The formula must refer to the one
   input cell that you designate in step 6. In the preceding figure, the
   formula is in cell C4.

3. Choose **R**ange, **A**nalyze, **W**hat-if Table. The What-if Table dialog
   box appears.

The dialog box used
for creating what-if
tables.

4. Choose 1 in the **N**umber of Variables list box.

5. In the **T**able Range text box, designate a range that includes the formula, the column of input values, and the column where the answers will appear.

6. In the Input Cell **1** text box, enter the address of the empty cell you used in the formula.

7. Choose OK. The values fill the empty cells in the right-hand column of the table.

Note: *You can create several one-way tables side by side with a formula at the top of each column where the answers will appear. Designate the input column and all empty columns as the table range.*

Creating a Two-Way Table

A two-way table uses two sets of changing variables. In the following figure, the variables are interest and principal amounts.

A two-way table.

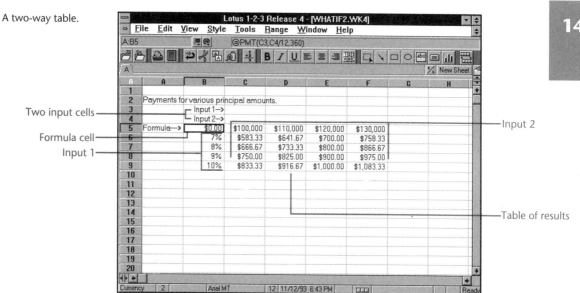

Two input cells

Formula cell

Input 1

Input 2

Table of results

14

To create a two-way table:

1. Enter one set of inputs in the left-hand column of the table area.

2. Enter the other set of inputs across the top row of the table area.

3. Enter the formula in the top left corner of the table area. The formula must refer to the input cells.

4. Choose **R**ange, **A**nalyze, **W**hat-if Table. The What-if Table dialog box appears.

5. Choose 2 in the **N**umber of Variables list box.

6. In the **T**able Range text box, designate a range that includes the formula, the column and row of input values, and the range where the answers will appear.

7. In the Input Cell **1** and **2** text boxes, enter the addresses of the two empty cells to which the formula refers.

8. Choose OK. The results appear in the empty cells of the table.

Creating a Three-Way Table

A three-way table uses three variables. In the loan example, those variables could be principal, interest rate, and term. The third value in this example is the term.

To create a three-way table:

1. Create a two-way table, as described in the preceding section.

2. Place the third variable in the top left corner cell of the table.

3. Write the formula anywhere outside the table range. Make sure that the formula refers to the three input cells you will designate in step 10.

4. Copy the table to the following worksheets, using one worksheet for each value in the third input.

   Note: *The first set of inputs is in a column; the second set is in a row. Enter variables for the third input across several worksheets.*

5. In the top left corner of the other worksheets, place the other values for the third input, one value for each worksheet.

6. Choose **R**ange, **A**nalyze, **W**hat-if Table. The What-if Table dialog box appears.

7. Choose 3 in the **N**umber of Variables list box.

8. In the **T**able Range text box, designate a range that includes the corner cell, the column and row of input values, and the range in the first worksheet where the answers will appear; then extend this range to the other worksheets.

9. In the Input Cell **1, 2,** and **3** text boxes, enter the addresses of three empty cells.

10. In the **F**ormula Cell text box, enter the cell where you placed the formula. Make sure that the formula refers to the three input cells.

11. Choose OK. The resulting values fill the empty cells in all worksheets.

Using Solver

Imagine that you are responsible for maximizing profits by adjusting production volume for the various items a company manufactures and the prices of those items. There is a huge number of permutations and combinations of all the possible values. Throw into the mix minimum production levels, resource allocation, or the need to ensure prices that are above a certain level relative to costs, and you have a bewildering problem, even if you use a what-if table.

Solver is the tool to use when the number of variables becomes too large for a simple worksheet. Create a worksheet that shows the relationship of data, but enter estimates for such variables as production levels and prices. Tell 1-2-3 for Windows the rules for calculating the best possible combination of answers to the variables, and then let the program do the thinking.

Defining a Problem for Solver

The example in this section involves a small company that manufactures two kinds of picture frames: simple and fancy. The following figure shows the company's production statistics.

14

The data that Solver will use to propose answers.

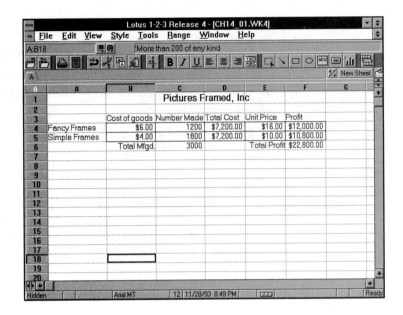

The numbers entered in columns C and E are estimates; Solver will not use those figures when it proposes answers to the questions. Total Cost is the cost of goods times the number of frames produced. Profits is unit price times the number produced minus the total cost.

The specific decisions you want Solver to make are how many frames of each kind the company should make and how much the frames should cost. Naturally, you want to keep an eye on profits—the higher, the better.

Defining Solver Terms

To understand Solver, you need to understand some definitions. Most of a worksheet is simply data. But certain cells will contain information that Solver may change (and fill with varying amounts) in its attempts to find a solution; another cell may be where you want Solver to put a maximum or minimum value; and a third group of cells will tell Solver the rules to follow in generating answers. These three types of cells are called *problem cells*.

The three types of problem cells are:

■ *Adjustable cells* are the cells that Solver may change to show possible answers. These cells must contain values, not text or formulas. Do not protect the cells; Solver will want to change them.

- An *optimal cell* is one in the worksheet for which you want Solver to find the maximum or minimum value. You don't have to designate an optimal cell, but if you do, make sure that it is a single cell based on adjustable cells. When Solver proposes answers, it does so in random order unless you designated an optimal cell, in which case the first answer is the one that will produce the desired optimal result. The optimal cell must contain a formula that relies on data in the adjustable cells.

- *Constraint cells* tell Solver the rules to follow in calculating the possible answers. The number of constraint cells you use will be determined by the complexity of your worksheet and will be limited by the amount of memory your computer has. The more constraint cells you have, the longer the calculating of the proposed answers will take. The constraint cells must contain logical formulas—ones that represent statements that are true or false. True is represented by 1; false, by 0. The formulas can use the following symbols: =, <, >, <=, or >=. They cannot contain such operators as #AND#, #OR#, #NOT#, or <>.

14

Solver can generate the following types of solutions, depending on circumstances:

- *Optimal answer:* the solution that most closely yields the optimal value in the optimal cell, if you designated one.

- *Best answer:* a solution that Solver cannot verify is an optimal answer. In complicated problems, Solver may not be able to determine whether a solution is truly optimal, so it labels the answer "best" if the optimal cell has the highest or lowest value of all proposed solutions.

- *Answers:* proposed solutions that do not necessarily produce optimal results but that satisfy all constraints.

- *Attempts:* proposed solutions that do not satisfy all constraints. Cells containing constraint formulas that are not satisfied will display zeros.

Caution
Although many
functions are
supported, adding
or multiplying
them; using nested
@HLOOKUP,
@VLOOKUP, or
@IF formulas; and
using large ranges
in those formulas
make a problem
difficult to solve.
Whenever possible,
stick with simple
functions such as
@SUM and @AVG;
convert formulas
to values when
you have many
formulas (use **E**dit,
Paste **S**pecial); and
keep relationships
among formulas
to a minimum.

Setting up the Problem

In creating the worksheet that will supply the information for Solver, be aware that not all cells need to be problem cells. Also be aware that Solver does not support certain functions.

Note: *To see the list of functions supported by Solver, choose **Help** and search for* Functions in Solver Problems.

To use Solver to generate answers:

1. Create a worksheet that includes all data you want Solver to process. Make sure that the adjustable cells where Solver will place solutions contain only values.

2. In a range separate from the worksheet data, enter logical formulas for the constraints.

   The formulas you enter will return 0 or 1 (if you entered them correctly). In the following figure, the formula cells were formatted as text, so you could see the formula rather than the answer.

   Note: *The best way to enter constraints is to write them in cells near the cells where you will place the formulas, and then write the formulas. This practice ensures that you will remember all constraints and what each formula does.*

Constraints added
to the basic
worksheet.

These are the
constraints

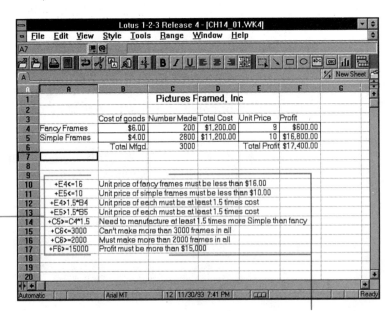

These are descriptions of the constraints

The preceding figure has eight constraints entered in cells A10 through A17. The Text format was applied to those cells so you can see the formulas. (Had the format been Automatic, each cell would contain 1 or 0, depending on whether the data in the worksheet met the criteria.) A description of each constraint appears in the cell next to the formula.

Note: *You probably will need to add constraints after you generate the first set of solutions. Situations that you did not anticipate will become obvious when you see the results, and you will have to run Solver again.*

3. Choose **R**ange, **A**nalyze, **S**olver. The Solver Definition dialog box appears.

4. Designate the **A**djustable Cells and the **C**onstraint Cells. If all the cells of one type are not adjacent, enter all the ranges in which those cells appear, using commas to separate the ranges.

Note: *The constraint cells are only the formula cells, not the comments to the right.*

The Solver Definition dialog box, with the ranges for the problem entered in the text boxes.

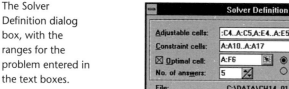

5. If you want Solver to generate a solution that gives a minimum or maximum answer, designate an **O**ptimal Cell. The optimal cell can be an adjustable cell.

6. If you designate an **O**ptimal Cell, choose Ma**x** or Mi**n**, depending on whether you want Solver to generate solutions that give the largest or smallest possible value in that cell.

7. To force Solver to generate more answers than one (the default), increase the number in the No. of Ans**w**ers box.

8. Choose **S**olve. The Solver Progress dialog box appears, showing Solver's progress and telling you which answer Solver is working on.

This box appears while Solver is calculating answers.

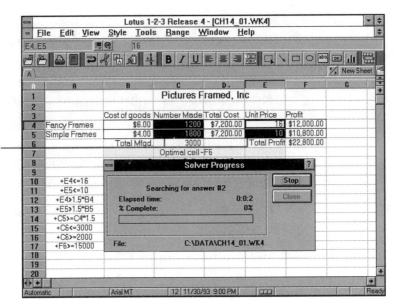

The adjustable cells are highlighted to show where Solver placed its solutions

---

If you have problems...

If you have many constraints and a large worksheet, and require many answers, you may have a bit of a wait for Solver to find all the answers. Choose Stop if you get impatient; Solver will retain all answers that it found up to that point.

When Solver finishes, the Solver Answer dialog box appears. Notice that we reformatted the formula cells in column A to show the effect of Solver's results on the constraint formulas.

The Solver Answers
dialog box.

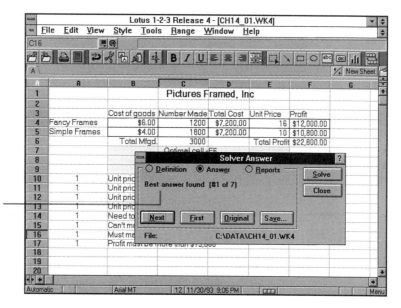

Dialog box shows
that the current
data in the
worksheet is the
best answer

In this dialog box, you can choose the next step. Choose **N**ext to see the next answer in order, **F**irst to see the first optimal or best answer, or **O**riginal to see the data you entered in the adjustable cells. As you cycle through the answers, the values that Solver generated appear in the adjustable cells. (You may need to move the dialog box so that you can see the adjustable cells.) If you choose Sa**v**e, you create a scenario that contains the data for the current solution. For more information on scenarios, refer to Chapter 13, "Making Use of Advanced Spreadsheet Features."

Choosing **S**olve in the dialog box causes Solver to generate more answers—if possible, as many answers as you designated in the No. of Ans**w**ers box in the Solver Definition dialog box.

Across the top of the Solver Answer dialog box are three additional options. A new dialog box is associated with each option. **D**efinition enables you to return to the Solver Definition dialog box to make changes and then generate new answers. **R**eports creates any one of seven reports about the answers Solver generated. Solver reports are covered in "Generating Reports" later in this chapter.

14

If you have problems...

Some answers may appear with the message `Roundoff error`. This message appears when Solver and the worksheet use different calculation methods and the answer that Solver generated does not satisfy some constraints. This problem usually occurs with very large or very small numbers and generally does not affect the validity of the answer.

If you have problems...

You may see the error message `Cannot find an optimal answer--The optimal cell is unbounded.` This message means that you did not supply sufficient constraints to the optimal cell.

Using the constraints shown in an earlier figure, Solver generated useful answers, several of which suggest that the company create a negative number of one type of frames or a decimal part of a frame. Clearly, those solutions are not possible. To force Solver to create more useful answers, you may decide to add more constraints.

Two added constraints force Solver to generate more sensible answers.

A table showing the three groups of problem cells

	A	B	C	D	E	F	G
1			Pictures Framed, Inc				
2							
3		Cost of goods	Number Made	Total Cost	Unit Price	Profit	
4	Fancy Frames	$6.00	1200	$7,200.00	16	$12,000.00	
5	Simple Frames	$4.00	1800	$7,200.00	10	$10,800.00	
6		Total Mfgd.	3000		Total Profit	$22,800.00	
7			Optimal cell -F6				
8			Constraint Cells -A10..A19				
9			Adjustable Cells -C4..C5,E4..E5				
10	1	Unit price of fancy frames must be less than $16.00					
11	1	Unit price of simple frames must be less than $10.00					
12	1	Unit price of each must be at least 1.5 times cost					
13	1	Unit price of each must be at least 1.5 times cost					
14	1	Need to manufacture at least 1.5 times more Simple than fancy					
15	1	Can't make more than 3000 frames in all					
16	1	Must make more than 2000 frames in all					
17	1	Profit must be more than $15,000					
18	1	Must make more than 200 of any kind					
19	1	Must make more than 200 of any kind					
20							

In the preceding figure, two constraints were added in A18 and A19 to force Solver to create solutions that involve at least 200 of either kind of frame.

Some of the new solutions will be useful; others will contain data that you are not interested in keeping. If one answer satisfies you and you want to make it a permanent part of the worksheet:

1. Use Solver to generate answers.

2. Cycle through the answers until the answer you want is in the adjustable cells.

3. Save the worksheet, using **F**ile, **S**ave.

If you want to keep several of the answers created by Solver:

1. Use Solver to generate answers.

2. Cycle through the answers.

3. When an answer that you want to save appears, choose Sa**v**e in the Solver Answer dialog box. The Save as Scenario dialog box appears.

4. Type a name in the **S**cenario name box.

5. Choose Sa**v**e.

> **Note:** *The ranges containing the adjustable cells where the scenarios are created are automatically named ADJ0, ADJ1, ADJ2, and so on.*

Caution

This procedure does not save the file— only the solution in a scenario. Make sure that you save the file itself; otherwise, you will lose scenarios and solutions when you close the worksheet.

Generating Reports

When the number or complexity of solutions makes creating scenarios impractical, you need to create a report. Some reports can be created only in a separate worksheet, which you can save; others can be placed in separate worksheets or can highlight cells in the current worksheet and show report data in a dialog box.

To create a Solver report:

1. Choose **R**eports in the Solver Answer dialog box. The Solver Reports dialog box appears.

2. In the Re**p**ort type box, choose the type of report you want Solver to create. (See the list that follows these steps for descriptions of report types.)

3. Choose **C**ell or **T**able, depending on the type of report you want to create. **C**ell shows the solution in worksheet cells and additional

14

information in the Solver Report dialog box; **T**able creates a separate file. (**C**ell is not available for answer-table or how-solved reports.)

You can create seven types of reports in 1-2-3 for Windows:

■ *Answer-table reports* list in table form all the answers that Solver found. These reports always are separate worksheets that are automatically named ANSWER01, ANSWER02, and so on; you can save these worksheets.

An answer-table report.

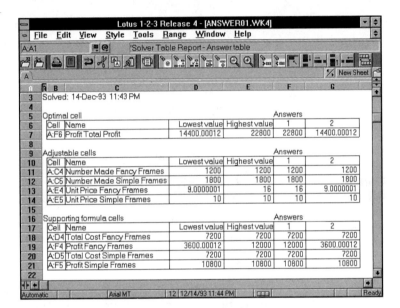

■ *How-solved reports* show what happened behind the scenes to generate the solutions, including information about the optimal, constraint, and adjustable cells. These reports always are separate worksheets that are automatically named HOW00001, HOW00002, and so on; you can save these worksheets.

A how-solved report. Blank rows were removed to make more of the report visible.

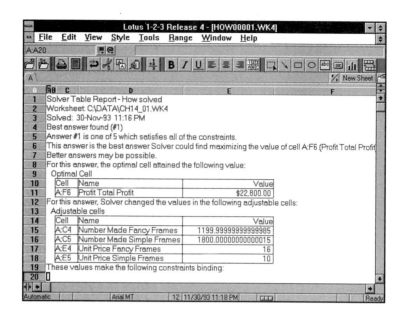

```
                    Lotus 1-2-3 Release 4 - [HOW00001.WK4]
   File   Edit   View   Style   Tools   Range   Window   Help
AA20
 A
   AB  C                D                        E                    F
 1  Solver Table Report - How solved
 2  Worksheet: C:\DATA\CH14_01.WK4
 3  Solved: 30-Nov-93 11:16 PM
 4  Best answer found (#1)
 5  Answer #1 is one of 5 which satisfies all of the constraints.
 6  This answer is the best answer Solver could find maximizing the value of cell A:F6 (Profit Total Profit
 7  Better answers may be possible.
 8  For this answer, the optimal cell attained the following value:
 9     Optimal Cell
10     Cell   Name                                       Value
11     A:F6   Profit Total Profit                     $22,800.00
12  For this answer, Solver changed the values in the following adjustable cells:
13     Adjustable cells
14     Cell   Name                                       Value
15     A:C4   Number Made Fancy Frames         1199.99999999999985
16     A:C5   Number Made Simple Frames        1800.0000000000015
17     A:E4   Unit Price Fancy Frames                         16
18     A:E5   Unit Price Simple Frames                        10
19  These values make the following constraints binding:
20

 Automatic              Arial MT           12  11/30/93 11:18 PM                    Ready
```

- *What-if limits reports* list the highest and lowest numbers for each cell in all solutions. These reports also list the highest and lowest values you can assign to one cell for the current solution (assuming that all other adjustable cells stay the same) and still satisfy all constraints. The purpose of this kind of report is to help you to make reasonable guesses about different numbers you can try in a given cell.

You can create a what-if limits report on a cell-by-cell basis or as a table. If you choose **C**ell, the program highlights each adjustable cell and displays the ranges of values in a dialog box. If you choose **Ta**ble, the program creates a separate worksheet named LIMITS01, LIMITS02, and so on. This worksheet lists the values for all adjustable cells in tabular form.

14

A what-if report in **C**ell format.

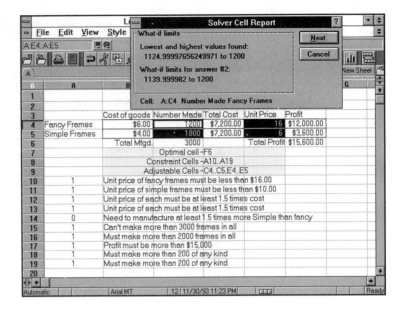

■ *Differences reports* show the differences between the values generated in two different solutions. Whether you specify T**a**ble or **C**ell, you must specify the two sets of answers you want to compare; you can specify the minimum difference you want the report to include.

A differences report comparing all differences greater than zero for answers 1 and 2.

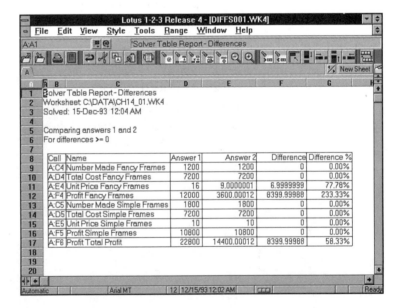

■ *Nonbinding-constraints reports* list all constraints that were satisfied with the current solution but did not affect the solution because the values placed in related adjustable cells did not reach a limit. A report of this type shows how you can rewrite the constraint formula to make it binding. If a constraint is not binding, it may be superfluous, a duplicate, or inconsistent with another constraint.

A nonbinding-constraint report in table form.

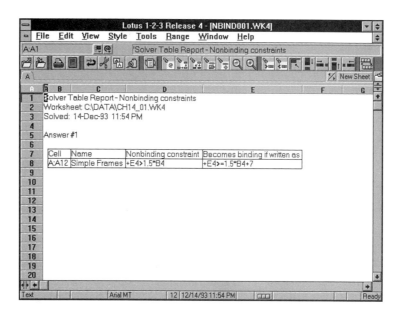

■ *Inconsistent-constraints reports* list all constraints that were not met by the current solution and show how you can adjust the formula to satisfy the constraint.

14

A cell-used report.

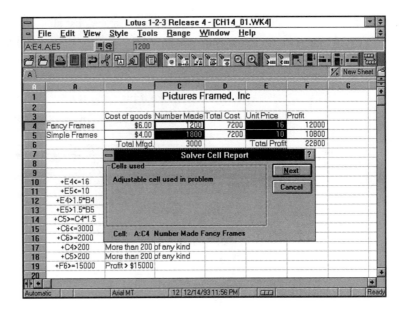

■ *Cells-used reports* list all cells involved in the solution to confirm that the cells you designated as problem cells were used.

A cells-used report
in table form.

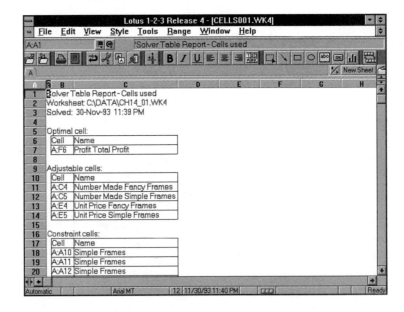

Using Backsolver

Backsolver starts with a desired outcome for a formula cell and places values in cells supporting that formula so that the desired outcome occurs. In the frame-company example, you could use Backsolver to find how many frames you would need to produce to raise your profit to $30,000.

Note: *The values you enter in the adjustable cells determine the ratio of the answers Backsolver generates. If you enter* **1000** *in cell C4 and* **2000** *in C5, for example, the answer that Backsolver generates in C5 will be twice the contents of C4.*

To use Backsolver to solve a problem:

1. Choose **R**ange, **A**nalyze, **B**acksolver. The Backsolver dialog box appears.

The Backsolver dialog box.

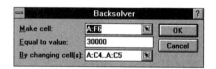

2. In the **M**ake Cell text box, specify the cell containing the formula for which you want Backsolver to change inputs.

3. In the **E**qual to Value text box, enter the value you want Backsolver to use.

4. In the **B**y Changing Cell(s) text box, enter the range of adjustable cells. (You can enter a cell or a range, but not a collection.)

5. Choose OK. Backsolver changes the values in the designated cells so that you achieve the desired result in the formula cell.

The result of Backsolver displayed in cells C4 and C5.

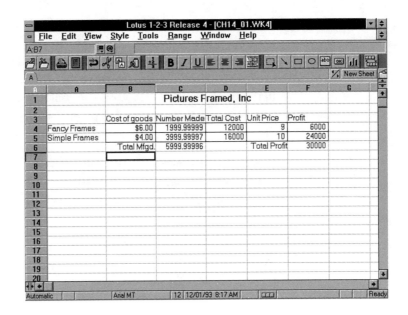

Caution

Any formulas that rely on data in the cells changed by Backsolver recalculate to reflect the new values. If the original data is valuable, make sure that you save the worksheet before using Backsolver.

Note: *Backsolver does not use constraint cells the way Solver does. The only information Backsolver uses is contained in the cells you designate in the Backsolver dialog box.*

Summary

To	Do This
Create a one-way what-if table	Enter range of values in a column; create formula; choose **R**ange, **A**nalyze, **W**hat-if Table; set **N**umber Variables at 1.
Create a two-way what-if table	Enter range of values in the left column and top row of table; create formula; choose **R**ange, **A**nalyze, **W**hat-if Table; set **N**umber Variables at 2.
Create a three-way what-if table	Enter range of values in the left column, top row, and top left corner of the table in each worksheet (one worksheet for each variable). Choose **R**ange, **A**nalyze, **W**hat-if Table; set **N**umber of Variables at 3.
Change inputs in a what-if table	Change data in top row, left column, or top left corner of each table; then choose **R**ange, **A**nalyze, **W**hat-if Table.

To	Do This
Generate Solver solutions	Create a worksheet; choose **R**ange, **A**nalyze, **S**olver; designate **A**djustable, **C**onstraint, and (optional) **O**ptimal cells; choose **S**olve.
Create a Solver report	Choose **R**eport in Solver Answer dialog box; specify type and form of report (**C**ell or **Ta**ble).
Use Backsolver	Choose **R**ange, **A**nalyze, **B**acksolver; specify the cell from which to backsolve, the amount to be used in the solution, and the cells that can be changed; choose OK.

On Your Own

Estimated time: 75 minutes

1. Create a one-way table for monthly payments on a principal amount of $50,000, with the interest rate ranging from 6.5 percent to 10.5 percent at half-point intervals.

2. Create a two-way table from the preceding example, using principal amounts ranging from $50,000 to $100,000 at $10,000 intervals.

3. Create a three-way table, using as the third variable terms of 5 to 30 years in five-year intervals.

4. Enter the worksheet used in this chapter, including constraints. Then generate five Solver solutions.

5. Change the profit constraint so that it must be larger than $20,000.

6. Save the optimal solution as a scenario.

7. Generate a Solver report showing the differences between solutions 1 and 2 in table format.

8. Use Backsolver to find out how much to charge for each type of frame if you produce 2,000 fancy frames and 4,000 simple frames and want a profit of $50,000. Start with values of $15 and $10, respectively.

14

Chapter 15

Working with Other Windows Applications

Among the advantages of using software that runs under Microsoft Windows is the capability to move data among various applications. To a certain extent, you can move information among all Windows applications.

This chapter covers the ways to have several programs active at one time and to move data among them.

Specific topics covered in this chapter:

- Running multiple applications under Windows

- Opening files from other programs

- Exchanging data among Windows applications

- Using SmartSuite and the bonus pack

- Sending electronic mail from 1-2-3 for Windows

Running Multiple Applications under Windows

At your desk, you probably do several things in rapid succession: work on one bit of paperwork, talk on the phone, and punch numbers into your calculator. Similarly, when you are working on your computer, you may need to work for a few minutes on a word-processing document, then update a worksheet, then look up a phone number in a computer-based phone book.

If you are working under DOS, you must close one application before starting another. In Windows, however, you can have more than one application going at once. You can switch among applications as your need to update documents occurs; you can display several applications' documents at the same time, if necessary; and you can exchange data among those documents. The number of applications you can have active is largely determined by the amount of memory (RAM) in your computer.

1-2-3 for Windows and Ami Pro sharing the screen.

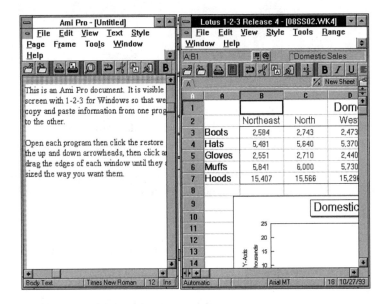

To have several applications active:

1. Start the first application.

2. Press Alt+Tab to return to Program Manager.

3. Double-click the icon of the other application you want to use.

4. Repeat step 3 until you have opened all the applications you want to work with.

To switch among the open applications, press Alt and tap Tab until the desired application name appears; then release the Alt key. Alternatively, press Ctrl+Esc and choose the application you want from the Task List.

Using Alt+Tab enables you to switch to an open application quickly. The names and icons of open applications appear one at a time.

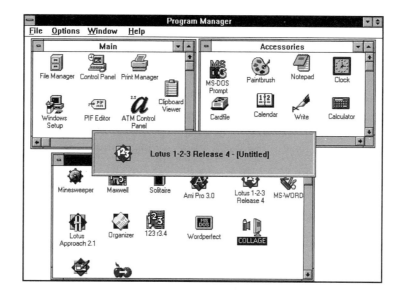

Opening Files from Other Programs

You can retrieve files from many programs into 1-2-3 for Windows. You can retrieve some files immediately, such as files from earlier versions of 1-2-3 for Windows or from 1-2-3 for DOS.

To retrieve a file from a program whose files are compatible with 1-2-3 for Windows:

15

1. Choose **F**ile, **O**pen.

2. In the Open File dialog box, select a file type from the File **T**ype drop-down list. This list shows the programs whose files can be retrieved or combined into 1-2-3 for Windows.

The drop-down File **T**ype list shows the formats you can immediately retrieve into 1-2-3 for Windows.

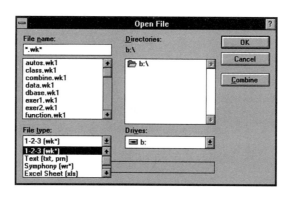

3. Change the drive or directory, if necessary; then highlight the file name and choose OK.

Before you can retrieve files from incompatible programs, such as dBASE, you must translate them in the Translate Utility that accompanies 1-2-3 for Windows. The Translate Utility is not a command in the 1-2-3 for Windows program; you must start it from its own icon in the Windows Program Manager. After starting this utility, you can use it to translate files to or from 1-2-3 for Windows Release 3 format.

Note: *Because the Translate Utility is an older utility, it translates files to Release 3 format.*

Files from the following programs can be translated into Release 3 format, and Release 3 files can be translated into the following formats:

> 1-2-3 Release 1A and 2
> dBASE II, III, and III+
> DIF Enable Version 2.0
> Multiplan 4.2
> SuperCalc4
> Symphony 1, 1.01, 1.1, 1.2, and 2

To translate a file to Release 3 format:

1. In the Windows Program Manager, double-click the 1-2-3 Translate icon in the Lotus Applications group.

2. In the From list on the left side of the screen, select the file format of the file being translated, and then press Enter.

3. In the To list, change the selection, if necessary, and confirm the destination format by pressing Enter.

    Some formats present a dialog box at this point. Press Enter to clear the box and continue.

4. By default, 1-2-3 for Windows looks in C:\123R4W\TRANSLAT\ for the file to be translated. If the file type is not there, an error message appears. Press Esc to clear the error message and continue.

5. Change the drive letter or drive name, if necessary, and then press Enter.

6. Highlight a file to be translated, and press the space bar to select it. Repeat this step for other files to be translated.

7. Press Enter.

8. Enter the directory name into which the translated file or files will be placed, and then press Enter.

9. A series of dialog boxes asks for confirmation. Choose Yes in each box to continue.

10. Message boxes appear, showing the progress of the translation. When the translation is complete, press Enter to translate more files or Esc to return to the main menu.

11. To quit, press Esc and then choose Yes.

After conversion to Release 3 format, the file can be retrieved into 1-2-3 for Windows and saved as a Release 4 file.

Including Data from Other Windows Applications in Worksheets

One way to bring data into 1-2-3 for Windows from other programs that run under Microsoft Windows is to use the Clipboard.

To copy data into 1-2-3 for Windows:

1. Enter the other application, and highlight the data you want to paste into 1-2-3 for Windows.

2. Use the application's Copy command to place the data in the Clipboard.

   Note: *Almost all Windows applications use the* **E***dit,* **C***opy command.*

3. Activate 1-2-3 for Windows, and place the cell pointer where you want to place the data.

4. Choose **E**dit, **P**aste. The data is pasted, without enhancements, into 1-2-3 for Windows.

15

Likewise, you can paste data from 1-2-3 for Windows into another application. Copy a range to the Clipboard, and paste the data from the Clipboard into the other application. The following two figures show a section of a 1-2-3 for Windows worksheet and the same section pasted into an Ami Pro document.

Data in 1-2-3 for Windows.

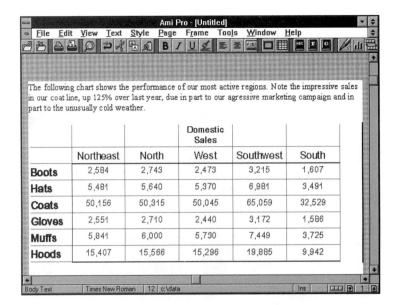

The same data pasted into Ami Pro.

Linking Data from Other Applications to 1-2-3 for Windows

Link
A communication set up between two files so that when you update the source file, the target file in the link is updated.

The next level of sophistication is to *link* a range in 1-2-3 for Windows with the original data in the other application so that if you update the original document, the range in 1-2-3 for Windows will automatically update. You create a link so you don't have to remember to update the same information in two places: the original document and the worksheet.

The file containing the original material being linked is called the *server*; the file containing the link to the original material is the *client*. A server can be linked to several clients, and a client can be linked to several servers.

Server
In links, the document in which the original text or data is located.

You can create two types of links: *DDE* (Dynamic Data Exchange) and *OLE* (Object Linking and Embedding). Among the differences between DDE and OLE are:

Client
The document that reflects changes made in the server document.

- DDE creates a replica of the data or drawn object in the client.

- OLE places an icon representing the server application in the 1-2-3 for Windows worksheet when the original data is text or an entire document. You can use OLE to embed a drawn object in a client application. You also can embed actual data from 1-2-3 for Windows into other applications, such as Freelance and Ami Pro.

- DDE-linked data in the client file is updated as soon as the server data is edited. Under OLE, changes to the server are not reflected in the client file.

  In either case, you can double-click the embedded or linked object to open the server application, where you can edit the original data.

- DDE requires that the *file* containing the original material be present so the link can be maintained. OLE requires that the *program* in which the original material was created be available so that you can click the object to see the original.

Note: *You cannot create a link between two files in 1-2-3 for Windows; you must use a formula to link spreadsheet files. For details about using formulas to link spreadsheet files, see Chapter 9, "Working with Multiple Worksheets and Multiple Documents."*

15

To link data in another program with the current worksheet:

1. Activate the other program, and create or open the document whose data you want to include in 1-2-3 for Windows.

2. You must save the document; otherwise, you cannot create the link.

3. In the other program, highlight the data you want to paste into 1-2-3 for Windows, and copy it to the Clipboard.

4. Switch back to 1-2-3 for Windows, and move to the cell where you want to paste the data.

Caution

Do not close the server application until you finish pasting and editing links. If you close the server too early, links will no longer be available, and correcting the problem can be frustrating and sometimes difficult.

5. You can use either of the following methods to place the data in the worksheet:

   ■ Choose **E**dit, Paste Lin**k**.

   ■ If you want to specify which Clipboard format to use in pasting the link, choose **E**dit, Paste **S**pecial, and then choose the format from the **U**sing Clipboard Format box. Choose Paste **L**ink to complete the step.

   Note: *Depending on the application from which the data is pasted and on the format you use for **E**dit, Paste **S**pecial, the pasted object may be embedded rather than linked.*

The **U**sing Clipboard Format box shows all formats that can be shared by the server and client.

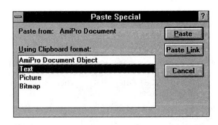

When you finish the steps, a DDE (Dynamic Data Exchange) link is created between the source file and the current file. The following figure shows a short sentence that was pasted from Ami Pro into 1-2-3 for Windows by means of a DDE link.

The Ami Pro server
and the 1-2-3 for
Windows client in
a DDE link.

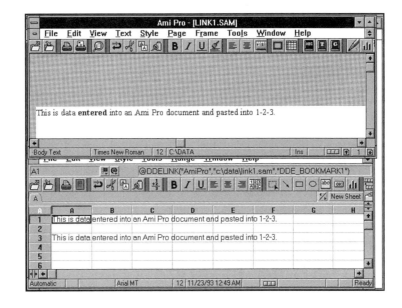

Caution

After you edit the
server document,
make sure you save
it so that the up-to-
date version is on
disk for the link.

In the figure, cells A1 and A3 seem to contain the same data, but there is
a difference: the data in cell A1 of the worksheet actually is a DDE formula placed with **E**dit, Paste Lin**k**. The formula is visible in the edit line.
The data in cell A3 was placed in the document with **E**dit, **P**aste. Therefore, cell A3 contains the actual text; A1 contains a formula.

You can edit the text in cell A3 right in the worksheet; to edit the data in
A1, you must open and edit the server document. On the other hand, the
data in A3 will not change when the server is changed because it is not a
link; the data in A1 will immediately reflect the changes made in the server
document.

15

**If you have
problems...**

You occasionally might see NA in a cell, meaning that the link is not available.
There are several reasons for this, the main one being that you closed the
server application or document and then tried to edit the client cell or paste
another link. To correct this problem, open the server document, delete the
NA cells, and repeat the **C**opy and Paste **L**ink procedures.

Keep the server application open while you are editing and pasting links in your document. To edit the original data that is linked to a cell in the current worksheet, double-click the cell. Both the server application and the document become active. Edit the text in the server. When you switch back to the client, you will see the changes reflected there.

If you work on the server document separately and retrieve the client document later, a prompt will appear, asking whether you want to update the links. Choose **Y**es to ensure that the client contains the current data from the server.

Note: *With DDE links, there is a difference between pressing F2 and double-clicking to edit a cell's contents. Pressing F2 enables you to edit the link formula, whereas double-clicking activates the server document.*

Caution

If the server application is on a floppy disk, make sure that the disk is in the disk drive when you retrieve the client so that the links can be updated.

You also can link data or drawn objects in 1-2-3 for Windows to another Windows application. 1-2-3 for Windows becomes the server, and the other application becomes the client.

To link 1-2-3 for Windows data to another application:

1. Open the 1-2-3 for Windows file that contains the data or object you want to link. If the file is a new worksheet, save it.

2. Highlight the data or object to be linked.

3. Choose **E**dit, **C**opy.

4. Keeping 1-2-3 for Windows open (you can minimize it to an icon, if you want), open the client application and the file into which you want to paste the link.

5. Use the Paste Link command in the client to create the link.

Note: *Most Windows applications perform paste linking through one of two standard commands. One common method is to choose **E**dit, Paste Lin**k**. The other is to choose **E**dit, Paste **S**pecial, and then choose **L**ink or Paste **L**ink. If a command sequence similar to this is not available, see the documentation for the application you are using.*

You can view and change several characteristics of the links you create in a worksheet. To edit a link:

1. Choose **E**dit, **L**inks. The Edit Link dialog box appears.

2. If necessary, select DDE/OLE Links from the **L**ink Type list box.

3. Highlight the link you want to edit. The data for the highlighted link appears in the Information box.

4. To change any of the listed data, choose **E**dit. A new Edit Link dialog box appears.

The **E**dit, **L**inks, **E**dit
dialog box.

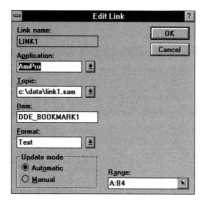

This dialog box contains seven separate pieces of information, all but one of which you can modify:

■ *Ap*plication: the name of the server program. To change the server application for the link, choose one of the open applications in the drop-down list box.

■ *T*opic: the path and file name of the server document. You can edit this information to create a link to a different document.

■ *I*tem: the location in the server document, such as a range in a worksheet or a bookmark in a word-processing document. The bookmark refers to the specific text included in the link. Change this information to link different data or objects of the server.

■ *F*ormat: the Clipboard format of the link. To change the format, choose one of the formats in the drop-down list box.

15

■ *Update Mode:* Aut**o**matic or **M**anual, depending on whether changes to the server appear immediately in the client or whether you need to use the menu to update them. If you choose **M**anual, you will need to update the links with **E**dit, **L**inks, Update **A**ll. Until you do, the linked data will not reflect changes made in the server.

■ *Link Status:* Active means that the link can be updated; Inactive means that the link cannot be updated until it is reactivated. Deacti**v**ate is located in the main **E**dit, **L**inks dialog box. If you Deacti**v**ate a link, you can reactivate it by choosing **E**dit, **L**inks, Update **A**ll or by selecting the link and choosing **U**pdate.

■ *Range:* The range or cell in the worksheet where the link is pasted. To copy the link to a different location, enter a different cell or range. Notice that the link is not removed from the original range.

You can delete a link in the main Edit Link dialog box, although it usually is much easier to go to the cell containing the link and then press Del. You also can create a link from the Edit Link dialog box by choosing **C**reate and then entering the appropriate information in the new Edit Link dialog box. The new dialog box contains the same information discussed in the preceding list.

Note: *You can see some of the information about a link by using F2 to edit a cell containing a link. The @DDELINK formula contains the name of the application, the topic, and the item described in the preceding list.*

Embedding Data in a 1-2-3 for Windows Worksheet

Embedding an object usually means placing in the current file an icon that represents the server application. You can double-click this icon to open the original document for viewing or editing. You can open the server, create the document or drawn object, and then paste it into the current worksheet without leaving 1-2-3 for Windows.

You might, for example, use Ami Pro to create a report that describes business trends in detail. Numerical data and charts in a 1-2-3 for Windows worksheet illustrate the trends, but you want the reader to be able to read the Ami Pro report to get the full picture. An OLE link enables the reader to click the object representing the document to call it to the screen.

The file into which the data is embedded can be saved to a floppy disk for use in another computer, as long as the other computer has the application in which the embedded data or object was created. It is not necessary to have the original server file, however. This is especially handy if objects from many embedded files are included in one client file.

To embed an object:

1. Open the 1-2-3 for Windows file in which you want to embed the object.

2. Choose **E**dit, Insert **O**bject. The Insert Object dialog box appears.

3. Choose the server application from the **O**bject Type list box, and then choose OK. The server application either opens or becomes active.

4. Create the object or text.

5. Choose **F**ile, **U**pdate to save the object.

6. Choose **F**ile, **E**xit or **F**ile, E**x**it & Return.

After the object is embedded in 1-2-3 for Windows, you may need to edit or read the object. You must edit in the server application. Double-click the embedded object to open or activate the server application, retrieve the server document, and then edit the original.

To embed a drawn object in 1-2-3 for Windows:

1. Select the object in the server application, and copy it to the Clipboard.

2. Activate the 1-2-3 for Windows file into which you want to embed the object.

3. Highlight the range, cell, or drawn object where you want to embed the object.

4. Choose **E**dit, Paste **S**pecial.

5. Choose the Clipboard format you want to use.

6. Choose **P**aste.

15

An Ami Pro docu-
ment embedded in
a 1-2-3 for Windows
worksheet.

Indicator of
embedded object

The embedded
Ami Pro document

Using SmartSuite and the Bonus Pack

SmartSuite is a collection of five Lotus applications sold in one package.
Included are 1-2-3 for Windows, Ami Pro, Organizer, Approach, and
Freelance. A bonus pack containing additional SmartIcons and macros is
included with the software. The 33 icons and 112 macros are intended
for use with Ami Pro as it works with the other applications, making
integration of the Lotus Windows applications even easier.

The icons launch macros that integrate the applications and that perform
such tasks as computing college costs, preparing presentations, creating
organizational charts, and searching on-line help for specified topics.

The macros streamline such activities as calculating house payments,
converting Ami Pro styles to 1-2-3 for Windows named styles, and
calculating savings and investment variables.

Sending Electronic Mail from 1-2-3 for Windows

If you have Lotus Notes Release 2.1 or later, or cc:Mail for Windows Release
1.1 or later, you can use a 1-2-3 for Windows command to send a 1-2-3 for
Windows worksheet as *electronic mail*.

Electronic mail
Also called *e-mail*, electronic mail is one of several programs that enable you to send documents or messages to other computers over a network.

You can send, as part of a message, a range of data, a chart, a drawn object, or any combination of these items. To send 1-2-3 for Windows data as *electronic mail*:

1. Choose **F**ile, Send **M**ail. The Send Mail dialog box appears.

2. Choose OK. If your electronic-mail program is not already open, 1-2-3 for Windows opens it.

3. In the dialog box that appears, specify the addressees in the **T**o text box, the carbon-copy addressees in the **C**C text box, and the subject of the message in the **S**ubject text box. Then, in the **M**emo text box, type a memo to accompany the file.

4. Attach the file and choose **S**end.

Summary

To	Do This
Open several Windows applications	Open an application; press Alt+Tab to return to Program Manager; double-click another program icon
Retrieve a file from another program	Choose **F**ile, **O**pen; select the proper File **T**ype; choose path and file name
Bring data from another Windows application into a 1-2-3 for Windows worksheet	In the other application, copy the data to the Clipboard; paste the data into 1-2-3 for Windows
Link data from another application to 1-2-3 for Windows	In the other application, copy the data to the Clipboard; Paste Lin**k** the data into the current worksheet
Change linked data	Edit data in original file
Prevent the link from updating when server is updated	Choose **E**dit, **L**inks; select the link; choose **E**dit, **M**anual
Send a file as part of an electronic-mail message	Choose **F**ile, Send **M**ail; fill in the addressee and memo information; choose **S**end

15

On Your Own

Estimated time: 20 minutes

1. Retrieve a file from another Windows application into 1-2-3 for Windows.

2. Copy some text from another Windows application, and paste it into 1-2-3 for Windows.

3. Paste data from another application into 1-2-3 for Windows as a link.

4. Edit the data in the server, and ensure that the data is updated in 1-2-3 for Windows.

5. Change the link to **M**anual, edit the server, and then update the link.

6. Embed an entire Ami Pro document in a 1-2-3 for Windows file.

7. Embed an Ami Pro drawing in a 1-2-3 for Windows file.

Part IV
Appendixes

Appendix A

Installing 1-2-3 for Windows

Installing the program means creating a copy of the program from compressed files on floppy disks and transferring the copy to the hard disk. You cannot run the program from floppies.

To run 1-2-3 for Windows on your computer, you need the following hardware and software:

- An EGA, VGA, or IBM 8514 monitor.

- An 80286, 80386, or 80486 processor certified for use with Microsoft Windows 3.0 or higher.

- A mouse is strongly recommended.

- 4M (megabytes) of RAM.

- As much as 13M of free hard disk space on a stand-alone computer or 7.5M on a laptop.

- Microsoft Windows 3.0 or higher. (The Guided Tour requires Version 3.1.)

- DOS Version 3.30 or later.

Steps for Installing 1-2-3 for Windows

To install 1-2-3 for Windows:

1. Insert the disk labeled Disk 1 Install into the floppy disk drive.

2. Start Windows, if it is not already running.

3. From Program Manager, choose **F**ile, **R**un. In the command line, type **a:install**. (Substitute the correct letter if the drive you are using is not the A drive.)

   A message appears, telling you that working files are being transferred to your hard disk. Then a welcome screen appears.

4. Choose OK in the welcome screen to continue with installation.

5. Type your name and company name in the appropriate text boxes, and then choose OK. The Confirm Names dialog box appears.

6. If the names are correct, choose Yes; if not, choose No.

   If you choose No, you will repeat step 5.

   If you choose Yes, the Main Menu dialog box appears.

The Main Menu dialog box.

7. Choose Install 1-2-3. The Type of Installation dialog box appears.

The Type of Installation dialog box.

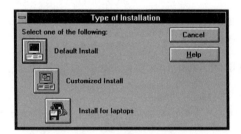

8. Choose one of the following options:

   ■ *Default Install* makes the decisions about which features to transfer and how the defaults will be set. Default Install transfers the following features: Audit, Solver, Backsolver, Dialog

Editor, Macro Translator, Translate, Version Manager (if Lotus Notes is installed on your computer), Spell Checker, all sample files, DataLens Drivers, Tutorial, Guided Tour, and detailed help files for functions and macros.

■ *Custom Install* enables you to choose which features of the program to install. This option also enables you to determine some program defaults. (See the following section for details on the options available in a custom installation.)

■ *Install for Laptops* uses the least disk space, installing only the basic 1-2-3 for Windows program.

9. If you choose Default Install, the following dialog box appears.

Determine the drive and directory for the default installation in this dialog box.

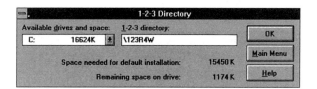

10. If the default drive and directory name are acceptable, choose OK. Otherwise, choose a different drive from the drop-down list of available drives and change the directory name; then choose OK. A confirm box appears.

11. Confirm your selections by choosing OK.

12. After you confirm your choices for custom or default installation, the transfer of files begins. Click Cancel to interrupt the process.

If the process runs to completion, a message appears to confirm that the file transfer is complete. Choose OK.

13. After you choose OK, a message box appears, offering you the opportunity to install Adobe Type Manager. Installing this program is not essential but highly recommended, because Type Manager improves the screen display of fonts and provides some additional fonts.

A

When the install process is complete, you can click the new program icon for 1-2-3 for Windows to start the program. Make sure that you store the program disks in a safe place so that they are available in case something happens to your hard disk or your computer.

Custom Installation Options

If you choose Custom Install in step 8 of the preceding section, the following dialog box appears. At the top of the dialog box, you can designate a different drive or directory for the program files.

The first Customized Install dialog box.

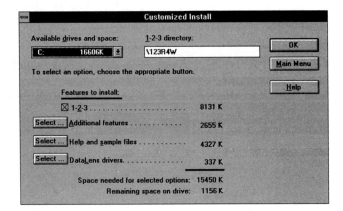

If you have already installed the program and want to install only parts of the program, deselect the 1-**2**-3 check box.

If you click the **A**dditional Features button, the Additional Features dialog box appears. Select or deselect individual items to determine whether they will be included in the transferred files.

Supplies values to make a
formula reach a specified
value (see Chapter 14)

Analyzes data and presents a series
of values, given constraints that
you specify (see Chapter 14)

Permits the creation
of audit reports (see
Chapter 13)

Permits the creation of
custom dialog boxes

This dialog box
enables you to
choose additional
features.

Converts files from other
programs to 1-2-3 for
Windows format
(see Chapter 15)

Permits use of the
Version Manager
(see Chapter 13)

Converts macros created in
1-2-3 for Windows Release
1 to Release 4 format

Amount of space
that will be used
on drive to install
selected features

Permits use of the
spelling checker
(see Chapter 4)

Free space that will remain
on drive after selected features are installed

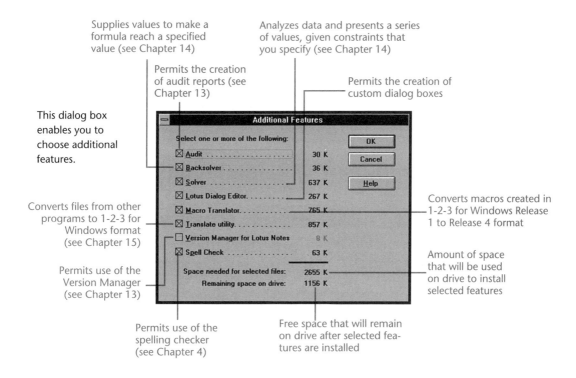

If you click the Help and **S**ample Files button in the Customized Install
dialog box, the following dialog box appears.

Installs files used by the
tutorial and help features

Use this dialog box
to choose the help
and sample files you
want to transfer.

Provides specific
help for each
macro command

Provides specific help
for each function

Provides an animated
orientation to many
features of 1-2-3 for
Windows

Provides an on-
line interactive
training program
for 1-2-3 for
Windows

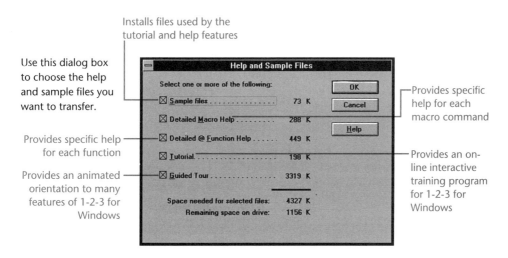

A

If you click DataLens Drivers in the Customized Install dialog box, the DataLens Drivers dialog box appears. This dialog box permits you to specify the database programs to which you can write and from which you can read database files without leaving 1-2-3 for Windows.

The choices available in the DataLens dialog box.

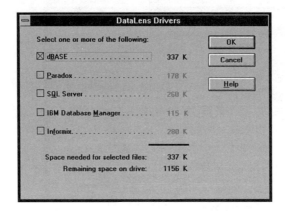

After you make the selections in these dialog boxes, you confirm the directory into which the files will be transferred. Then the 1-2-3 Application Icons dialog box appears. In this dialog box, you select the program group in Windows where the icons you select will be placed. The icons start the various additional features you selected earlier.

Select the icons and program group to be added to Program Manager in this dialog box.

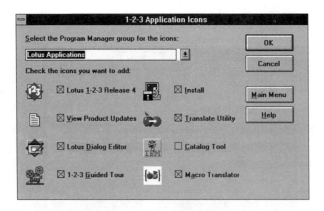

The next dialog box enables you to determine the defaults for several features of the program. Each checked feature will be added to the program.

The User Setup dialog box enables you to set defaults for the features listed.

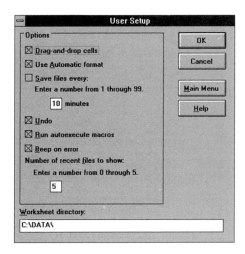

Note: *For details on the use of these options, see Chapter 12, "Customizing 1-2-3 for Windows."*

After you confirm your choices in Custom or Default Install, the transfer of files begins. Click Cancel to interrupt the process.

If the process runs to completion, a message appears, confirming that the file transfer is complete. Click OK.

Next, a message box appears, offering you the opportunity to install Adobe Type Manager. Installing this program is not essential but highly recommended, because Type Manager improves the screen display of fonts and provides some additional fonts.

When the install process is complete, you can start 1-2-3 for Windows by clicking the new program icon.

Make sure that you store the program disks in a safe place so that they will be available in case something happens to your hard disk or your computer.

A

Appendix B

Commonly Used Functions

Describing all 220 functions would take too much space for this book. This appendix, therefore, lists only the most useful and most frequently used kinds of functions, along with examples. The list is by no means complete. For a complete description of functions, use the help feature or see Que Corporation's *Using 1-2-3 for Windows Release 4, Special Edition*.

Mathematical Functions

Used for standard arithmetical operations

- *@ABS(**number**)*. Computes the absolute value of the argument. *number* can be a cell or a number. If the argument refers to more than one cell, the function returns ERR. The function returns the positive value of a number, regardless of whether the *number* argument is positive or negative.

    @ABS(-145.990)=145.99

- *@FACT(**number**)*. Calculates the *factorial* of a number: the product of all numbers from 1 to the value of the *number* argument. If the argument refers to more than one cell, the function returns ERR.

    @FACT(7)=5040

- *@INT(**number**)*. Returns the integer portion of a number.

    @INT(123.4567)=123

- *@MOD(**number,divisor**)*. Calculates the modulus, or remainder, when *number* is divided by *divisor*. If *divisor* is not a number, the function returns ERR.

How much money will be left over if you have $45.67 and buy as many items priced at $5.99 as you can?

```
@MOD(45.67,5.99)=3.74
```

- *@RAND.* Generates a random number. @RAND returns a decimal between 0 and 1 but never generates 1. To generate a random number between 1 and 10, therefore, use @RAND*11. To eliminate the decimal part of the result, use @INT(@RAND*11). To generate a random whole number between 100 and 200, use 100+@INT(@RAND*101).

   Note: *Every time you enter data into the worksheet or perform a command, the @RAND function returns a new number.*

Calendar Functions

Generate dates or perform date math

- *@DATE(**yr,mo,da**).* Converts the date entered to its serial-number equivalent so the date can be used in date arithmetic.

   ```
   @DATE(93,10,31)=34273
   ```

- *@DATEDIF(**start-date,end-date,format**).* For the first two arguments, you can use serial numbers or refer to cells. The third argument must be one of the following, including the quotation marks:

Argument	Meaning
"y"	Number of years
"m"	Number of months
"d"	Number of days
"md"	Number of days, ignoring months and years
"ym"	Number of months, ignoring years
"yd"	Number of days, ignoring years

If **January 1, 1980** is entered in A1 and **January 30, 1985** in A2, @DATEDIF(A1,A2,"dy")=29; it is 29 days more than the number of years that have elapsed.

■ *@DATEINFO(**date-number,attribute**)*. Returns the attribute selected for the date entered. The date can be a serial number or a cell that contains a date.

attribute is a number and returns the following information:

Number	Result
1	Day of the week as an abbreviated label (Sat)
2	Day of the week as a label (Saturday)
3	Day of the week as an integer (1=Monday, 7=Sunday)
4	Week of the year as an integer (1 to 53)
5	Month of the year as an abbreviated label (Sep)
6	Month of the year as a label (September)
7	Number of days in the month specified in *date-number*
8	Number of days left in the month specified in *date-number*
9	Last day of the month specified in *date-number*
10	Quarter of the year for the date in *date-number* as an integer
11	1 if the year in *date-number* is a leap year, 0 if it is not
12	Julian date for *date-number*, from 1 to 366
13	Days remaining in the year after *date-number*. Enter **01/01/94** in cell A1. @DATEINFO(A1,1)=Sat

■ *@TODAY*. Returns a number that represents the current date. If unformatted, the cell in which the function is entered shows the result as a five-digit serial number representing the number of days that have elapsed since January 1, 1900. Give the cell a date format to display the number as a date.

B

`@TODAY-@DATE(50,11,21)` shows how many days have elapsed since November 21, 1950. (Substitute your birthdate in the argument to see how many days old you are.)

- *@NOW.* Returns the same five-digit number as @TODAY, except that a decimal is added to show how much of the day has passed.

Statistical Functions

Process and interpret data

- *@SUM(**list**).* Returns the sum of all numbers in the highlighted range. The *list* argument is a cell or range address or name. If the numbers 5 through 9 are entered in cells A1 through A5, `@SUM(A1..A5)=35`.

- *@AVG(**list**).* Returns the average of all numbers in a range. The sum of all values in the range is divided by the number of filled cells, so a label in a cell in the range will cause the results to be wrong. If the numbers 5 through 9 are entered in cells A1 through A5, `@AVG(A1..A5)=7`.

- *@COUNT(**list**).* Counts the number of filled cells in a range, whether the cells contain labels or values. Type a cell entry in each of the cells in A1 to A5A: `@COUNT(A1..A5)=5`.

- *@MAX(**list**).* Returns the highest value in the range named in *list*. If the numbers 5 through 9 are entered in cells A1 through A5, `@MAX(A1..A5)=9`.

- *@SUBTOTAL(**list**).* Totals the numbers in the range specified in *list*. Used in @GRANDTOTAL. See the figure following @GRANDTOTAL.

- *@GRANDTOTAL(**list**).* Totals the subtotals in the range specified in the *list* argument. Even if you highlight a large range, the function only adds @SUBTOTAL results. See the following figure:

In this figure, the numbers in row 9 result from @SUBTOTAL functions. The figure in row 11 is @GRANDTOTAL (D9..B1).

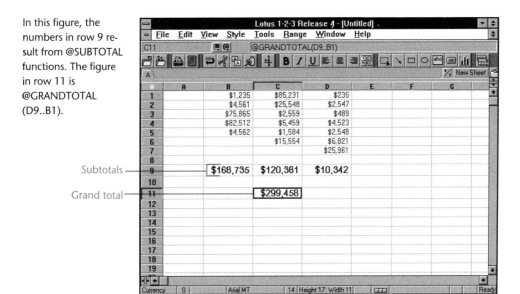

Subtotals —— (row 9)

Grand total —— (row 11)

Engineering Functions

Used for advanced numerical operations and numerical conversions

- *@HEX(**decimal**).* Converts a decimal number to a hexadecimal number. The argument must be a decimal number, a formula that returns a decimal number, or a cell that contains a decimal number.

    @HEX(27)=1B

- *@DECIMAL(**hexadecimal**).* Converts a hexadecimal number to a signed decimal number. The argument must be a hexadecimal number entered as a label or a cell that contains a hexadecimal number.

    @DECIMAL("FE")=254

- *@BETA(**value,value**).* Returns the @BETA function to within at least six significant digits.

    @BETA(4,0.6)=0.66773504

B

Lookup Functions

Compare a given value with a table of values and return an associated value

Note: Lookup functions are the equivalent of making decisions when there are many options.

■ *@HLOOKUP(**reference,table,offset**)*. The *reference* argument is a cell that contains some information; *table* is a range that contains data including the information in *reference*; and *offset* is the row offset in the table. @HLOOKUP uses a horizontal table; @VLOOKUP uses a vertical table.

In the following figure, the discount is determined by the total. The @HLOOKUP function uses the value in C1 and interpolates it into the table in rows 3 and 4. Because the total is in row 3 and the discount is in row 4, you want the function to look one row below the total for the discount, so the offset is 1. The discount increases when the total reaches the next higher amount. The @LOOKUP function can interpolate into tables when values are used as the initial value.

This is an example of a lookup table.

The amount looked up

Corresponding discounts (offset of one row)

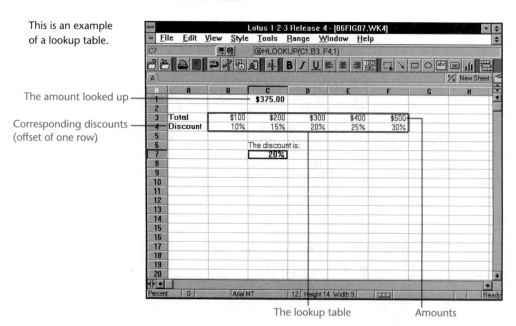

The lookup table   Amounts

- *@CHOOSE(**offset,list**)*. Chooses an item from a list according to the item's position in the list. (Remember that the first position in the list is number 0, not 1. Therefore, the second item is 1, and so on.) The *offset* argument can be a number or formula contained in another cell.

  `@CHOOSE(2,"Winter","Spring","Summer","Fall")=Summer`

Information Functions

Return answers about the cells and ranges in a worksheet or about the status of the program

- *@COLS(**range**)*. Counts the columns in a range.

  `@COLS(J1..AK1)=28`

- *@RANGENAME(**cell**)*. Returns the name of the range, if any, in which the cell is located. If you give the range A1..200 the name "Table", `@RANGENAME(A175)=Table`.

- *@CELL(**attribute,reference**)*. Returns the attribute listed for the current cell. The *attribute* argument must be in quotes.

  If cell C5 contains the formula @SUM(A1..B25), @CELL("contents",c5)=@SUM(A1..B25).

  The following table lists the acceptable attribute arguments used with @CELL and what those functions return:

attribute	Result
"address"	The absolute address
"col"	The number of the column (A=1, IV=256)
"color"	1 if negative numbers are formatted in color, 0 if not
"contents"	The actual contents of the cell
"coord"	The full cell address, including worksheet letter
"filename"	The name of the path and file containing the cell

B

(continues)

(continued)

attribute	Result
"format"	The format of the cell*
"parenthesis"	1 if negative numbers are displayed in parentheses, 0 if not
"prefix"	Shows label prefix ('=left aligned, ^=centered, "=right aligned, \=repeating)
"protect"	1 if cell is protected, 0 if not
"row"	Row number (1 to 8,192)
"sheet"	Worksheet name or letter (A=1, IV=256)
"type"	b if blank, v if value, l if label
"width"	The width of the column

* Consult the help feature for a complete list of numbers and format equivalents.

Financial Functions

Used for business-related operations such as depreciation or interest, principal, time, and payment calculations

- **@FV(*payments,interest,term*)**. Calculates the future value of a series of payments made over a period of time and earning a fixed interest rate. In the following formula, payments of $100 are made into an investment that pays 10 percent per year (10%/12) per month (see note) and involves 120 monthly payments over 10 years.

    ```
    @FV(100,10%/12,120)=$20484.50
    ```

    Note: *In financial calculations, the* payments *and* term *arguments must represent the same period. If you use the figure 10% as an annual percentage rate, the term must be expressed in years, not months, and the payment must be the annual payment.*

- **@PMT(*principal,interest,term*)**. Returns the payment for a given principal amount, interest amount, and time period. Make sure that all three arguments represent the same period. The following example calculates the monthly payment on a mortgage of $100,000 at 9.5 percent annual interest (divided by 12 for the monthly rate) over 30 years (360 payments):

```
@PMT(100000,9.5%/12,360)=$840.85
```

- *@RATE(**future-value,present-value,term**)*. Calculates the interest rate required for *present-value* to appreciate to *future-value* over the period represented by *term*. The following example calculates the rate required for $10,000 to appreciate to $50,000 after 10 years:

```
@RATE(50000,10000,10)=17.46%
```

Logical Functions

Generate a decision based on a test of a condition

- *@IF(**condition,x,y**)*. Checks the condition to see whether it is met or not. If the condition is met, the function takes the action specified in the *x* argument; if the condition is not met, the function takes the action specified in the *y* argument.

    Enter **100** in cell A1. `@IF(A1>50,"Yes","No")`. The cell where the formula is placed shows the word `Yes`.

Database Functions

Return an answer based on certain criteria or perform query functions

- *@DSUM(**input,field,criteria**)*. Adds numbers in cells that fit the criteria.

B

In this database, @DSUM added the salaries only for members of the sales department.

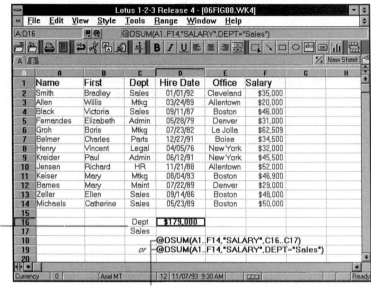

The sum of salaries paid in the sales department

Two possible ways of writing the formula

- ■ *@DCOUNT(**input,field,criteria**)*. Counts the filled cells if they conform to the criteria. In the preceding figure,

  `@DCOUNT(A1..F14,"NAME",C16..C17)=4`.

Text Functions

Return the requested information about text strings or convert text strings

- ■ *@UPPER(**string**)*. Displays an entire string in uppercase letters. The *string* argument can be a text string, a cell that contains a string, or a formula that returns a text string. If cell A1 contained "coke," for example, `@UPPER(A1)=COKE`.

- ■ *@PROPER(**string**)*. Converts a common noun to a proper noun by capitalizing the first letter of each word, making all other letters lowercase.

  `@PROPER(A1)=Coke`

■ *@LENGTH(**string**)*. Returns the length of the string or the cell in which the string is located. `@LENGTH(A1)=17` (it counts the space).

■ *@EXACT(**string1**,**string2**)*. Compares two strings or cells where the strings are located. If the strings are the same, the function returns 1; otherwise, it returns 0. If "george washington" were in cell A1, `@EXACT(A1,"George Washington")=0` because the second argument contains initial capital letters.

Index

1-2-3 Release 4 for Windows QuickStart DiskPack Order Form

Use this form to order the *1-2-3 Release 4 for Windows QuickStart DiskPack*, which contains additional exercises that build on the examples presented in the chapters and in the Visual Index. These hands-on exercises enable you to further your learning of 1-2-3 Release 4 for Windows by practicing with existing worksheets (rather than creating new worksheets from scratch). The *1-2-3 Release 4 for Windows QuickStart DiskPack* includes a 1.4K HD 3 1/2" disk that contains the following items:

- Sample files used in the chapters of *1-2-3 Release 4 for Windows QuickStart*. These files include the examples shown in the Visual Index at the beginning of the book.

- Practice files that you will use in the exercises supplied with the *1-2-3 Release 4 for Windows QuickStart DiskPack*.

The easiest way to order your *1-2-3 Release 4 for Windows QuickStart DiskPack* is to pick up the phone and call

(800) 428-5331

between 9 a.m. and 5 p.m. EST.

For faster service, please have your credit card available.

ISBN	Quantity	Item	Unit Cost	Total Cost
1-56529-618-4		1-2-3 Release 4 for Windows QuickStart DiskPack	$7.99*	TOTAL

* The unit price *includes* the shipping and handling charges for domestic orders. For overseas shipping and handling, add $2 per DiskPack. (Price subject to change.)

If you need to have the DiskPack *now*, we can ship it to you so that you will receive it overnight or in two days for an additional charge of approximately $18.

Que Corporation
201 W. 103rd St.
Indianapolis, IN 46290

Orders: (800) 428-5331   Sales Fax: (800) 448-3804   Customer Service: (800) 835-3202